PENNY PINCHER'$ ALMANAC

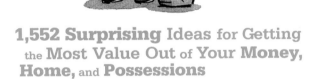

1,552 Surprising Ideas for Getting the **Most Value Out** of Your **Money, Home,** and **Possessions**

From the Editors of Reader's Digest

Reader's Digest

The Reader's Digest Association, Inc.
Pleasantville, NY

A READER'S DIGEST BOOK

This edition published by The Reader's Digest Association, Inc.

Copyright © 2007 The Reader's Digest Association, Inc.

ISBN 13: 978-0-7621-0849-7
ISBN 10: 0-7621-0849-5

The content for the *Reader's Digest Pocket Guide: Penny Pincher's Almanac* was compiled from the original *Penny Pincher's Almanac* (ISBN 0–7621–0444–9)

PENNY PINCHER'S ALMANAC PROJECT STAFF
Senior Editor: Don Earnest
Senior Design Director: Elizabeth Tunnicliffe
Production Technology Manager: Douglas A. Croll

Contributors:
Writer: Kim Elliott
Illustrator: Elwood Smith
Cover Designer: George McKeon
Interior Designer: Susan Bacchetti
Copy Editors: Susan C. Ball, Denise Willi
Indexer: Andrea Chesman
Manufacturing Manager: John Cassidy

Address any comments to:
The Reader's Digest Association, Inc.
Adult Trade Publishing
Reader's Digest Road
Pleasantville, NY 10570-7000

For more Reader's Digest products and information, visit our website: www.rd.com

Printed in China

1   3   5   7   9   10   8   6   4   2

welcome to the world of the

Penny Pincher

**you'll know the real joy
of penny pinching when:**

- **You eat amazing dinners for next to nothing** ...
  because you use grocery-store ads to pick out your
  meats and vegetables.

- **Your car runs like a dream year in and year out** ...
  because you regularly invest in smart maintenance.

- **Your house is sparkling fresh and smells divine** ...
  because you know the cleaning power of vinegar and baking soda.

- **Your heating bills are half those of your neighbors** ...
  thanks to the caulking, weather-stripping, insulating,
  and window maintenance you've done.

- **Your family has exciting weekends** ...
  thanks to your diligence in scoping out discount tickets
  for museums, concerts, plays, and events.

- **You drink luscious, deeply aromatic coffee** ...
  but never pay exorbitant coffeehouse prices.

- **You do all the travel your heart desires** ...
  because you've learned the tricks to find the most frugal
  flights, hotels, and meals.

- **You have lots of cash and home equity for your future** ...
  thanks to smart choices to pay off your mortgage quickly.

living well for less 6

(1) good eats 8
for less
- savvy food shopping 9
- frugally fresh 14
- the penny pincher's pantry 22

(2) beauty on 26
a budget
- dressing for less 27
- chic looks
  for little investment 38
- cosmetic caper... 44

(3) frugal health 56
and fitness
- home remedies from a to z 57
- exercise economics 72

(4) home 76
sweet home
- cleaning house 77
- laundry for less 86
- decorating on a dime 90
- frugal furniture facts 94

1,552

(5) penny-smart parenting   102

- bargain-basement babies   103
- lower cost kids   111
- free-time fun   117

(6) cent-sational special occasions   124

- penny-wise parties   125
- the well-planned wedding   130
- happy homemade holidays   140
- all good gifts   146

(7) going out and spending wisely   150

- discount fine dining   151
- bargain culture   154
- sporty savings   158
- cheap thrills   162

(8) thrifty travel   166

- up in the air   167
- discount detours   172
- savings at sea   178
- frugal family fun   181

(9) thrifty home improvements   184

- cost-saving home care   185
- do-it-yourself damage control   190
- reduce, reuse, recycle   198

(10) cheap car talk   204

- the best car buy   205
- car care   210

(11) money-savvy medicine   214

- medical insurance   215
- doctors and hospitals and HMOs, oh my!   219
- drugs for less   222

(12) frugal finances   226

- the working life   227
- home accounting 101   234
- retire like royalty!   243

index   250

living well for **Less**

Stop for just a minute and look around. Everywhere you turn you can probably see examples of folks who have a clear understanding of their priorities, who know what they want now and who have a solid understanding of what they want in the future. These people understand the importance of living well. But unfortunately living well usually takes money. Or does it? This book will show how you can maintain a good life while putting something away for the future by adopting simple penny-pinching strategies. After all, why should you pay full price for something when you can get the same high quality at a lower price simply by remaining aware, prioritizing, and choosing carefully? Penny pinchers aren't cheap; they're smart, and they enjoy the process of spending money— wisely. These are the words they live by, their mantra: **Don't live in denial; live well for less, and have fun doing it.**

it's not just about money

Each generation is faced with challenges—making the most of economic highs and digging in to weather economic lows. Penny pinchers know how to meet these challenges with humor, courage, and creativity, always keeping an eye on the long-term goal of living well.

That's the most important reason to practice the art of pinching pennies—to enable you to live the life you want. Sometimes it means creative budgeting so a parent can stay at home with small children. Sometimes that means saving small amounts throughout the year to take one stupendously big trip abroad. Sometimes it means socking away now to leave a legacy to your loved ones in the future. Whatever your personal reason for choosing to be a penny pincher, thrift as a way of life can give you the freedom to really live.

a budget is not a straitjacket

Budgeting is an art. It should embrace who you are and what you value. Most important, budgeting should become such a well-ingrained part of your life that you are hardly aware you are doing it. It doesn't mean practicing constant self-denial, being a martyr, or fleeing from life's comforts and niceties. We penny pinchers truly enjoy the process of spending money—wisely. We dive into researching the best deal for car insurance. We think nothing of checking all the consumer information to buy the highest performing dishwasher for the most reasonable price. We never feel better than when someone is wowed by our "new" leather coat—which we picked up at a garage sale and carefully restored with face cream. We find bargains beguiling, delight in a discount, and positively gush over a really great deal.

learn the real value of things

Living well for less means not only knowing the price of things but also knowing the value. What's the difference? Costs fluctuate depending on all sorts of factors. Value remains more constant. Buying a cheap sofa costs less money up front, but if the poor construction and inferior fabric wear badly, you'll end up spending more money to repair or replace it—bad value. A high-quality sofa that is structurally well made with sturdy fabric and that will continue to look good despite hard use may cost more at first, but the savings over time are considerable—good value. Of course, being a penny pincher also means that you found that good sofa for the absolute best price. The price was higher than the cheap sofa's, but your good-value sofa still looks great and provides comfortable seating 10 years down the line while the bad sofa couldn't even be donated to charity.

THE PENNY PINCHER'S ALMANAC covers all the main aspects of penny pinching your way to the Good Life—from caring for your body, your home and car, to travel and entertaining, with a little money management thrown in for good measure. But every penny pincher is unique—no one model will work for everyone—so as you read, assess how these ideas can be modified to fit into your lifestyle. If you can't give up Starbucks every morning, can you cut out the health-club costs and start exercising with tapes at home? Keep a pad and pen handy while you read, note aspects that resonate—driving to save gas, finding the cheapest flights, buying designer children's clothing at consignment stores, saving on prescription drugs—and always keep your eyes on the prize: learning to spend less on daily living to afford you the luxury to live as you like.

CHAPTER 1

Good Eats for Less

- savvy food shopping
- frugally fresh
- the penny pincher's pantry

savvy food
Shopping

BUYING GROCERIES IS A REAL TEST
OF THE PENNY PINCHER. GO ARMED WITH
SHOPPING LIST, COURTESY CARD, AND COUPONS.

strategies for supermarket savings

Never underestimate a grocery store manager's marketing savvy. No other store is organized so cunningly to get you to buy things you don't need. Only need milk? Funny how you have to walk by the fresh-baked cookies, cheese crackers, and discount videos to get it. At the register, you're surrounded by muffins, candy bars, magazines, and tabloids. So here's how to manage a supermarket frugally and happily:

have a sense of purpose Know what you are going to buy when you enter the store, and leave the store with just that. It's so obvious, yet we so often go astray.

shop the perimeter Food essentials (produce, meats, dairy, and bread) are usually on the store's perimeter. The middle aisles have the more costly prepared foods. The more you concentrate your shopping on the edges of the store, the healthier and cheaper your food-buying will be.

turn your head Eye-catching displays of cookies, chips, and convenience foods are everywhere. Ignore them. Unless they are truly staples of your home, they should be off limits.

know your aisles Every store has an aisle or two that has no temptations for you (pet food, paper goods, baby supplies, cosmetics, and so forth). Make that aisle your passageway to the departments you need at the back of the store.

study sales patterns Grocery store sales often occur in patterns. For example, we know of a grocery store that puts our favorite ice cream on a "buy one, get one free" sale one week every month. Many items regularly rotate between on sale and off. Learn the patterns, and never buy at full retail!

look up, look down, look all around Generally, the most expensive brand-name items are on shelves at eye level. Less expensive store brands are on the upper and lower shelves.

weigh it yourself Preweighed produce is convenient, but reweigh them, just in case. A 5-pound bag of carrots will end up being anywhere from 4.5 pounds to 6 pounds!

calculated savings When comparing prices, always always always compare price per pound. It's the only objective way to do it. Most stores put that number on the shelf product tags. But the tags are often missing. And always have a calculator with you. It makes comparison shopping a breeze.

twenty-four hours a day If your store is a 24-hour operation, try shopping during off hours. Just being able to take your time can help you make better choices and save money.

cashing in on store courtesy cards

A relative newcomer in the savvy shopper's arsenal, store courtesy cards (also dubbed club or thank-you cards), issued by a supermarket, give you additional savings on certain items. The store offers the cards in an effort to make you a regular shopper, but the savings can actually be significant, and there are no rules restricting how many stores you can have a card from. In a recent supermarket flier, we spotted Old Orchard 100% Juice, often $1.99 per can, at five for $5 using the courtesy card, and three Tombstone Pizzas (usually between $4 and $5 apiece) at three for $10 with the card! As with coupons, you will need to keep an eye on the going prices of things, but courtesy cards can help in your fight to contain food costs.

using the newspapers

Few of us have the time (or the gas) to go tooling around town checking prices from one store to the next. Many local newspapers devote a section one day a week to food, and that is also the day the grocery stores really go to town on ads or inserts. Use that day to sit down and armchair-compare prices before you go shopping.

making coupons work

Ah, the joy of the Sunday newspaper, with its enticing sheets of coupons. The dollars off! The cool stuff! The traps, the tricks, the truth: Used wisely, coupons can truly save you money on certain items, if you know how to make coupons work for you.

- Organize your coupons the way you organize your shopping list: in the same order as the store aisles. You'll find the coupons you want more quickly and will be less likely to overlook a useful coupon. As you clip them, put each coupon in a product category. Within a category, put them in expiration order, with the soonest to expire first.
- Seek out stores that regularly offer to double or triple coupons, saving you twice or three times the face value.
- If there is a special on any food on your list, be sure to check for a coupon that will give you even more savings. Combining shopping specials with coupons will reward you the most.
- Though buying the largest size of most items is usually thriftiest, you may be able to buy several smaller sizes with coupons and actually get a better price per pound.

You can also find coupons on the Internet, often with a novel twist. At nesteggz.com, you can save money at the register and put money into a savings account. With its "Account Credit" coupons, you only get about 10 cents off at the supermarket register, but the full value of the coupon is deposited into an online interest-bearing savings account and you can withdraw the cash value at any time. The site also offers regular "Instant Cash" coupons on all kinds of items. The valupage.com site offers register-redeemable coupons for "wish list" items. So surf for savings before you shop.

coupon catches and hidden costs

Although coupons can indeed save you money, they can also fool you into spending money on foods you normally wouldn't buy—and doing that may actually cost you. Some money-saving maneuvers for using coupons:

- Big dollar-off coupons look good, but those coupons are generally for an already expensive item. Do the math before you grab it off the shelf.
- Think twice before switching brands. There may be a significant saving between the sale brand and your regular one, but your family may not like the product. Result? A product that sits on the shelf and wastes your money.
- Don't forget to check the cost of the store brands. Even with the price reductions offered by coupons, brand-name items may still be more expensive than store brands.
- Many foods that offer coupons are highly processed, expensive, and low in nutrients. You may pay a fancy price for foods that don't provide good nutrition.
- Sometimes a tie-in offer gives you an item free or at a bargain price if you

stock up on another product at a regular price. But if the freebie isn't exactly what you want, it can take a large bite out of your week's budget, and it may never be used.

bulk bargains

- Preshredded and pregrated cheeses are usually more expensive than blocks of cheese. Buy the blocks and grate your own. Then make your own convenient packages of grated cheese in self-sealing plastic bags. Most grated hard cheese can be frozen without any problem, so grate extra and freeze it.
- Ask the deli if it has lower prices on end pieces of block cheese. If so, buy the ends, grate them, and freeze.
- Bologna, salami, and other cold cuts bought in bulk and sliced at home are less expensive than packaged meats.
- If there's a great sale on milk (and you have the freezer space), buy extra and freeze it. Whole containers will take about two days to thaw in the refrigerator.

dollarwise do-it-yourself items

- Don't buy packages of seasoned rice and noodles; they cost more and contain too much salt. Cook plain rice in low-sodium broth and add fresh or dried herbs or spices. Cook fresh noodles and toss with a little olive oil or butter and herbs. For a really quick fix, toss pasta with a little salad dressing. Or make your own seasoned rice mix to keep on hand for quick fixes.
- Buy plain cottage cheese and plain yogurt and stir in fresh or canned fruit or even a little homemade jam.
- Bags of salad are extremely popular and convenient, but they are also expensive per pound, and it is easy to prepare your own. Tear a head of lettuce into bite-size pieces and wash and dry the pieces in a salad spinner (a good cheap investment). Wrap the pieces in a dish towel or paper towels and store them in self-sealing plastic bags, preferably ones intended for storing greens. Consider adding sliced or diced carrots, sweet peppers, radishes, and so on. For best taste and nutritional benefit, combine several types of lettuce and add some raw spinach.

the value of price clubs

We all know those big box stores where you can buy a pack of 40 rolls of toilet paper, but do they really save you money? Yes, they do, if you use them well. You have to know the price per pound or the price per item of things you formerly bought in other stores, such as traditional supermarkets or drugstores, so you can compare costs at a price club. And you have to buy things that you use and that you have room to store. But you can net yourself a tidy savings by buying in bulk such things as meat and poultry, canned and other shelf-stable items, paper goods, toiletry items (body soap, shampoo, toothpaste, and sunscreen), juices, breakfast cereals, and coffee. You just have to be an informed consumer.

buy frozen juice

Save from half to three-fourths the price of juice by purchasing frozen juice concentrates and reconstituting them. They are just as nutritious, you'll find a wide variety, and they are smaller to store, so you can buy in bulk when they're on sale. Look for those that are made from 100 percent juice and avoid juice "drinks"—they have way too much added sugar.

choice beef is cheaper

When buying beef, select choice cuts instead of prime. Prime cuts are more marbled, which makes them fattier and more expensive. To ensure flavor and tenderness in leaner (and cheaper) cuts of meat, marinate them before cooking. To really lower the fat content, trim all visible fat from meats and skin poultry before cooking.

egg economy

Always buy large eggs; they are the size most often called for in recipes and are usually a good value. The outside color of eggs doesn't affect the inside quality.

make your own oil spray

Buy a small spray bottle and fill it with vegetable or olive oil (or one of both), and you'll be spending a lot less than if you bought the prepackaged spray cans. You will also use less oil, cut calories, and do the environment a favor!

frugally
Fresh

LET'S FACE IT: FRESH FOOD TASTES BETTER.
HERE ARE SOME TIPS ON BUYING AND PREPARING ITEMS
FROM ASPARAGUS TO ZUCCHINI.

admirable asparagus

Though it is rarely cheap, asparagus is delicious, nutritious, and less costly if purchased in season. If you see it at a good price, buy a bunch with firm stems and heads intact. At home, place the asparagus with the ends in water (like a bouquet of flowers). Dampen a paper towel or washcloth and drape it gently over the asparagus tips. Place a piece of plastic wrap (or the bag the asparagus came in) over the towel and store in the refrigerator. The asparagus will keep for almost a week this way.

a hill 'o beans

Beans, dried or canned, are one of a penny pincher's best friends. A remarkably inexpensive source of protein, naturally low in fat, and containing no cholesterol, beans are easy to use in soups, stews, chili, and salads.

- If you are using dried beans, be sure to pick through them first to remove any pebbles or shriveled beans. Place the beans in a large pot and fill with cold water. Skim off anything that comes to the surface, drain in a colander, and rinse under cold running water.
- To soak or not to soak? Dried beans are usually soaked before cooking. Place them in a large bowl or pot and cover (by about 2 inches) with cold water. The length of soaking time will vary with the type of bean.
- To help beans keep their shape, do not soak them. Instead, place them in a pot with cold water and, very slowly, bring them to a boil. Reduce the heat and simmer until the beans are tender. Then continue with the recipe.
- If you are using canned beans, be sure to rinse them well in a colander under cold running water to remove the excess salt. Then use as directed.

berry good

Don't let fresh berries get soggy! Store them in the refrigerator in the open-weave baskets from the store or in a colander, if you picked them yourself. Do not wash berries until just before you are going to eat them.

● Chill berries before washing them, because cold berries are less likely to bruise or bleed during washing than those at room temperature.

● To freeze berries, wash them and pat them dry. Lay the berries in a single layer on a baking sheet lined with a paper towel and freeze until the berries are hard (about one hour). Transfer the frozen berries to self-sealing plastic bags, label, date, and return to the freezer. Use within nine months.

best bread

Fresh bread will generally keep for five to seven days, depending on the texture; the lighter the bread, the more quickly it dries out. To keep bread and rolls fresh longer, put them in one heavy-duty or two regular plastic bags and store the bags in the freezer. Slice a whole loaf before freezing it, so that you can easily remove just the amount you need.

● If you really love the taste of fresh crusty bread—and frequently find yourself spending $3.50 or more on a loaf of fancy bread—you'll find that it pays to invest in a breadmaking machine. These appliances sell for about $100 and the cost of the ingredients for a loaf run less than $1, so, with regular use, you should recoup the cost within a year. Best of all, you get bread that's fresher and tastier than any store-bought loaf—and the house will be filled with a wonderful aroma as it bakes.

cheesy chat

● To inhibit mold growth on cheese, wrap the cheese in a paper towel that has been dampened with vinegar. Then seal it inside a plastic bag. Keep the towel moist with additional vinegar as needed.

● Cottage cheese will keep fresh longer if it's refrigerated upside down in its original carton. And you can freeze cottage cheese, though it will break down when thawed. After thawing the cheese, just whip it until it is creamy; then use it in cooking.

citrus spectaculars

When lemons, limes, oranges, and grapefruits are at their peak, they are also least expensive. Buy in bulk, store some for eating and using in recipes, and use the rest to make a large batch of each kind of juice.

● Before juicing oranges, lemons, or limes, grate the rind and store the zest in the freezer. The next time a recipe calls for grated zest, you'll be good to go.

● After the zest is removed, submerge the fruit in hot water for 15 minutes and then roll it on a counter, pressing down as you roll; this releases the juice before squeezing.

● Pour the juice into ice cube trays and freeze it. Transfer the cubes to labeled and dated self-sealing plastic bags. Whenever citrus juice is called for, thaw one cube for each 2 tablespoons of juice you need.

● If you need only a drop or two of juice, don't squeeze the citrus—jab it with a toothpick and squeeze out the amount you need. Put the toothpick back in the hole to close it, and store the fruit in the refrigerator.

coffee talk

Save dollars a day by brewing your own gourmet coffee instead of purchasing coffee or coffee drinks at a high-priced coffee boutique.

● Invest in good quality coffee (you'll get more flavor per scoop), preferably beans. The best buy we've spotted is at Costco: They sell their store brand, Kirkland, in 2-pound bags for $8.99. The bags are marked with the Starbucks logo and say "Roasted by Starbucks." A 2.5-pound bag of Starbucks French Roast, however, sold for $15.99. Makes you wonder. Costco also had Seattle Mountain Drum-Roasted coffee beans at $7.99 for a 3-pound bag. Some so-called world market stores, such as Cost Plus or Pier One, also offer gourmet coffee beans at a reasonable price. And supermarkets are now selling their own beans in bulk for a relative bargain.

● Depending on where you live, you'll find other good buys. Latin-brand coffee, coffee imported from Mexico, and the coffee-and-chicory blend from Louisiana will all brew a cup of tasty dark-roast coffee for a lot less than you'd pay at a trendy coffee shop.

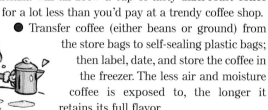

● Transfer coffee (either beans or ground) from the store bags to self-sealing plastic bags; then label, date, and store the coffee in the freezer. The less air and moisture coffee is exposed to, the longer it retains its full flavor.

- Add a pinch of salt to your ground coffee before brewing a pot to reduce bitterness and enhance flavor.
- Give your coffee that boutique touch for pennies by adding a teaspoon of ground cinnamon or a grating of orange zest to the grounds before brewing. (It smells great, too!).
- Love flavored coffees but don't want to pay $3 a cup? Cost Plus had Torani syrups on sale for $2.49 for a 6.3-ounce bottle and $4.99 for a 750 ml bottle. Available in both regular and sugar-free versions, they have vanilla, hazelnut, Irish cream, and chocolate.
- For a special coffee topping, keep a can of light whipped cream in your refrigerator. Or invest in a device to froth your own milk for a cappuccino (we found a Bodum milk frother at Bed, Bath and Beyond for $9.99!).

egg-axtly!

There is really nothing like the flavor of farm-fresh eggs, if you're cooking them by themselves. From-the-nest quality is a bit less crucial if you are using eggs in a recipe. Check the dates on cartons carefully. There is no nutritional difference between brown and white eggs, so buy whichever you prefer. If you are in doubt about the freshness of an egg, place it in a deep container of cold water. If it floats to the top, it's too old to use.

- Store eggs in their carton, not on the refrigerator egg shelf. This helps preserve moisture and prevents the eggs from absorbing the flavor of other foods.
- If a recipe calls for just egg whites or egg yolks, don't toss the other part of the egg down the drain. You can freeze both yolks and whites for future use.
- To freeze egg whites, use a plastic ice cube tray. Put one egg white into each cube space and freeze until hard. Pop the egg-white cubes out of the tray and store them, labeled, in a self-sealing plastic bag in the freezer.
- To freeze egg yolks, add a pinch of sugar or salt to each yolk to prevent them from coagulating. Freeze them as you do egg whites.

fresh fish on ice?

Retain the flavor of your freshly caught fish by putting it in a clean, empty milk carton. Fill the carton with fresh water and put it in the freezer. After thawing the fish for a meal, use the water to fertilize house plants.

gingerroot

Many recipes call for a little fresh gingerroot, but the root loses its flavor if stored for long in the refrigerator. Instead, buy a larger piece and store in a self-sealing plastic bag in the freezer. When you need a little, take it out and grate what you need, then return the unused portion to the freezer. Another plus: Frozen gingerroot grates more easily.

got milk?

When you buy milk, pick a carton or jug with the latest sell date, but keep in mind that the date does not indicate when the milk will go bad, only the date by which the store has to sell it. If properly chilled, milk should last for at least a few days past the sell date.

● Use evaporated milk as a convenient substitute for fresh milk. Regular, low-fat, or skim, it has a long shelf life. To reconstitute, add an equal measure of water. Evaporated milk works well in sauces, gravies, and baked dishes. (Condensed milk is a sweetened form; use it only when specifically called for in a recipe.)

● For richer texture without extra fat, add 1 or 2 tablespoons of nonfat dry milk to skim milk, cream soups, omelets, or puddings. The powdered milk also provides extra calcium and protein.

herbal essence

Growing your own herbs is easy and economical. Here's how to store them for future use:

● For herbs you will use in the next few days, make a bouquet and set the stems in a cup of water. Cover the leaves loosely with a plastic bag and refrigerate. Change the water regularly, and your fresh herbs will last from a week to ten days.

● To quick-dry herbs, place them on a baking sheet and warm them in a 100° F oven until they are dry. If you have a gas oven, preheat it to 200° F, turn it off, and set the sheet of herbs inside until dry.

● Parsley, chives, and basil all freeze well. Wash the leaves and pat them dry, then finely chop and store each herb in a small labeled and dated self-sealing plastic bag.

● For other herbs, wash, dry, and chop them. Place the chopped herbs in an ice cube tray, add just enough water to cover the herbs, and put the tray in the freezer. When the cubes are frozen, store them in self-sealing bags. If you need some oregano, for example, for spaghetti sauce, just drop a cube of the oregano into the pot.

mushroom magic

Button or white mushrooms can often be bought on sale, but the more exotic varieties tend to stay on the pricey side, so make a little go much longer this way: Mix a small amount (about 1/2 ounce) of dried specialty mushrooms with a much larger amount (about a pound) of button mushrooms. The intense flavor of the exotic dried mushrooms will saturate the mild, inexpensive button variety.

● Store mushrooms in paper bags in the main section of the refrigerator. Plastic bags and produce drawers reduce air circulation, leading to slimy, quickly spoiled mushrooms.

● Clean mushrooms with a damp towel or mushroom brush just before preparing them. Never soak mushrooms; it robs them of flavor and nutrients, such as phosphorus, magnesium, potassium, and selenium.

● Save your stems! Chop the mushroom stems and add them to stock, stuffing, or soup.

nut know-how

To keep nuts fresh longer, store them in airtight jars or cans in the refrigerator. If you will not be using them for a few months, store them in the freezer. For longer-lasting nuts, buy them in the shell. Plan to use them within a month or two, though, because they can turn rancid if stored longer.

pick a peck of peppers

Sweet peppers, with the exception of green, can often be high-priced. If you spot a good sale on yellow, orange, or red peppers, buy them and freeze the extras.

● Peppers are among the few vegetables that require no blanching before freezing. Cut, seed, and slice or dice them, and freeze them in dated, self-sealing plastic bags.

● Don't spend money on jars of roasted peppers; do it yourself! Broil whole peppers about 4 to 6 inches from the heat, turning them often, until the skins are well charred. Remove the peppers from the broiler and transfer them to a paper bag; close the bag and let sit for about 15 minutes. The skins should be loosened by then and come off easily. Then cut, remove the seeds and membranes, and rinse. Let the roasted peppers dry completely, then cover and refrigerate them. They should keep for up to two weeks.

rootin' tootin' root veggies

When shopping for root vegetables, such as onions, potatoes, carrots, and beets, look for firm surfaces with no cracks. Store onions and potatoes in a totally dark, cool, dry place. Other root vegetables can be refrigerated.

sugar is sweet

Buy store brands, not national brands, unless there's a sale and the price per pound for the national brand is better.

● Don't use sugar substitutes when baking; the taste and texture will disappoint you. And don't try to use confectioners' sugar and granulated sugar interchangeably; the weight and volume are completely different.

● There is no real difference between light brown sugar and dark brown sugar, although the darker the color, the more intense the flavor. To revive caked brown sugar, sprinkle it with water and set it in a 200° F oven for 10 minutes, or microwave it for 20 seconds. If you place a slice of apple in the sugar container and close it tightly, the sugar will soften in a few days.

tutti fruity

● Size matters: If you are planning to eat fruit raw, buy the smallest pieces you can find. You'll probably be able to buy more pieces of fruit per pound this way. But if you are planning to cook with the fruit, buy larger (and fewer) pieces, so you will have less fruit to wash, peel, core, pit, and chop.

● Sneaky shoppers: When a fruit is in season, check for sales on its frozen counterparts. For example, when peaches are in season, the demand for frozen peaches drops, and the market may want to sell them. Stock up and take advantage of the lower prices.

you say tomato

Loaded with vitamin C, tomatoes are delicious raw or cooked. Recent studies suggest that consumption of cooked tomatoes may reduce the risk of some cancers, particularly those that are more likely to plague men. Whether you grow your own or take advantage of seasonal specials and farmers' markets, tomatoes are a good buy.

● Ripen tomatoes at room temperature in a bowl with other fruit or in a closed brown paper bag. Tomatoes will not ripen in the refrigerator and actually turn pulpy and lose flavor in cold temperatures.

● At season's end, use the last of your homegrown tomatoes to make (and freeze) tomato sauce, purée, or tomato soup. You can also freeze ripe tomatoes, whole or cut up, in plastic freezer bags. After they thaw, use them for cooking.

z is for zucchini

Enjoy this vegetable with the peel on, as that's where you'll find the beta carotene and other vitamins. If you're cooking zucchini, look for firm, bright-green squashes no longer than 6 inches. But if you're planning to stuff them, then the larger the better.

● If you have a bumper crop or want to take advantage of seasonal sales, shred the zucchini and freeze in self-sealing bags. Use shredded zucchini in soups or breads.

● Fresh uncooked zucchini, sliced crosswise or cut into strips, makes a welcome addition to a crudités plate.

● Zucchini are great on the grill. Cut them into thin slices, brush the slices with some olive oil and balsamic vinegar, sprinkle with some herbs or garlic, and grill until the edges are slightly charred.

● Slice 1 pound of zucchini into long strips. Dredge the strips in flour, shaking off the excess, and dip each strip in a batter of 1/2 cup flour and 1/2 cup water or beer. Deep-fry in 3 inches of hot vegetable oil and drain on paper towels. Serve with low-fat ranch dressing for dipping, or sprinkle with balsamic vinegar before serving.

the penny pincher's
Pantry

SETTING UP YOUR KITCHEN THE RIGHT WAY
WILL SAVE YOU TIME AND MONEY.

in with the new (or nearly new)?

You can pick up small appliances at many places, and it pays to shop around. We found the Cuisinart Automatic Grind & Brew coffee maker, which freshly grinds and brews coffee using a timer, at Cooking.com and at Chef's Catalog online **(www.chefscatalog.com)** for $99.95, but Costco was offering it for only $69.99!

- Garage sales can net you fabulous finds for your kitchen and dining room. We recently picked up two brand-new, in-the-wrapper Pyrex pie plates for $3 and a beautiful set of four never-used linen place mats with matching napkins for $2! We've spotted a Crockpot slow cooker, knife sharpeners, bread makers, ice-cream makers, and all those gadgets people get for wedding gifts that often are never used, all on sale for a song at garage sales. You can also pick up china, silverware, and glassware, some of which has never been used or is gorgeous collector stuff.

- After you've assessed your kitchen, make a list of the things you'd like to have or need. Keep that list with you whenever you go out. You never know when you'll spot a sale that might have exactly what you want for much less than what it cost new.

cookware 101

There are few things more frustrating than trying to cook with lousy pots and pans. But how do you invest in good cookware without going into debt? Folks who purchase the good stuff rarely part with it, so you won't often find it at garage sales or resale shops (but always check anyway, just in case). Not to worry. We found some decent prices by doing a little digging.

on the web The Chef's Catalog **(www.chefscatalog.com or 1-800-884-2433)**

has long been known as a source of high-quality cooking items at decent prices. Recently, they were offering a seven-piece set of Le Creuset (enamel-coated cast iron) cookware for $229.99, down from $470. They also had a ten-piece set of Emerilware stainless steel cookware for $199.99, originally $350. Both came with free shipping (on orders of more than $99)—quite a savings when you consider how heavy cookware can be. But the real deal was in their clearance section: A commercial-quality covered saucepan in heavy-gauge anodized aluminum was just $19.99, down from $65! How's that for a bargain?

back to betty Remember Betty Crocker coupons? They're boxtop coupons—each worth a certain number of points—on Betty Crocker–brand products that you can redeem when purchasing products from the company's catalog (or now its Web site, too).You can still save money with them. At **www.bettycrocker.com/bettystore** we found an eight-piece set of anodized cookware for $199.95 (plus 400 points), originally priced at $399.95. In their clearance section, they had beautiful French copper cookware with stainless steel interiors. A 9.5-inch sauté pan was $119.99, originally $200, and a 2.7-quart covered saucepan was $79.99, originally $150.

web discounter Costco online (**www.costco.com**) was showing a ten-piece set with copper exteriors, aluminum centers, and stainless steel interiors by Cuisinart for $249.99. They also had a Circulon commercial cookware 12-piece set for $199.99 and a Sitram stainless steel 11-piece set for $199.99.

discount superstores Stores like Target, Kmart, Walmart, Bed, Bath and Beyond, Linens 'N Things, and Tuesday Mornings all offer cookware, often at very good prices.

department stores Don't ignore traditional outlets like Marshall Fields, Macy's, Dillards, and Bloomingdales. They all have sales and clearance shelves. Check them out. You can pick up great stuff for half price or even less!

wood cutting boards are back

A few years ago, there was a huge fuss about using plastic cutting boards instead of wooden ones because you could sterilize the plastic. Turns out to be wrong. Bacteria don't incubate on wooden boards, but they grow rapidly on plastic boards at room temperature. Always wash any cutting board with soap and hot water after using it.

● To remove odors and dirt from a wooden cutting board, make a paste of baking soda and water. Rub the paste into the board, then rinse and allow the board to air dry.

- To clean a butcher's block, coat it with coarse salt and let it sit for several hours or overnight. The salt absorbs fats and oils, and when you brush off the salt, you brush off the greasy stuff, too.

the cutting edge

Good-quality knives are not only much safer to use but will save you money and time. How much does quality cost? Costco was offering a 12-piece set in a block by J. A. Henckles (high quality) for $168.99. Sound pricey? A  seven-piece Henckles set at Target was going for $149.99 and an 8-piece set of Wusthof (top quality) was selling for $299.99 on the Chef's Catalog website **(www.chefscata-log.com)**, and that was the discount price!

- You actually need only four knives: a small paring knife, a larger chef's knife, a curved-edge cleaver, and a serrated bread knife. Buy the best quality you can afford (and use them for 25 years or more). Cheap tip: Check in Chinese shops for a time-saving curved-edge vegetable cleaver, usually priced around $25.
- Sharpen your good knives after each use. Run the blade along a butcher's steel for ten or so strokes. Your knives will stay sharper much longer. A whetstone or electric sharpener can also be used to keep knives sharp.
- Store knives in a wooden block or on a magnetic strip with the tips pointing up. Use a wooden cutting board, because hard plastic and stone tend to dull knife blades.

do-it-yourself kitchen tools

- Make a sturdy funnel by cutting a clean plastic 1/2- or 1-gallon jug (milk, orange juice, or the like) in half with a sharp, heavy knife or kitchen shears. Use the half containing the spout for your funnel. (Use the bottom half as a saucer for a potted plant, to start seeds in, to store cleaning products under the sink, as a portable dog water dish, or for just about anything else.)
- If you need a temporary funnel for dry ingredients, clip one corner of a small paper bag. For cool liquids, cut off the corner of a heavy plastic bag.
- Don't spend money on a cake-decorating bag. Spoon icing into a self-sealing plastic bag and seal it. Squeeze all the icing to one corner and cut a small opening in the corner. Practice your design on the side of the icing bowl or another test surface before working on the cake.

- The same technique can be used for making melted chocolate designs. A big plus is that you can melt the chocolate right in the bag (immersed in a bowl of hot water), making cleanup a breeze.

- Old herb and spice bottles with shaker tops are invaluable. Wash them well and let them dry thoroughly. Then fill them with flour, cornmeal, cinnamon sugar, confectioners' sugar, cocoa powder, or anything else you might need for sprinkling on baked goods or coating surfaces where dough will be rolled out.

- Don't have a flour sifter? You don't actually need one: Sift flour through a kitchen sieve.

hand blender

Most kitchen gadgets are just a waste of money and precious kitchen storage space. But one real time-saver is the hand held blender. You can use it to puree foods—from spaghetti sauce to baby food—right in the pot. (Of course, you have to let the food cool a bit first.) You can also use the blender to make instant milkshakes and smoothies right in the glass.

the right baking pans

If you bake, getting the right baking pans can make a huge difference in the results you get. What you want are heavy duty, shiny metal pans. They won't warp like lighter weight pans. And they'll produce cookies, cakes, pastries, and breads that are golden in color. With dark-colored pans, which absorb heat, you are more like to get burnt or dry results. Also look for pans that have a nonstick finish.

honey: don't toss it out

If that jar of honey has crusted over (called sugaring), place the open jar in boiling water until the original texture is restored. You can also liquefy honey in a microwave.

Beauty on a Budget

- ● dressing for less
- ● chic looks for little investment
- ● cosmetic caper...

dressing for
Less

fashion-plus musts

For a dynamic working wardrobe, you'll need a well-made blazer or two, two skirts, and two pairs of slacks. The skirts and slacks should not be all the same color, but they should all go well with the jacket. Solid colors are more versatile and date less quickly than patterns or plaids, but you don't have to think only in dark solid colors. Look for fabrics you can wear year-round, such as lightweight wool, challis, sturdy cotton, linen, and silk, and buy the highest-quality basic pieces you can. By investing in well-made basics, you'll actually save money, because the clothes will last longer and look better even after numerous cleanings. Always check the label on a new garment for the care required to avoid spending more on dry cleaning than you have to. It's well worth the money to dry-clean a suit, but do you really want to pay to clean shirts and blouses, too?

the rule of three

When you're considering a clothing purchase, be sure each piece passes the rule of three: Can you think of 3 things to wear it with, 3 places to wear it to, and 3 ways to accessorize it?

For example, you spy a poppy-red, washable silk blouse on sale. You can wear it with your linen suit and a scarf for the office, with a paisley challis skirt and your antique gold earring and necklace set for dinner out, and with black wool slacks and a brocade vest for casual entertaining (three outfits, three places, three accessories). If you can't quickly come up with three pairings, places, and presentations, forget it! It's just not worth the cost.

time to shop: stores galore

Clothing stores are much more varied than they once were. At both high-end department stores (such as Nordstrom and Saks Fifth Avenue) and discount stores (such as Kohl's and T. J. Maxx), you can find bargains and less-than-bargains—it's your job to be a savvy shopper.

high end These stores (Nordstrom, Saks, Barneys, and the like) cater to the well-to-do and carry designer labels with correspondingly high prices. Does that mean a penny pincher should never shop at them? No! Even the priciest department stores have sales, including clearance sales, where you can pick up extremely well-made clothing at reduced prices.

mid-range These department stores (Macy's, Dillard's, and the like) also have designer sections, but they carry a large inventory of mass-market designer labels, such as DKNY (Donna Karan), Chaps (Ralph Lauren), and Lizwear (Liz Claiborne). These stores sometimes have fabulous sales. (At Macy's post-Christmas sale, we picked up an $80 cocktail dress for $19.99!)

discount clothing chains These stores (T.J. Maxx, Kohl's, Daffy's, and the like) carry a hodgepodge of clothing, including designer fashion, all at significant discounts. For example, T.J. Maxx sells brand names at 20 percent to 60 percent off retail. On their Web site recently, Kohl's was selling Gloria Vanderbilt stretch capris for $21.99, discounted from about $36. And Daffy's was advertising men's Italian sports shirts for $26.99 to $29.99, discounted from about $98 to $118. So the savings can be terrific.

specialty stores In these stores (Gap, Banana Republic, Abercrombie & Fitch, and the like), the retail prices, like those in high- and mid-range department stores, are often fairly steep, but their clearance racks can yield fantastic finds and are well worth a visit.

outstanding outlets

Are factory outlet stores and malls really full of great bargains? Sometimes. Are they worth the trip? That depends—on how close they are, on what you're shopping for, and on how astute you are about prices. You can find some outstanding bargains at outlets (up to 75 percent off the retail price), but a designer or upscale item is still going to cost you, even if it's deeply discounted. At an L.L. Bean outlet, for instance, we found that the clothes weren't much of a bargain (half off, but still $60 for a casual dress), but Teva sandals (normally $40 to $80) were priced at $29.99. That's still not cheap, but it's not bad for a high-end product. Unfortunately, what you find will be the luck of the draw, but for a major shopping trip, try the following:

O Know the general prices of the merchandise before you go.

O Look for outlet malls that are anchored by a few well-known names (Gap,

Burlington Coat Factory, Saks) and that have at least three stores you're interested in.

O Get there early and walk the stores to get an overview of what they carry and the prices, making notes to yourself so you won't forget to go back later.

O Examine the merchandise carefully. Some big-name companies produce special lines just for their outlets, and the quality isn't always as high as their retail counterparts.

O Wear comfortable shoes and bring snacks and water. You'll last longer and won't have to stop to eat.

how super are superstores?

Stores such as Target, Kmart, and Wal-Mart can be super sources of inexpensive clothing, but you have to know how to use them. Although these stores sell mostly casual clothing, they are also good places to pick up trendy gear at a minimal cost. Both Target and Kmart have their own house brands (Cherokee, Route 66), which tend to cost less than national name brands and are quite well made. All three chains have contracts with celebrity designers (such as Kathy Ireland, Jaclyn Smith, Mossimo), allowing them to offer more trendy looks at lower prices. Always make a point of checking the clearance racks (usually toward the back of the department) at the end of a season. You can pick up stuff for 75 percent off or more (say, a $16 sweater for $4.99).

price clubs

These big box stores may surprise you. Price clubs offer a variety of clothing, including major clothing lines, often at fantastic bargains. On a recent expedition to Costco, we spotted women's Speedo swimsuits for $21, crinkle-cloth dresses for $15, and designer shorts for $12. SAM's Club offered Polo jeans for men at $24.99 and their store brand, Members Mark, men's jeans for $11.98. The only drawbacks to clothes shopping at price clubs are that you can't count on seeing the same merchandise from one visit to the next, there often aren't any dressing rooms, and the stock tends to be strictly seasonal.

thrift stores

Although your local Salvation Army or Goodwill shop can still delight or disappoint, there are a few new wrinkles.

consignment stores These are popping up all over (especially for children's clothing), and you can score excellent deals at them. You can find them in the Yellow Pages under Consignment Shops—often with cute names like Once Again or Second Time Around. Although they sell mostly used clothing, their standards are pretty high. The clothing must be in good condition for sale. At a consignment store, you can sell, buy, or trade gently used, good-looking clothes. Buffalo Exchange, a consignment chain thriving in the Southwest and West, hires "trendspotters" to ensure the fashion aspects of the inventory. You'll find a lot of vintage 1960s, '70s, and '80s clothing at consignment stores, but you'll also discover traditional looks and even some new clothing.

thrift stores These range from Goodwill warehouses to opera society stores, and the merchandise can be just as varied. In high-end thrift stores, located in upscale neighborhoods or run to benefit a charity or cultural institution (such as an opera company) that attracts a fairly well-to-do clientele, you may find Armani, Valentino, or other designer clothing—some of it barely worn. The downside is that you will pay more for the clothes; the upside is that what you pay will still be a fraction of the full price. You also have the other end of the thrift-shop spectrum—stores that offer well-worn, uninspiring collections of rags.

coupons for clothes?

Now here's some good news: Coupons are not just for food.

○ Check major department-store ads in your newspaper. They often have coupons for 10 to 20 percent off. Combine that with a sale, and you can snap up some dazzling duds at truly bargain-basement prices.

○ Outlet malls also frequently offer books of coupons (sometimes for a small fee) for their stores.

○ If you have a store credit card, check the inserts with your bill each month. You may find a coupon tucked in there to lure you back to the store. And department stores sometimes have special sales offering an extra 10 to 20 percent off for using their card.

getting discounts on discounted items

Some tips to save you even more at the checkout counter:

button-off bargains If you find a garment you really like and a button or two is missing, you may be able to buy the piece at a discount, especially if it is an end-of-season item. A good discount can more than pay for new buttons.

highly irregular Items marked as irregular may not be perfect in size or color, but they are usually free of substantial damage and are often a real deal. Those marked as seconds or thirds should be examined with a fine-tooth comb, however, as they may have serious flaws. You may still decide to buy such items; just look carefully first to see whether you can live with, cover, or repair the flaws.

life extenders for new clothes

Check all the stitching before wearing a new piece of clothing. If you see any loose thread ends, fasten or trim them or pull them to the wrong side of the garment and secure them.

○ Reinforce stitching on patch pockets by sewing a tiny triangle at each top corner of the pocket.

○ Use iron-on patches on the inside of the knees of pants, especially jeans. You can use this trick on shirt or jacket elbows that will get a lot of rough wear, too. Hidden iron-on patches are particularly useful for kids' clothing.

○ Use cotton underarm shields to protect your favorite dresses from perspiration stains. Either tack the shields on or sew on snaps to secure them.

○ Check the stitching on all fasteners—buttons, hooks and eyes, snaps—and resew them securely if any are loose. Machine-stitch around the edges of Velcro pieces to keep them from pulling away from the fabric.

○ Let your clothes air out or dry before you put them away. Don't wear the same items day after day; allow at least 24 hours for moisture to evaporate.

○ Use a cotton ball soaked in witch hazel to wipe away body oils around your neck and wrists before getting dressed to avoid staining collars and cuffs.

GETTING THE MOST FOR YOUR MONEY

To get the best value, look for pieces that are of as high quality as you can afford. Here are some signs of quality:

☑ Fabric that doesn't hold wrinkles after being crushed by hand

☑ Fabric cut on the straight grain (or on the bias, if that's the style of the garment)

☑ Linings that are smooth and invisible from the outside of the garment

☑ Plaids, stripes, and cross seams that match evenly

☑ Flat, smooth seams with finished edges

☑ Straight, smooth, unbroken stitches

☑ Hems and seams that are even in width and allow for alterations

☑ Collars and lapels with even points that do not curl upward

☑ Zippers that lie flat and work smoothly

☑ Securely sewn trims, pockets, buttons, and fasteners

the right coat

Coats can end up costing you big bucks unless you're a smart shopper. When you shop for a coat, keep in mind that this item will get a lot of wear and tear, so pick a coat that is well made. Try these coat-buying tips:

○ Buy at the end of the season. Department stores often have great sales on high-quality coats they want to get rid of before the new season starts. Depending on where you live, January and February are often the best months.

○ Make your coat do double duty. Instead of buying a wool coat for warmth and a raincoat for wet weather, buy a raincoat with a zip-out lining. It will see you through all but the worst cold weather (when you can wear a sweater underneath). In fact, any waterproof shell with a warm, removable lining can easily get you from fall through spring. At the Burlington Coat Factory site (www.bcfdirect.com), we found a Bill Blass microfiber rain jacket with removable lining for $79.99, originally priced at $175!

○ Check out thrift stores. They sometimes have great coats, especially if you like a funky, retro look.

bathing beauty

A good-quality swimsuit can be a good investment. Cheap bathing suits usually don't last very long, but if you don't swim often or plan to wear a suit only a few times, quality may not matter that much to you. Here are some buying tips:

○ Look for end- or beginning-of-season sales (typically May and August).

○ If you find a suit you love at a bargain price, buy two. You'll double your savings and won't have to shop again soon.

○ Take care of your suit. Rinse it in cold water after each use to remove salt or chlorine and hand-wash or machine-wash it on the gentle cycle. Do not twist or wring it out.

making leather last

A brand-new leather coat is a hefty investment, which is why dedicated penny pinchers often buy used ones at thrift or consignment stores or garage sales and clean them up. But a new leather coat will usually last for years (especially if you stick to a classic style) and can truly keep the wind out (which is why bikers wear them). Besides, for many people they are the ultimate in cool. So if you make the investment, protect it!

○ Waterproofing your leather garment can protect it from minor staining. The products sold for waterproofing leather work fine on shoes and boots, but for soft leathers, you might be better off using a temporary fluorocarbon spray such as 3M Scotchguard every few weeks.

○ Cold cream is as good for leather as it is for your face. Rub it in with your fingers and wipe off excess with a cloth or paper towel.

○ Removing stains from leather is tricky, so it's best to leave them to an expert.

○ If you want to darken leather, use a cloth dipped in ammonia. Apply as evenly as possible to avoid streaks.

new clothes from old

If you have some old favorites stashed in your closet or drawers that are no longer in style or are worn out in places, try overhauling them in one of these ways:

○ Transform a too-tight pullover sweater into a classy cardigan. Measure the exact center of the front, mark it, and machine-stitch down each side of the centerline. Cut from top to bottom between the lines of stitching. Finish the edges with ribbon or decorative sewing tape.

○ If the sleeves of a sweater are stretched out of shape or are too short, use the above stitch-and-cut idea around each armhole to turn the sweater into a sweater vest! Then use the cut-off sweater sleeves to make leg warmers for kids!

○ If you've been a bridesmaid more times than you care to think about and have a slew of essentially unusable dresses clogging the back of your closet, look closely at each: Can it be made into a cocktail dress by taking up the hem and removing some decoration? Or might removing the sleeves or altering the neckline do the trick? A trip to the notions area of a fabric store can often provide just the right touch.

○ How about that outdated dress in a great fabric? Cut the top from the bottom and, with a little stitching here and there, you can have a great blouse or a great skirt.

○ Denim, wool, or corduroy dresses can be transformed into jazzy jumpers. Cut away the collar or reshape the neckline into a V or a scoop. Be sure to cut the armholes slightly larger to accommodate a blouse underneath. Cut facings from the sleeve fabric or face the new neck and armholes with bias binding.

○ Turn a full slip that just doesn't work anymore into a half-slip: Cut off the bodice, stitch a casing at the top, and insert elastic. If the top is in decent shape, hem the bottom of it to make a new camisole.

stalking perfect stockings

It may sound crazy, but your panty hose will last longer if you freeze them when they're brand new. After wetting them thoroughly and wringing out excess water, put the panty hose in a plastic bag and store them in the freezer. When you need stockings, thaw them out and let them dry.

○ Panty hose resist runs much better and go on more easily if you starch them very lightly first.

○ To stop a run in a stocking, rub the run with wet soap, spray it with hair spray, or dab on clear nail polish.

○ When you see a really good sale on microfiber tights, buy, buy, buy! They last much longer than panty hose, keep your legs warmer in winter, are easier to clean, and are almost always in style. You can find tights made from other fabrics that are less expensive than microfiber tights, but the cheaper tights tend to lose their shape rather quickly, and no one wants to wear baggy tights.

if the shoe fits . . .

Don't buy shoes strictly by size. Walk around in them for several minutes before making a final decision. A size 7 shoe, for example, can vary in size, depending on the style and manufacturer, or your feet can swell up to a half size larger if you've been walking a lot. If you're shopping for shoes that you'll be wearing regularly to work or for sports, buy the best-quality shoes you can afford. They will last longer and look better longer, if you take care of them.

○ Coat good shoes with a stain-repellent product or even plain shoe polish to protect them.

○ Don't wear the same shoes every day. Wear them one day and let them air the next.

○ If the heels are starting to wear down, take the shoes to a repair shop—and consider putting protectors on the heels.

○ Don't spend a bundle on shoes or sandals that you will be wearing without stockings or socks. Your sweat will wear the shoes out faster. And summer styles tend to change rapidly. So save on summer footwear and get a really great pair of leather boots for the fall and winter.

○ Avoid wearing your good shoes on the streets. Keep your nice shoes at the office and wear a pair of inexpensive sports shoes to and from work or when you're going outside on an errand. Your shoes will thank you and so will your feet, ankles, and legs, not to mention your back!

○ New shoes can be slippery. To avoid slippage, lightly sand the soles or apply nonslip bathtub appliqués, strips of adhesive tape, or bicycle tube repair patches to the soles.

twice as nice

If the collar of a shirt is starting to fray, don't get rid of the garment. Carefully remove the collar at the seam where it is joined to the shirt, turn the collar over, and reattach it with the unworn side showing. Or sew the seam closed and leave the shirt collarless. If the cuffs are fraying, cover them with bias or satin binding (depending on the style of the shirt). If you use a contrasting color for the binding, also bind the edges of the collar.

old reliable denim

Turn that pair of old jeans into a skirt. Cut the jeans to the desired skirt length, leaving an inch for hemming. Then remove the inseam stitching. For a straight skirt, just sew those edges together and hem the bottom. To add flair, cut triangular pieces from the leg material you cut off and sew the triangles into the openings formed by the inseam edges.

○ Keep jean hems from unraveling by attaching a wide strip of iron-on mending material inside the bottom hem.

○ Gussy up a plain denim jacket with decorative stitching, buttons, braid, or any other trim.

○ Give your old straight-leg jeans a new flare or bell-bottom effect. Working from the bottom up of each outside leg seam, remove 6 to 12 inches of stitching. Cut two triangular pieces from old jeans or contrasting fabric to add the amount of flare you want to each leg. Stitch the triangles to the edges of the outside seams.

SAVE THOSE HOSE!!

Before you toss out that old pair of panty hose, check out some of the ways you can reuse them:

☑ Stuff 'em: Cut up old panty hose and store them in a plastic bag. Now you have FREE stuffing on hand for making or repairing toys, dolls, pillows, or seat cushions.

☑ String 'em: Use panty hose to secure boxes, stacks of newspapers and magazines.

☑ Tie 'em: Use panty hose to tie up plants such as tomatoes, beans, and other climbers.

☑ Scrub 'em: Put a sponge inside sections of panty hose to make scrubber sponges.

☑ Rag 'em: Old panty hose make terrific lint-free cloths for dusting and other chores. They're also great for applying finishes to unstained wood.

☑ Repel 'em: Fill panty hose with clippings of your hair or your dog's and hang the hose in the garden to scare Bambi & Co.

- Add eye-catching stripes of colored rickrack, embroidered braid, or metallic ribbon to the bottom of your jean legs. Use several stripes of varying trims for extra pizzazz.

shoe shine

- To remove salt stains from winter boots, wipe them with a solution of 1 cup water and 1 tablespoon white vinegar.
- Cover ugly scuff marks with a matching color of acrylic paint, indelible felt marker, or crayon. Typewriter correction fluid makes a great cover-up for scuff marks on white shoes; try a bit of India ink on black shoes.
- Remove light scuff marks with an art-gum eraser. To remove tar and grease stains from white shoes, try a little nail-polish remover.
- To speed-clean patent leather, rub a little petroleum jelly over the shoes and buff. Or try a spritz of glass cleaner.
- Don't throw out hardened shoe polish. Put the metal container in a bowl of hot water until the polish is soft again.
- If you need a quick shine, rub hand lotion or cream over your leather shoes and buff with a tissue.

smooth suede shoes

- Perk up the nap on suede shoes by rubbing a dry sponge or a stiff upholstery brush over them after each wearing. To get rid of stubborn scuff marks on suede, gently rub with very fine sandpaper. (An emery board works great.)
- Steam-clean suede shoes by holding them over a pan of boiling water. Once the steam has raised the nap of the shoes, stroke the suede with a soft brush in one direction only. Let the shoes dry completely before wearing them.

on canvas

- Extend the life of canvas shoes by spraying a fabric protector or starch over them before wearing.
- Clean canvas sneakers quickly with a spray-on carpet cleaner. Scrub with a toothbrush, let dry, and then brush with a dry brush.
- Help your canvas tennis shoes keep their shape longer: After washing and drying them, stuff the shoes with paper towels, cover them with liquid starch, and let them dry.

purse perfection

Purses, like shoes, can be a major investment. Again, before you buy, consider how you will use the purse, the season in which you'll use it, and the wear and tear it will face. Also consider what you will put in it; do you need a pocket for a cell phone, for example?

○ For your everyday purse, which gets the most use, invest in a high-quality leather purse in a neutral color. (Black is always good, as is cream.) Check out holiday sales at department stores, factory outlets, price clubs, and shoe stores. A high-quality purse in good condition is hard to find at a thrift store, but it is not impossible.

○ Microfiber purses can take a lot of abuse and maintain their good looks.

○ Save on summer bags. They usually don't last more than one season, so buy straw or canvas bags on sale and wear them till they fall apart. (Superstores sometimes offer good variety and great sales on casual purses.)

○ Evening bags that are real gems can often be found at thrift stores and garage sales. Clutch purses from the 1940s, '50s, and '60s can be picked up for a pittance and can add swank to an outfit.

○ If you have a special occasion and can't find the right purse, pick up a cloth purse in the right color and decorate it yourself with trims.

pamper your purses

If you've spent serious money on a high-quality leather purse, it will last a long time, if you take care of it.

○ When you're storing the bag, gently stuff it with tissue paper or newspaper to maintain its shape. Then place it in an old flannel or cotton pillowcase to protect the exterior.

○ Clean and condition your leather purses by wiping them with a damp cloth and mild soap, or apply a colorless leather conditioner with a dry cloth.

○ Keep the metal trim on your bag from tarnishing by coating it with clear nail polish.

○ Bring the shine back to a patent-leather purse by spraying it with a little glass cleaner and gently drying and buffing it with cotton cloths or paper towels.

○ Replace a broken purse strap with a heavy chain necklace or belt.

chic looks for little
Investment!

hats off

Try a few simple tricks to keeping nice hats looking like new (or to perk up second-hand steals):

○ Brush interior leather hatbands with a little melted paraffin to prevent oil and dirt from accumulating.

○ Brush and sponge a straw hat regularly. If it's especially dirty, run a hand vacuum over it.

○ Add sheen to a dull straw hat by applying a light coating of glycerin or hair spray.

○ After laundering a beret, slip it over a dinner plate to dry. Just be sure you use a plate that's the same size as the hat!

○ Keep a felt hat looking fresh by using a soft brush on it after each wearing. Store the hat in a plastic bag.

○ If you're caught in the rain with your best felt hat, blot the raindrops with a tissue. Then rub a wad of tissue paper over the rain spots using a smooth, circular motion. A coffee can works great as a hat stand while your hat dries.

○ Revive a tired felt hat by holding it over steaming water for a second or two and then brushing with the nap.

be sure to wear some flowers in your hair

Fresh flowers are among the simplest—and, if you have a garden, cheapest—ways of adding glamour and elegance to an evening ensemble. You can wear flowers in your hair, on your clothing, attached to a ribbon tied around your wrist, or pinned to a hat.

○ A white gardenia pinned next to a chignon not only looks lovely but also adds a wonderful fragrance.

- Roses, either single large blossoms or sprigs of tiny tea roses, are always in fashion.
- Daisies last for hours and create a summery look.
- A nosegay of chrysanthemums in rusts, browns, and yellows will signal the advent of autumn.
- Variegated ivy, either tucked behind a flower or on its own, can be a real eye-catcher.
- Be daring: Fresh sprigs of herbs, such as thyme, rosemary, purple sage, bay leaves, and lavender, are quite ornamental.
- For a Christmastime adornment, use sprigs of holly, preferably with berries. Just be careful not to prick yourself.

fits like a glove

When trying on new gloves, clench your fist to see how comfortable the glove feels. Make sure the glove opening falls right at your wrist and palm joint and that the seams are well sewn.

- To keep gloves looking as good as new, always pull them back into shape right after removing them.
- Remove stains on leather gloves by rubbing them with an art-gum eraser or white cornmeal.
- If you get an oily stain on leather gloves, dust them with cornstarch and leave it on overnight. In the morning, brush off the residue.

belt up

- Fix a belt that is too small by adding another hole. With a pen, make a dot where you want the hole. Lay the belt on a piece of scrap wood. Place the point of an awl, ice pick, or large nail on the dot and tap it vigorously a few times with a hammer to pierce the leather.
- As with metal purse trimming, keep metal belt buckles bright with a coat of clear nail polish. The polish also helps prevent scratches.

special scarf effects

Scarves and shawls are a simple, quick way to add color and flair. They can also provide just the right finishing touch to a simple outfit. But they can be pricey when bought at department stores. Keep a lookout for bargains at garage sales and flea markets. Search the remnant bins at fabric stores for beautiful pieces of silk, rayon, challis, gauze, lace, or any other fabric that hangs well. Take the pieces home, cut them to size, hem them, and voila! Gorgeous designer scarves at penny-pincher prices.

- Wear a large silk or lace scarf as a shawl over a cocktail dress for an elegant evening look.
- Tie a brightly colored oblong scarf around the band of a straw hat, letting the ends hang down your back, for that country-fair charm.
- Brighten up a solid-color T-shirt dress by tying a scarf around your waist or a shawl around your hips.
- To dress up a plain winter coat, drape a scarf or shawl around the shoulders and partially under the lapel.
- Do you have an heirloom lace tablecloth you never use? Fold it in half and use it as a shawl.
- Twist together or braid two to three oblong scarves in contrasting colors to use as a belt.

button, button

You can use interesting buttons in an endless variety of ways. Be on the lookout for them at garage sales and flea markets, and don't pass up big bags o' buttons at fabric stores.

- Sew buttons around the band of an old denim or plain fabric hat. Buttons are a particularly useful decoration for a kid's hat, making it instantly identifiable without putting the child's name in it.
- Trim a plain vest or jacket with a set of buttons along the bottom edge or the lapel. Group buttons of the same color but different styles for added interest.
- Transform a plain blouse, dress, or jumper by changing the buttons from drab to dazzling. You'll get a custom look for very little cost.
- Make buttons stay on longer by dabbing a bit of clear nail polish over the threads to strengthen their hold.
- Instead of sewing on buttons with thread, use dental floss; it's stronger and keeps the buttons in place much longer.

new looks from old

Try the following to give old jewelry a rebirth or to create new pieces out of found objects:

○ Hang a baby's ring on a chain for an instant heirloom necklace.

○ Drill holes though coins collected on a special vacation and string them on a bracelet or necklace chain. Or use an inexpensive craft-store kit to create unique earrings.

○ Collect subway tokens from foreign travels and hot-glue them to a pin backing.

○ Use a single stud-type pierced earring as a lapel pin.

○ Stitch single earrings to hatbands for eye-catching decorations.

pinups

If you own or find a brooch with the pin on the back broken, don't toss it:

○ Stitch it to a hatband.

○ Put it on a chain to make a necklace.

○ Sew it to a jacket (but remember to clip it off when cleaning the jacket).

○ Repair the brooch yourself by using hot-glue or superstrength glue to attach it to a new pin backing.

beaded beauties

Beading is a simple craft, and the variety and modest price of beads make beading a skill worth learning. Look for beads at craft or fabric stores or specialty bead stores. You can find bags of beads and bead kits on the markdown aisle. When you see a good price, stock up and keep them on hand for a variety of projects.

QUICK FIXES FOR JEWELRY

● To repair chips on gold- or silver-plated jewelry, use a fine-pointed paintbrush and a can of gold or silver spray paint. Spray a small puddle of paint on a piece of cardboard, dip in the brush, and touch up your jewelry.

● To unknot a chain, lay your necklace on a piece of wax paper. Put a drop or two of baby oil or salad oil directly on the knot. Use a pair of needles to gently untangle the knot.

● If the post on a pierced earring has broken off, use a nail file to smooth off any residual glue on the earring back; then apply superstrength glue, and mount a new post.

GET A
GLUE GUN

If you like to do your own trimming or make your own jewelry, a hot-glue gun is one of the best investments you can make. You can buy glue guns in craft stores, fabric stores, drug stores, and superstores at a variety of prices, generally not expensive. Most come with a small supply of the glue sticks that they use. Make sure you can buy extra glue sticks for a particular gun easily, because different guns sometimes require different-size sticks. Follow the manufacturer's instructions carefully, and get crafting!

○ Sew or glue beads to formed or stretchy fabric headbands.

○ Sew tiny pearl-like beads along a blouse or jacket edge.

○ Buy an inexpensive black or white cloth clutch purse and cover it with matching beads for an instant antique.

○ Dig out that old felt beret from your closet and create a pattern of contrasting beads all over the top and edges.

string of beads

Go one step further with beads and make your own necklaces. If you're using thread or string, dab clear nail polish on one end and let it dry before starting to string beads.

○ To keep the whole strand from coming apart if the string breaks, tie knots between the beads.

○ Out of string? Use waxed dental floss, nylon fishing line, or yarn coated with beeswax.

some classy combinations:

○ Thread wooden beads on a leather thong.

○ Alternate long silver beads with small, round dark blue or turquoise beads.

○ String beads in different shades of the same color for a subtle effect.

keeping your ice in trays

Use plastic ice cube trays to organize your earrings and rings. The trays don't cost much to start with, but if you keep an eye out, you'll find them at garage sales for pennies.

TWINKLE, TWINKLE, LITTLE JEWEL!

Jewelry is simple to clean and restore to its former beauty. Here's how:

- **Amber:** Put 2 drops linseed oil on a cotton ball and rub; wipe off residue.

- **Amethyst, aquamarine, emerald, garnet, jade, sapphire, ruby, topaz, tourmaline:** Immerse in 1/2 cup warm water with 1 tablespoon ammonia; scrub.

- **Costume jewelry:** Sprinkle a layer of baking powder; brush off. Shine pewter with silver polish. For brass, copper, chrome, or steel, use brass cleaner.

- **Diamond:** Soak in 1 cup hot water with 1/4 cup ammonia and 1 tablespoon detergent for 20 minutes; scrub with a toothbrush. Rinse, dip in rubbing alcohol, and air-dry.

- **Gold:** Soak in 1 cup warm water with 1/2 cup ammonia for 10 to 15 minutes. Then gently scrub with soft toothbrush and rinse. Air-dry.

- **Ivory:** Rub with denatured alcohol.

- **Lapis lazuli, malachite:** Use detergent in cool water and soft toothbrush.

- **Pearl:** Soak in mild soap and water solution. Rinse and buff with a flannel cloth. Do not soak a string of pearls; clean each individually with a soapy cloth.

- **Silver:** Wash in a mild detergent; then use silver polish.

- **Turquoise:** Shine with a chamois; then polish with a dry toothbrush.

cosmetic Caper...

WHAT YOU REALLY NEED
VS. ALL YOU REALLY DON'T

Rx: H₂O

One of the best things you can do for your skin—and for your overall health—is also one of the cheapest and easiest things to do: Drink water. Not juice, not soft drinks, not coffee, not sports drinks. Good old plain water. At least six 8-ounce glasses a day. Eight glasses would be better. To make it easy on yourself, buy a sports bottle that holds 24 ounces, fill it with water, and drink it down three times a day.

a clean face on the cheap

You don't need to buy special cleansers to achieve healthy, clean skin. A mild, unscented soap with a neutral pH (such as Dove or Basis) is the best bet for every member of the family. And you can use it on your face as well as your body, saving you money on extra products. If you want to exfoliate, simply rub soap over a washcloth, then gently rub the soapy cloth over your skin.

go for yogurt

If you want to treat yourself to a special facial cleanser, boil 1/3 cup of water and pour it over 1 teaspoon of either chamomile tea (for dry or normal skin) or peppermint tea (for oily skin). Let the mixture steep until it is completely cool; then strain it and discard the solids. In a small bowl, beat together 5 tablespoons of plain yogurt with the tea mixture until they are well mixed. For dry to normal skin, stir in 1 teaspoon of wheat-germ oil or sesame oil; for oily skin, stir in 1 teaspoon of lemon juice. Pour the mixture into a sterilized jar with a tight-fitting lid. The mixture will keep in the refrigerator for up to five days. Always shake before using.

do-it-yourself cleansing cloths

A hot item in drugstores and beauty shops is prepackaged cleansing cloths for your face. You pull out one of these little guys, get it wet, wash your face, then toss it. Now we can see immediately that this is a waste of resources and money (these cloths are not cheap), but the convenience factor woos us against our better judgment. What to do? Make your own. For "at home" wipes, cut up those old, very soft but stained T-shirts into 4-inch squares. Keep them in an old, clean butter tub near your bathroom sink and use them with your pH-balanced soap. You won't find a cloth that is gentler on the face. If you make or purchase a net washing bag, you can toss the used cloths in there and then just throw the bag in with your regular washing.

- For cleaning cloths on the go (when traveling), purchase cotton gauze pads in bulk. When you want to wash your face, wet a pad, rub it over a bar of pH-balanced soap, apply to your face, rinse, then toss the pad.

- If you want a bit more exfoliation, sprinkle a little cornmeal on your dampened cloth and wash as usual; the cornmeal will provide just the right amount of friction without being too harsh on your delicate facial skin.

skin to beat the band

Save money on moisturizers: Baby oil or plain mineral oil can be just as effective as expensive cosmetics in softening your skin or removing makeup. For daytime use, sunscreen with a sun protection factor (SPF) of at least 15 can do double duty as your moisturizer and your skin protector.

peaches-and-cream complexion

Did you know you can use peaches and cream to help you get a peaches-and-cream complexion? Blend one ripe peach with enough heavy cream to make a soft, creamy mixture. Massaged into the skin once a day, this stimulating, rich moisturizer can help you achieve a real peaches-and-cream complexion. Store it in the refrigerator.

making up is hard to do

You don't have to spend a small fortune on makeup. The brands sold in drug-stores or discount stores will give you ample variety to choose from as to skin type and personal preference and will be much cheaper than similar products sold at a department-store cosmetics counter. Clip coupons for brands you really like (October and May are good beauty coupon months) and watch for newspaper ads about sales.

must haves:

- Foundation: to even out the complexion and cover flaws
- Blush: to give a healthy glow
- Mascara: to enhance the eyes
- Lipstick: to enhance the lips

nice to haves:

- Eyeliner pencil
- Eye shadow
- Face powder
- Lip liner
- Concealer for under-eye circles or blemishes

Makeup is perishable, especially eye makeup. Bacteria from your eyes can be introduced to the product and vice versa. Replace your shadows and pencils every six months; your mascara, every three months.

double duty does it

Makeup can really add up, so look for products that do two things to get double your money's worth. For example, buy a foundation or moisturizer with sun-block, a combination foundation-and-powder compact, an eyeliner pencil that can also tend to your eyebrows, or an extra-moisturizing lipstick or lip liner for color and comfort.

toned up

A toner tightens the pores temporarily. You don't actually need a toner for good skin care, but many people like the feeling of cool, tight skin after they use a toner. Instead of shelling out for commercial products, keep a bottle of witch hazel in the refrigerator and get the same fresh feeling for a whole lot less. If you want to pamper yourself a bit (and who doesn't?), try this herbal milk toner:

○ Bring 2/3 cup of milk to a boil and pour it over an herbal teabag in a cup or bowl. Cover the cup and let the mixture steep while it cools. If you have dry to normal skin, use whole or 2 percent milk and chamomile tea; if you have oily skin, use 1 percent or skim milk and peppermint tea. When the mixture is completely cooled, strain it through a piece of cheesecloth or unbleached muslin. Pour the mixture into a sterilized jar or bottle with a tight-fitting lid. The toner will keep in the refrigerator for up to five days. To use: After cleaning your face, soak a cotton ball in the toner and wipe it over your skin.

acne

Though instinct might tell you otherwise, acne-prone skin needs to be treated extremely gently. If you are using a harsh exfoliation method or are rubbing too hard and long with a washcloth when you clean your face, you will actually increase oil production and eruptions, so easy does it. Follow these acne-treatment tips:

○ Avoid the sun. Although exposure to sun seems to clear up acne, the results are temporary. A week or two later, the oil-producing sebaceous glands go into high gear, often increasing breakouts.

○ A paste of baking soda and water applied at bedtime will help dry up and draw out pimples overnight.

BAG BUSTERS (AND OTHER EYE SOLUTIONS)

● Store used tea bags in a self-sealing bag in the refrigerator to use on mornings when your eyes are puffy. Place a damp tea bag on each eye for about 10 minutes.

● Cut two slices of raw potato. Lie down and put a slice over each eye. Rest for 15 minutes, then wash away any filmy residue. For red, swollen eyes, substitute cucumber for the potato slices.

● Soak a clean cloth in weak chamomile tea. Then hold the compress over your eyes for 10 to 15 minutes to soothe itchy eyes.

frugal facials

Although a wonderful way to make your skin feel renewed and revitalized, a professional facial can set you back quite a bit. The good news: Homemade facials are every bit as good, and you probably have the ingredients on hand.

◯ Start by filling a bowl with hot water. Drape a towel over your head and keep your face directly over the steam for about 10 minutes.

◯ Next, gently blot your wet face. If you wish, apply a mask (see Make Your Own Masks, below) and let dry. Wash off the mask with cool water.

◯ Soak a cotton ball or soft cloth in witch hazel and gently rub over your face.

◯ Finish by moisturizing.

make your own masks

◯ To help relieve inflammation and irritated facial skin, apply a compress of cool skim milk for 10 minutes, rinse it off with cool water, and then apply a thin coating of face cream.

◯ For a deep-cleansing mask, stroke milk of magnesia on your face with cotton balls, avoiding the eye area. Leave the mask on for 10 minutes. Then gently remove with a warm washcloth and apply a moisturizer.

Good Old Ways

Take a tip or two from days gone by to make your own hair rollers:

• Cut narrow strips of cotton cloth and knot each strip in the middle. Roll a section of your damp hair around the knot and use the loose ends of the cloth to tie the curl in place, or secure it with a bobby pin.

• For a permed look, bend pipe cleaners into U shapes. Section your damp hair into thin strands. With the bend in a pipe cleaner toward the top of your head, weave a strand of hair around the pipe cleaner, going in and out and around both sides of the pipe cleaner. Then twist the pipe-cleaner ends together to secure it.

• For larger curls, cut a paper-towel roll into four sections. Roll damp hair around each section and pin in place.

◯ For dry skin, combine 1 egg yolk with 1 teaspoon of honey and 2 tablespoons of plain yogurt. Apply to clean skin with cotton balls, being careful to avoid the eye area. After 15 minutes, rinse thoroughly with cool water.

◯ For oily skin, make a paste of honey, oatmeal, and lemon juice (use about 2 tablespoons of each). Apply the paste to your face and leave on for 10 minutes. Rinse with warm water. If you're out of oatmeal but have a box of Cheerios or a generic version of it on hand, just grind up a small amount of the cereal and substitute it for the oatmeal in this mask.

○ For normal skin, make a paste of 1/3 cup of finely ground almonds and enough witch hazel to moisten. Apply to face, being careful to avoid the eye area. Leave on for 15 minutes. Then wipe off the mask with tissues and rinse your face with warm water.

the eyes have it

○ Before putting on eye shadow, apply a light coating of cream foundation makeup over the area, blending with your little finger. Be careful not to get the foundation in your eye. Then brush on your eye shadow. The powdery shadow will bind to the foundation and stay in place a lot longer than if you apply it directly to the skin.

○ Tame unwieldy eyebrows by using a dab of petroleum jelly on a clean, soft-bristled toothbrush. Gently brush your eyebrow hairs up and out.

lasting lipstick

○ Your lipstick will last much longer if you use the following method of application: Pat face powder over your lips, apply the lipstick, blot and powder again, then apply a final layer of lipstick.

○ To repair a broken lipstick, use a lighter or long fireplace match to slightly melt the bottom of the broken piece and the top of the remaining lipstick. Press the melted pieces

TEN TRICKS FOR AN OLD TOOTHBRUSH

Never throw out a toothbrush! It still has many uses. (Run it through the dishwasher to clean and sterilize it if needed.) Here are a few ideas:

☑ Use to clean jewelry, with or without a cleaner.

☑ Use to clean small appliances, such as hair dryers, food processors, and juicers.

☑ Use as a mustache or beard brush.

☑ Use as an eyebrow brush.

☑ Use as a cleaning brush for shoes.

☑ Use as a cleaning brush for carpet spots.

☑ Use to scrub grout between tiles.

☑ Use as an infant's hairbrush.

☑ Use as a nailbrush.

☑ Dip in kerosene and use for cleaning oily gunk from motors.

together gently and seal the edges with a clean match or a toothpick. Place the lipstick in the refrigerator until it is completely cool.

a cut above

The key to good-looking hair is almost always a good haircut. Sometimes it pays to spend a little more at a salon for a professional style. (Skip the blow-dry.) But a fancy (expensive!) salon is not the answer. That $60-a-cut stylist could give you just as bad a cut as a $12-a-cut stylist. If you see someone with hair like yours (thick and curly, fine and straight, flyaway, and so forth) whose style you like, make a point of asking her where she got her hair cut; the answer may surprise you.

○ If you live in a city with a professional training salon for hair stylists, check their prices and hours. These are not schools for novices; they are places where professional stylists go to learn a new or specific technique. If you have time to seek out such places, you can often get an excellent cut for a small fee.

○ To lengthen intervals between haircuts, trim your own bangs (if you have them). Spray your hair with water and use a comb to bring down a fine layer of fringe. Holding your comb just above the length you want and trim off the excess hair. Keep bringing down layers, using a comb and fingers, trimming each layer as you go.

shampoo stretch

Commercial shampoos are highly concentrated and much stronger than you really need, especially if you wash your hair every day. Try diluting shampoo by about half with water. Your hair will get just as clean, and you'll save money, too.

highlights for hair

dark hair Simmer 1 teaspoon of allspice, 1 teaspoon of crushed cinnamon, and 1/2 teaspoon of ground cloves in 1 cup of water. Strain the mixture, discarding the solids, and let it cool. Pour the mixture over freshly shampooed hair. Then rinse well.

red hair Brew a cup of regular orange pekoe tea, or dilute some strained beet juice. Pour the cooled liquid through your freshly shampooed hair, wait five minutes, and then rinse well.

brunettes or redheads Pour cooled black coffee over your freshly shampooed hair and then rinse well.

blondes Combine 1 cup of chamomile flowers with 2 cups of boiling water;

simmer for 30 minutes. (Do not bring to a full boil.) Remove the pan from the heat and let the mixture cool for about two hours. Strain the mixture, discarding the solids. Pour the liquid through your hair several times, catching the excess in a bowl. The lightening effect will be increased if you dry your hair in full sunlight and use the rinse regularly.

dandruff destroyers

○ Shake 1 tablespoon of table salt into dry hair. Massage gently into your hair before shampooing. Don't use this treatment if you have any cuts or abrasions on your scalp!

○ Yogurt is reported to help even difficult cases of dandruff. Work a liberal quantity of plain yogurt into your scalp and hair and let it set for an hour. Shampoo as usual.

kitchen hair care

cornstarch For a fast, dry way to clean your hair, just sprinkle some cornstarch over it, especially along the part. Leave the cornstarch in your hair for about five minutes. Then brush it out.

vinegar To add shine to dark hair, stir 1 tablespoon of vinegar into 1 cup of water. Pour the mixture over your hair and then rinse well with plain water.

lemon juice To lighten and brighten blond hair, combine the juice of 1 lemon with 1 cup of water. After shampooing, work the lemon mixture into your hair and then rinse it out well with plain water.

mayonnaise For an old-fashioned conditioner that leaves hair smooth and shiny, coat your hair with mayonnaise, pin it up, and wrap it in plastic wrap or use a shower cap or plastic bag. Leave the mayonnaise on your hair for 30 minutes, then shampoo as usual.

olive-oil combo Combine 3/4 cup of olive oil, 1/2 cup of honey, and the juice of 1 lemon. Rinse your hair with water and towel it dry. Work a small amount of the conditioner into your hair (store the remainder in the refrigerator), comb to distribute evenly, and cover your head with a plastic bag, plastic wrap, or shower cap. Leave on for 1/2 hour. Then shampoo and rinse with water.

pool rules for hair

○ Before swimming in a chlorinated pool, wet your hair thoroughly and work some conditioner through it. The water saturates the hair shafts, making them less likely to absorb the chemicals, and the conditioner protects the exterior of the shafts.

○ Always rinse your hair completely after getting out of the pool—not just at the end of the day, but every time you get out of the pool.

○ If your hair starts looking like you're from the Emerald City (green, that is), mix the juice of a lemon in a pint of water. Pour the mixture over your hair and rinse. Or try rinsing with club soda, tomato juice, or several aspirin dissolved in warm water.

happy hair dryer

Keep your hair dryer working better and longer with regular maintenance. First, unplug the dryer. Then use an old toothbrush to remove dust, lint, and hair from the air-intake filter at the back of the dryer. This helps prolong the motor's life.

glad hands

The key to keeping hands soft and young-looking is moisturizing and protecting them regularly. Creams are more effective than lotions, because lotions contain a high amount of water and preservatives; creams do not. Instead of spending money on several different products, find a thick sunscreen cream (SPF 15 or more) and use that as your daily hand moisturizer. This is a good idea for a body moisturizer, too, especially if you live in a sunny climate. Sun damages the skin more than anything else does.

○ For an inexpensive fix when you won't be going outdoors, slather petroleum jelly, baby or olive oil, or vegetable shortening on your hands. Do this before bedtime and wear cotton gloves while you sleep for a real hand saver.

○ A cost-effective moisturizer is the beauty secret of farmers and fishermen— and cows! Bag Balm is a highly concentrated ointment used to soothe and soften cow udders. Though you can find it in feed-and-seed stores, its growing popularity has moved it into many drugstores, too.

bathing beauty

For the perfect bath, be sure the water is neither too hot nor too cold. If you want to add oil to your bathwater, do so after you've soaked for five to 10 minutes. The presoak period allows your skin's pores to open and absorb the water. Then, when you add the oil, it will coat your skin, creating a barrier to hold in the moisture.

O To soothe dry skin, add a few tablespoons of olive or vegetable oil to your bathwater instead of expensive purchased bath oils.

O Add a cup of lemon juice to your bathwater to give it a clean, fresh scent and to tone and tighten your skin.

O For a winter warmup, add a couple of tablespoons of ground ginger to your bathwater. The ginger will intensify your feeling of warmth.

O Relieve dry, itchy skin by adding 1 cup of salt to your bathwater and letting it dissolve completely before bathing. If you want added luxury, use sea salt instead.

OIL ESSENTIALS

Throughout this book you will see formulas or recipes calling for essential oils. These highly concentrated oils are obtained by distilling leaves or flowers. They are volatile and flammable and evaporate at low temperatures. Essential oils are potentially toxic if inhaled or used incorrectly. Most of them must be diluted in a fixed oil (fatty, nonvolatile oil) before they are applied to the skin. Lavender and tea-tree oils are exceptions but should be used sparingly. You can find essential oils at health food stores and often at craft stores, since they are used in making perfumes and scented bath products. They come in very small bottles, and the cost may give you pause. (They are not cheap!) However, in any given recipe, you use only a drop or two of essential oil, and the products you can make with essential oils can compensate for the investment.

O If you're lucky enough to grow your own roses, toss some fresh rose petals into your bathwater. The oils from the fragrant petals will leave your skin feeling velvety smooth.

scents for cents

Make your own cologne or perfume, and you'll smell sweet at a fraction of the cost of purchased scents.

classic cologne Pour 1 cup of rubbing alcohol into a jar that has a tight-fitting lid. Add 1/2 cup of dried lavender flowers and 1 tablespoon of olive oil. Cover and let the mixture sit for two days, shaking occasionally. Strain the liquid into a bottle, discarding the solids, and add 1 cup of distilled water and 3 drops bergamot essential oil (see Bonus Tip box, previous page). Cap tightly and shake to mix.

lemon-fresh splash Combine 1/2 cup of rubbing alcohol with 3 teaspoons of lemon extract and the juice of 1 lime in a bottle that has a tight-fitting lid. Cover and shake well. Store in the refrigerator. Makes 5 ounces.

spicy scent Combine 1/2 cup of rubbing alcohol with 1/4 cup of whole cloves in a small jar with a tight-fitting lid; add 1 teaspoon of orrisroot (available at health food stores). Cover and shake well. Let the mixture stand for two days, shaking occasionally. Strain the liquid into a spray bottle, discarding the solids. To use, dab on behind your ears or on your wrists or spray lightly over your skin. Store out of the reach of small children.

odor eaters

Instead of using pricey deodorants, try one of these homemade solutions to unwanted body odors. But remember none of these controls perspiration.

○ Pat a little baking soda on freshly washed and dried skin under your arms. The moisture still on your skin will help the soda stick. If the soda isn't soft enough, mix it with a little cornstarch.

○ Pat a mixture of equal parts of white vinegar and water under your arms. Or just pat cider vinegar, either diluted or full strength, under your arms and let dry.

○ Mash a dark-green leaf of romaine lettuce to extract a drop of chlorophyll. Spread it under your arms and let it dry.

○ Combine a few drops of lavender essential oil (see Bonus Tip box, previous page) with a teaspoon of water and apply the mixture lightly to freshly washed skin.

powder power

Cornstarch makes a good substitute for talcum powder, and it's safe if you happen to breathe a bit in. Rice powder is also wonderful, especially for use on the face.

sharp shaving

Using a sharp blade to shave is just the beginning. The following can help you make the most of your shaving time.

⊙ Ouch! If you nick yourself while shaving, wet a tea bag with cold water and press it on the cut.

⊙ Apply sunscreen instead of aftershave to smooth your skin and shield it from the harmful rays of the sun.

after your shave

This mixture soothes shaved skin and smells just wonderful:

⊙ Combine 2 cups of rubbing alcohol, 1 tablespoon of glycerin (available at health food stores and some drugstores), 1 tablespoon dried lavender, 1 teaspoon dried rosemary, and 1 teaspoon ground cloves in a jar with a tight-fitting lid. Put the jar in the refrigerator and let the mixture steep for three to four days, shaking the jar occasionally. Strain the mixture into a second jar or bottle with a tight-fitting lid and discard the solids. The aftershave will keep in the refrigerator for up to two months.

CHAPTER 3

Frugal Health and Fitness

- home remedies from a to z

- exercise economics

home remedies
from A to Z

DON'T WASTE MONEY AT THE DRUGSTORE
FOR EVERY LITTLE ACHE AND PAIN. RELIEF IS
AT HAND, OFTEN IN YOUR KITCHEN PANTRY.

allergies

The best way to cut down on airborne allergies is to keep the air in your home as clean as possible. Before investing in expensive machines, try the plant approach: philodendrons, ferns, and dracaenas filter many allergens from the air naturally. For maximum benefit, have one plant for every 100 square feet of space.

arthritis

If you suffer from the daily pain of arthritis, here are a few tricks you can try:

- If your knees are swollen and painful, fill four small, self-sealing bags with ice. Hold or secure one bag over and one bag under each knee and keep it there for 15 to 20 minutes. Repeat several times a day until the swelling goes down and the pain is relieved.
- Try rubbing a little plain mustard over the afflicted joints as a pennywise alternative to costlier creams.
- Wear stretch gloves at night to reduce morning arthritic pain, stiffness, and joint swelling in your hands.
- If your arthritis causes you to have difficulty holding a pen, push the pen through a small rubber ball. Or wrap masking tape around and around the pen until it's large enough for you to hold.
- Exercise may be your most important weapon against the effects of arthritis. Physical activity strengthens the muscles and prevents the joints from stiffening further. Ask your doctor about an exercise program specifically designed for your needs, or see page 72 for great low-impact, low-cost workouts.

colds and flu

The common cold and influenza (the flu) are both viral diseases, and you cannot take something to cure them once you have them. What you can do is treat the symptoms.

Good Old Ways

Are you suffering from chest congestion resulting from a cold? Make an old-fashioned mustard plaster for relief: Sift together 1 tablespoon of dry mustard and 1/4 cup of flour. Slowly stir in just enough lukewarm water to form a paste. Spread the plaster on a piece of cotton cloth big enough to cover the chest area. Cover with another piece of cloth. Then place the mustard plaster on dry skin covering the chest. Check frequently and, when the skin begins to turn red (in about 10 to 20 minutes), remove the plaster. Do not use the plaster for more than 30 minutes at a time. Rub petroleum jelly over the reddened skin to hold in the heat. Use the plaster twice a day until the congestion clears up.

NOTE: Do not to use the plaster on the eyes, face, or open skin and make sure that the person isn't allergic to mustard. Do not use on young children.

cold symptoms Fatigue, a scratchy or sore throat, hoarseness, coughing, sneezing, a runny or stuffy nose, watering eyes, and a headache. Colds do not usually cause a fever over 100° F. Cold symptoms usually last from five to seven days.

flu symptoms Initially similar to those of a cold, but symptoms can become more severe, causing fever in adults and even higher fever in children. Flu often causes muscle and joint pain, weakness, and loss of appetite. Flu symptoms may disappear in a few days to one or two weeks, but full recovery can take from two to three weeks.

medical prevention People in high-risk groups—such as those older than 50 years old, adults and children who suffer from chronic illnesses such as diabetes or asthma, and people with weakened immune systems—should get flu shots every year between October and mid-November. People in high-risk fields, such as teaching or health care, should also consider getting flu shots. Flu vaccination will usually protect a person from the most common flu strains expected in a particular year.

what you can do

- Go to bed! Don't go to school or work, because you will likely prolong your illness and will spread the virus.

- Drink plenty of fluids, especially liquids that don't contain caffeine. Water is the best choice, but juice, low-sodium broth, or sports drinks are good, too. One 8-ounce glass per hour will help flush your body tissues and keep you well hydrated so that your body can fight the virus. (To encourage a child to keep hydrated, freeze different kinds of fruit juices on wooden sticks to create homemade Popsicles.)
- Wash your hands often with warm soapy water, whether you are the patient or the caregiver. Be sure to wash all glasses and utensils in hot, soapy water and either boil the family toothbrushes to sterilize them or use this opportunity to replace toothbrushes.

congestion

- Make your own saline nose drops to fight nasal congestion: Mix 1/4 teaspoon table salt in 1 cup water. With a dropper, place two or three drops in each nostril 1/2 hour before meals and at bedtime.
- Use a humidifier: Purchase an inexpensive model and follow the manufacturer's instructions for use and cleaning. Or place pans of water around your house, especially on radiators if you have them.

constipation

If you're eating enough high-fiber foods, constipation shouldn't be a frequent problem. Whole-grain breads, bran cereals, fresh or dried fruit (especially apples), and leafy vegetables are all good choices. If you suffer from chronic constipation, see your doctor. For the occasional bout, include more high-fiber foods in your diet and avoid "binders," such as rice, bananas, and yogurt, for a few days. Also remember to drink water, which keeps the digestive system lubricated. Don't spend your money on laxatives and enemas—they sometimes tend to make the problem worse. If you find you do need a laxative, here are two natural, cheap remedies:

homemade laxative Combine 2 cups tomato or vegetable juice, 1 cup sauerkraut juice, and 1/2 cup carrot juice. Drink 1 cup of the mixture at a time. Store the rest in the fridge.

fruit and fiber Soak about five prunes in orange juice or water overnight. Eat the prunes and drink the soaking liquid before you eat breakfast.

corns and calluses

Soften corns and calluses by soaking your feet in 2 gallons of warm water with

1 tablespoon of Epsom salts for 15 minutes. Then use a pumice stone to rub off the top layers of dead skin. Apply moisturizing lotion (or petroleum jelly) to the feet while still damp. Then put on thin cotton socks.

coughs

Few things are more exhausting than a hacking cough. Try a homemade cough syrup or cough drop to relieve this annoying problem.

cough syrup Combine 3 tablespoons lemon juice and 1 cup honey; slowly stir in 1/4 cup warm water. Take 1 or 2 tablespoons once every three hours to relieve coughing. Store in the refrigerator.

caution Never give honey to a child under the age of one; to be safe, wait until the child is at least two years old.

cough drops In a medium-size saucepan, boil 1 quart washed and chopped horehound leaves and stems (available at health food stores) in 2 cups water for 30 minutes. Strain the mixture and discard the solids. Stir in 3 cups sugar. Place a candy thermometer in the mixture and boil to the hard crack stage (300° to 310° F). Stir in 1/4 cup (1/2 stick) butter and remove the pan from the heat. Pour the mixture into a greased shallow pan and let it cool completely. When cool, break into pieces. Wrap each piece in waxed paper, twisting the paper ends, and store in a tightly covered jar.

dazzling dentures

If you wear dentures, don't waste your hard-earned money on fancy cleaners. Combine 1 tablespoon of household bleach and 1 teaspoon of water softener in 1 cup of water. Place removable full dentures (those with no metal parts) in the solution and soak for 1/2 hour. Remove the dentures and brush and rinse them thoroughly with plain water. Store your dentures in plain water when you're not wearing them.

- To get rid of calcium deposits on dentures, soak them overnight in 1/2 cup of white vinegar every two weeks. Then brush and rinse thoroughly.

ear problems

- For temporary relief of an earache, hold a hot compress against your ear. Leave it in place until the compress has cooled. Repeat as often as needed.
- Remove earwax safely and gently by flushing with a 50-50 mixture of hydrogen peroxide and warm water. Lie on your side and use a dropper to fill your

ear with the solution, then turn your head, holding a towel at the ready, and let the ear drain. Repeat twice a day until the wax softens and washes out.

● If an insect becomes trapped in your ear canal, try to float it out with water. If this doesn't do the trick, try rinsing your ears with drops of vegetable or mineral oil to kill the bug. Then have a doctor remove it from your ear.

feet that ache

Add 3 tablespoons of plain mustard to a pan of warm water and stir until the mustard is completely dissolved. Soak your feet in the warm mustard-water mix for at least 15 minutes, or until the water has completely cooled.

halitosis

Chronic bad breath may indicate a more serious disorder, but for everyday problems try one of the following:

chew herbs Chewing fresh parsley or fresh mint leaves helps freshen breath.

mouthwash Bring 2 cups of water to boil in a small saucepan. Remove from the heat. Add 3 teaspoons fresh or dried parsley, 2 teaspoons whole cloves, 2 teaspoons ground cinnamon, and 2 teaspoons peppermint extract. Let the mixture steep for about an hour. Strain the mixture into a jar or bottle with a tightly fitting lid; discard the solids. Will keep for two weeks in the refrigerator.

hangovers

Naturally, it's better never to have one of these, but . . . Here are some tried-and-true preventive measures and remedies.

● Drink water! Many hangover symptoms are actually caused by dehydration. A glass of water between each alcoholic drink will help slow down and dilute your overall alcohol consumption and prevent dehydration. And don't forget to drink one last glass of water just before bedtime.

● When finished drinking, take two ibuprofen tablets with a big glass of water. This may help stave off a headache. **caution** Never take acetaminophen when drinking alcohol; it can cause liver damage.

● Get some fresh air. Twenty minutes of walking outdoors and breathing deeply can do wonders. Though it may be the last thing you want to do when hung over, a little aerobic exercise (carefully done) can provide relief.

- Pump a little caffeine—it constricts the arteries dilated by alcohol and may relieve your headache.
- A vitamin C supplement or a couple of spoonfuls of honey may help your body eliminate the alcohol more quickly.

headaches

Try easing a tension headache with a gentle facial or neck massage or by applying a heating pad or hot compresses to the forehead and the base of the skull.

heartburn

- Tight garments and belts increase pressure on the abdomen. Don't wear them or loosen them after meals.
- Avoid lying down right after a meal. It can take several hours for the stomach to empty its contents into the intestine. Once that happens, regurgitation—and heartburn—are less likely. Don't eat near bedtime for the same reason. If you must lie down, try to lie on your left side. In this position the esophagus is above the stomach, so that gravity helps keep the stomach acids down. (Lying in this position is helpful during pregnancy as well.)
- Try not to consume effervescent substances, such as soda water, which cause belching. Belching allows acid from the stomach to flow back into the esophagus.
- Avoid bending over soon after meals; bending can cause the stomach contents to back up into the esophagus.
- Obesity increases pressure on the abdomen. Losing weight may help heartburn.
- At the first sign of gastric distress, eat a banana! Bananas contain natural antacids, which can provide fast relief for people with sensitive stomachs who suffer from heartburn pain.

heat rash

Heat rash, or prickly heat, occurs when pores become blocked and perspiration can't be released. Young children are prone to it, but adults can be affected too. To ease itching, steep 3 rounded teaspoons (1/2 ounce) fresh thyme leaves or 1 rounded teaspoon dried thyme leaves in 1/2 cup boiling water for five to ten minutes. Strain through a fine sieve and discard solids. Pour into bathwater and soak yourself.

heat relief

As you can probably guess, the best way to stave off heat exhaustion is to stay out of the sun and drink plenty of water whether you feel thirsty or not!

● If your home doesn't have air-conditioning or an evaporative cooler, head to cool public places during the hottest part of the day: libraries, malls, museums, or even a well-chilled supermarket.

● A tepid shower or bath can help lower your body temperature, but don't take a cold bath or shower, because that will signal your body to warm itself up.

● Small, light, cool meals are a better choice than hearty ones, and avoid junk food.

hiccups

● A spoonful of sugar will make the hiccups go away. Just quickly swallow 1 teaspoon of granulated white sugar for fast relief.

● A teaspoonful of bartender's bitters, followed by the juice of a fresh lemon wedge, can get rid of hiccups.

● Drink ten sips of water, swallowing after each. Don't take a breath until after the tenth sip.

● Hold your breath for as long as you comfortably can, then exhale very slowly. Repeat this exercise several times.

hives

Take an antihistamine and then rub the affected area with an ice cube or take a cool bath. Apply calamine lotion, witch hazel, or zinc oxide to relieve itchiness as well.

insect bites

prevention Try to avoid going outside early in the morning and one to two hours after sunset, the times when insects are most active. If you do go out, try the following:

● Wear clothing that is light in color, such as pale green, tan, khaki, or white.

● Wear long sleeves, long pants, socks, and shoes when outdoors during prime insect time.

● Rub baby oil or imitation vanilla extract on your skin as a nontoxic way of repelling mosquitoes and other biting insects.

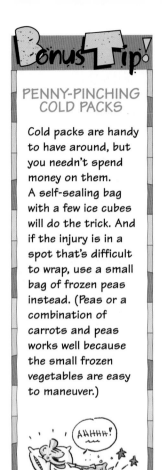

PENNY-PINCHING COLD PACKS

Cold packs are handy to have around, but you needn't spend money on them. A self-sealing bag with a few ice cubes will do the trick. And if the injury is in a spot that's difficult to wrap, use a small bag of frozen peas instead. (Peas or a combination of carrots and peas works well because the small frozen vegetables are easy to maneuver.)

AHHHH!

FROZEN PEAS

● Look for oil of pennyroyal, eucalyptus, and citronella at a health food store; they are all natural mosquito repellents. Mix about 10 drops of oil with an ounce of olive oil, sunflower oil, baby oil, or almond oil and spread the mixture on exposed skin.

● Mosquito repellent: Combine 3 cups rubbing alcohol, 1-1/2 cups red cedarwood shavings (available in pet stores), and 1/2 cup eucalyptus leaves in a large jar or bowl. Cover and let stand for five days. Strain the mixture and discard the solids. Apply the mixture to the skin as needed. Store in a tightly sealed jar. Makes two cups.

● Be careful of the normal products you use on your skin. Suntan lotions, perfumes, and colognes, as well as scented soaps, lotions, shampoos, deodorants, shaving lotions, and hair sprays, may actually attract mosquitoes.

once bitten . . .

● If you get bitten by an insect, first wash the affected area with soap and cold water. Then use cold compresses and elevation to ease the swelling.

● Make a paste of 1/4 tablespoon meat tenderizer and 1 to 2 teaspoons water. Rub the paste over the stung area as soon as possible. Repeat in an hour if it still stings. Meat tenderizer contains papain, an enzyme from the papaya fruit that breaks down insect venom.

● For a quick fix, dab a little ammonia or vinegar on the bite.

caution Allergic reactions to bites and stings can be severe. If you or a family member has a serious allergy, have your physician prescribe an insect-bite kit and carry it with you at all times. If you don't know whether you are allergic (and remember that you can develop allergies later in life), call 911 if you develop hives, shortness of breath, or any other potentially life-threatening symptoms.

menopause

Vitamin E to the rescue! Some doctors recommend 200 to 400 mg of vitamin E a day to reduce night sweats and hot flashes. Check with your doctor because vitamin E can intensify the effect of blood thinners, such as Coumadin and aspirin. Take a vitamin E supplement or eat foods that are high in vitamin E. Some E-rich foods include sunflower oil, safflower oil, wheat germ, mayonnaise, whole-grain cereals, nuts (especially hazelnuts), seeds, egg yolks, and some leafy green vegetables.

● Dress in layers that you can take off or put on as needed to reduce the discomfort of hot flashes. Keep your home cool, especially your bedroom. Keep consumption of caffeine, alcohol, and spicy foods to a minimum.

motion sickness

Instead of buying costly motion sickness drugs, which can cause drowsiness, dry mouth, or blurry vision, try chewing candied ginger.

nausea

stress-induced Soak in a warm bath. If desired, put four to eight drops of lavender essential oil or sandalwood scent into your bathwater.

queasy stomach Sip peppermint tea or eat peppermint candy after you comsume a large meal. Menthol in the mint can help soothe a sensitive stomach.

pregnancy-related Try eating several small meals during the day, rather than three big ones. Avoid heavy or greasy foods. Before going to bed, have something starchy, such as rice pudding or soda crackers.

ER USES FOR EVERYDAY ITEMS

Do you know how many things you already have on hand that can be used in an emergency?

☑ Cloth or disposable diapers: Use as compresses to control bleeding, bandages for large cuts, or padding for splints.

☑ Sanitary napkins: Use as compresses, bandages, or padding.

☑ Linens: Tear into strips for bandages or slings.

☑ Diaper pins or large safety pins: Use to secure bandages.

☑ Magazines and newspapers: Roll up and use as splints.

☑ Large handkerchiefs or scarves: Use for bandages or slings.

☑ Tap water: For flushing eyes, irrigating wounds or burns, washing cuts, and rehydrating someone who is dehydrated.

☑ Wrapping and duct tape: Use to secure bandages and apply pressure to wounds.

flu-related Ginger ale or other clear sodas may help, and they'll act to replenish the fluids that your body has lost. Avoid caffeinated sodas; caffeine functions as a diuretic and further dehydrates your body.

after nausea subsides Stick to bland, fat-free foods until you feel better. Good choices include dry toast, bananas, applesauce, rice, clear soups, and soda crackers. Drink lots of water and fruit juices. (Be wary of citrus juices, because they contain a considerable amount of acid and may cause indigestion in an already sensitive stomach.)

nosebleeds

Nosebleeds are often the result of dry, cracked nasal membranes, so keep the air in your house humidified, especially at night. During dry times of the year, when you plan to be outdoors, dab a little petroleum jelly in your nostrils. To stop a nosebleed:

- Sit in a chair and lean forward slightly. Gently pinch the nostrils together and hold them in this position for five minutes. Check to see whether the bleeding has stopped; if it has not, repeat the gentle pressure until it does stop.
- Once the bleeding has stopped, don't blow your nose for several hours, try not to lean over or lift anything heavy, and don't exert yourself any more than is absolutely necessary.
- If the bleeding is particularly heavy or pressure is not working quickly enough, apply a cold pack (see page 64) to the nose and cheeks. Or hold a little crushed ice in a washcloth directly on the upper lip under the nose until the bleeding stops.

osteoporosis

This "brittle bone" disease has no cure, so your best defense is a strong offense. The sooner in life that you begin to address the possibility, the longer you can stave off the disease. There appears to be a genetic link, and certain people seem more prone to it, so if the condition is in your family history or if you feel yourself to be at risk, ask your doctor about a bone-density test. This painless X-ray procedure can tell you if you have the disease or if you are at risk for it.

- Get enough calcium from food and supplements.
- Get enough vitamin D in your diet. It allows the body to absorb calcium and stimulates the growth of bone cells.
- Participate in weight-bearing exercises, such as brisk walking, jogging, tennis,

and weight lifting, to build dense bone tissue before menopause and to delay bone loss afterward. See pages 72–75 for some great exercise ideas.

● For an inexpensive supplement that does double duty, chew some sodium-free antacid pills, which consist mainly of calcium carbonate. These are just as effective—and less expensive—than traditional calcium supplements.

pill-taking

If a pill sticks in your throat, chew a bite of a banana thoroughly, then swallow it. The banana should dislodge the pill.

poison oak or ivy

"Leaves of three, let them be." Recite this simple rhyme every time you go into the woods. It's also an easy way to teach children how to recognize poison ivy. But if you have a close encounter with poison ivy or poison oak, try this:

● Soak the affected area in a mixture of 1 quart warm water and a cup of uncooked oatmeal. Pat dry and apply calamine lotion to the area.

premenstrual syndrome (pms)

Be assured, this is not in your head. Many women suffer from varying degrees of PMS, ranging from mildly annoying to completely debilitating. Here are tips to help with mild symptoms. If you find yourself unable to function at certain times of the month, see a gynecologist immediately and bring a detailed list of what happens to you and when.

● Two weeks before your period, cut down on (or cut out) caffeine and alcohol and try to limit your intake of sugar, salt, and fat. These foods can promote water retention, mood swings, and other unpleasant symptoms of PMS.

● Eat at least every three hours. Fruits, vegetables, complex carbohydrates, and low-fat dairy are good choices.

● Evening primrose oil, sold in health food stores, is thought by many to relieve breast soreness and other PMS symptoms. To try it, take the herb three days before you expect symptoms to start and continue until your period begins. The usual dosage is 1,000 mg twice a day.

● Exercise regularly, even if you don't feel like it! Aerobic exercise releases endorphins into the bloodstream. These proteins can help relieve pain and lift your mood. Exercise can also help relax your body.

● Generic ibuprofen can relieve menstrual cramping because it targets those specific pain receptors and also works as an anti-inflammatory. Aspirin can also relieve inflammation. Acetaminophen is not an anti-inflammatory, so it is less likely to help.

sleep

Although getting enough sleep is one of the most important things you can do for your health, it can be elusive for many people. How much you need depends on your age and genetic predisposition, but aiming for eight hours is still a good general rule. (Children need more, so consult with your pediatrician to determine a child's sleep schedule.) The following tips may help you get to sleep, and they don't cost a thing!

● Set and maintain a sleep routine: Go to bed and wake up at about the same time every day. Staying up later and sleeping later on weekends disrupts your sleep rhythm.

● Exercise aerobically four to six hours before you go to bed. If you exercise right before bedtime, you'll be too stimulated to sleep. Swimming is a great, relaxing choice.

● Stop any intake of caffeine six hours before bedtime. Caffeine takes that long for the body to process. Nicotine is also a stimulant and should be avoided.

● A drink of alcohol can make you feel relaxed and sleepy initially, but a few hours later the sugar kicks in and can wake you up or make you sleep restlessly. Try to stop intake of alcohol about four hours before bedtime.

● Wind down before going to bed by reading or watching television. Sit in a comfortable chair or couch and wear comfortable clothing.

● Take a warm bath to further relax your body.

● Too much sleep can be as disturbing to your body's rhythms as too little sleep. Short naps during the day are better than trying to sleep longer at night.

● Use your bedroom only for relaxing activities; don't do work there. Your body reacts to very subtle cues, and if your bedroom is a calm, quiet place used for relaxing, your body will react appropriately.

● If exterior noise is a problem, use good earplugs. White noise, such as running a fan or something similar, works well, creating a consistent background sound that blocks out unwanted noise.

snoring

- Sleep on your side. Most people who snore sleep on their backs. Tuck pillows in strategic places to keep you on your side. Or sew a pocket into the back of a T-shirt and put a tennis ball in it. When you roll onto your back, the discomfort will force you to turn back to your side.

- Check your weight. Being overweight is a major factor contributing to snoring. Even losing 5 or 10 pounds can dramatically reduce snoring frequency and intensity.

- Use a cool-mist humidifier in your bedroom at night to keep your nasal passages from drying out.

- Avoid drinking alcohol and smoking before bed. Alcohol relaxes the muscles of the throat, and smoking promotes nasal congestion, both of which can cause snoring.

sore throat

Here are three gargles that can help:

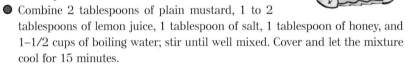

- Dissolve a teaspoon of table salt in a cup of warm water.

- Add 3 tablespoons of cider vinegar, 2 drops of hot red pepper sauce, and a pinch of salt to 1 cup warm water.

- Combine 2 tablespoons of plain mustard, 1 to 2 tablespoons of lemon juice, 1 tablespoon of salt, 1 tablespoon of honey, and 1–1/2 cups of boiling water; stir until well mixed. Cover and let the mixture cool for 15 minutes.

splinters

- If you can see the splinter but it is too deeply embedded to pull out with tweezers, try soaking the affected area in warm water for 10 to 15 minutes. As the wood swells, it may push the splinter out far enough for you to grab it.

- Coat the splinter with white, nontoxic glue. After the glue has dried, peel it off slowly. The splinter may pull out with the dried glue.

- If the splinter is small and there is no sign of infection, leave it alone. Most small splinters will break down or come out on their own over time.

sports injuries

A simple formula to keep in mind for sports injuries is **RICE**. This stands for Rest, Ice, Compression, and Elevation, and it is remarkably effective.

rest Stop whatever it was you were doing immediately. When you injure a muscle, it needs time to heal or you will keep reinjuring it—leading to costly doctor visits. A minor injury usually needs to heal only a day or two before you can resume gentle exercising. More severe injuries need longer and it is crucial not to resume exercising until you are fully healed. If you are taking ibuprofen or another pain reliever, don't let that mask the fact that your injury has not yet healed. You could do yourself permanent, expensive damage.

ice Ice reduces pain and swelling, helps stop bleeding, and encourages the body to begin the healing process. For comfort, wrap your ice pack in a towel or old T-shirt.

compression Use a stretch (Ace) bandage to wrap the injured area just tightly enough to support it, without cutting off circulation. This will also help reduce pain.

elevation If you've injured a limb, raise it above the level of the heart, if at all possible, or at least above hip level. Elevation helps to limit swelling and keeps you from accidentally moving the injured part.

sunburn

The best choice is to avoid sunburns altogether. Slather on sunscreen every day and reapply it as needed. Stay out of the sun from 10 a.m. to 3 p.m. if at all possible. Sunburn in childhood can lead to skin cancer in later life, so start a sun protection program while you or your children are young and stick with it throughout life.

- Soothe sunburns by putting ice wrapped in a towel on the burned area several times a day. The ice will reduce swelling and ease the burning sensation.
- Liquid from a leaf of aloe vera can both soothe burns and speed the healing process. The plants are very easy to grow, so you can supply your own.
- Combine 4 tea bags (cheap black tea), 2 cups fresh mint leaves (or 1 cup dried mint), and 4 cups water in a saucepan. Bring the mixture to a boil; reduce the heat and simmer for five minutes. Remove the pan from the heat and let the mixture steep for 15 minutes. Strain the mixture into a jar and discard the solids. To use: Dab the mixture on sunburned areas with cotton balls or a washcloth.

toothache

If you have persistent tooth or gum pain, see a dentist to fix the problem. Here are some strategies for quick relief:

- Soak a sterile cotton ball or piece of cotton gauze with oil of cloves (available at drugstores and health food stores), or make a paste of finely ground cloves and water. Pack the cotton or paste in the aching tooth's cavity or place it over the sore area. Cloves will naturally numb the area, but you may also feel a stinging in your lips and tongue.
- If your tooth has just started to ache, try drinking a hot liquid. For an ongoing ache, try sucking on an ice cube.
- Mix a teaspoon of salt in warm water and gargle once an hour, swishing the solution over the aching area.
- Try a form of acupressure: Massage the web of skin between your thumb and index finger with an ice cube. Rubbing that part of the right hand will affect the right side of your mouth; the left hand, the left side.
- If a filling has fallen out, make a temporary replacement by combining eugenol and powdered zinc oxide (both available at most drugstores) into a stiff paste. Pack the paste into the cavity, then bite down hard to further force it in and shape it. Then get to a dentist as soon as possible.

exercise Economics

TO KEEP DOCTOR'S BILLS AT BAY,
FIND AN EXERCISE YOU LIKE AND CAN STICK WITH.

exercise exchange

If you love working out at a gym—using the equipment or the pool—and enjoy the opportunity it gives you to meet people but are alarmed by the cost (even the YMCAs and YWCAs are getting pricier these days), think about a work exchange. Can you teach an aerobics dance class? A stretching for seniors group? Beginning swimming for tadpoles? People who work at these places, even part time, get a significant discount on membership or can use the facilities free of charge! And if you expand your horizons to the parks and recreation departments of most cities, the classes you could teach are practically limitless (art, crafts, languages, mechanics, and so forth). Check it out!

walk the walk

If an exercise exchange doesn't appeal to you, there's great news, penny pinchers! One of the best aerobic exercises is free and easy to do at any age: walking. Although higher-impact aerobics may burn more calories per hour, such exercises are often harder on the joints. Lots of people quit because of injuries incurred while running or doing step aerobics. Walking, on the other hand, can help keep you fit painlessly.

● Motivate yourself with an incentive. Plan walk dates with a good friend and catch up on each other's news while you get fit. Or listen to exciting books on tape while you walk so that you look forward to the next chapter.

ride a bike

Riding a bicycle is great for your body and great for the environment. It saves you money on gasoline and wear and tear on your car. If you don't own a bike, investing in one will be money well spent—and there are some bargains out there!

● Call your local police department information number and ask when confiscated bikes are auctioned off. This can be an outstanding way to pick up a pretty good or excellent bicycle for very little money. If the bike is a bit on the battered side, just pick up a can of bright spray paint for metal and make it look like new.

run for your life!

Running is a fantastic aerobic exercise—if you don't have joint or back problems. You'll need to invest in good running shoes (see below), but that should be the only major cash investment. You can run at home or on vacation, alone or with a partner. The roads and sidewalks are free.

in the swim

OK, this one does require a pool and a swimsuit. But it's worth mentioning because swimming is such great exercise!

pools for the parsimonious Check with the parks and recreation department in your area. These community-run pools usually offer classes and free-swim times, and are usually cheap. Another source can be YMCAs and YWCAs, or similar clubs, though they may require memberships, which can end up costing more than you want to pay regularly.

the economics of equipment

If you absolutely have to have equipment to work out with, don't buy new and don't buy on impulse. Check and see whether you can rent a piece of equipment for a month before deciding to buy, because you need to know you will use it before spending the money. Then scour the ads, go to garage sales (often a gold mine for practically new sports stuff), and bargain, bargain, bargain. In a local shopping paper, we spotted a triple-action bike for $20, a CardioGlide machine for $60, a Life Fitness treadmill for $250, and a health-club quality StairMaster, originally bought at $3,200, for $700. The last two items may still sound expensive (and they are), but those represent considerable savings over brand-new machines.

if the shoe fits . . .

The most important piece of exercise equipment that you can invest in is a good pair of athletic shoes. Notice that we don't say expensive athletic shoes. Anyone who pays $70 or more on shoes to exercise in probably shouldn't be reading this book. The more high-impact the exercise (running, tennis, and the like), the more you'll need to pay for shoes. But you should be able to pick up a decent pair of athletic sneakers for under $40. If you check the ads in the newspaper, comparison shop, and see what's available at outlet stores and discount stores, you should be able to whittle the price down to about $20 or even less.

sweat clothes?

Why would anyone pay $80 for a set of clothes to sweat in? People do, but penny pinchers are not among them. We're talking about clothes to get really hot, dirty, and sweaty in. Stick to cheap cotton (or cotton blends) for T-shirts, shorts, tank tops, and sports bras. Most discount stores now offer women's sets of bras and bike shorts for $7. Look for clearance sales to lower prices even further. And don't forget to check out the men's and boys' departments to pick up higher quality merchandise at a penny pincher's price, especially for sweatpants and sweatshirts.

dance fever

If you hate to do what is commonly called exercise but love to dance, you're in luck! Dancing can be one of the best aerobic exercises possible, but you have to get your heart rate up and keep it up for at least 20 minutes—so save the slow dancing for another time. Besides the so-called serious dance workouts, ballet and jazz, you can also keep fit with swing dancing, Latin dancing, line dancing, square dancing, ballroom dancing, just about any type of folk dancing, and even dancing to good old rock n' roll. Check your local paper, especially the entertainment section or the community calendar, for dance events or clubs. Lots of recreation centers sponsor all kinds of dances, some on a regular basis. Some require a partner, but many will try to pair up singles if possible. And if you like the kind of dancing you can do alone, just put on some music and get grooving—and keep moving!

do-it-yourself equipment

Don't spend money on things you can easily make yourself.

hand weights Use 1-pound cans of soup or vegetables or fill clean 1-liter soda pop bottles with water or sand.

ankle weights Fill an old athletic sock (no holes) with dry sand, raw rice, dried lentils or beans, or clean cat litter. Keep weighing the sock as you fill it until it reaches 2 to 3 pounds. Tie or sew the ends closed, leaving room in the toe and the top of the cuff. Either use the empty ends to tie the weights to your ankles or sew pieces of Velcro to each end to use as fasteners. (If you want to be sure the filling won't leak out, fill a plastic bag first, then put the bag in the sock.)

mats A folded beach towel or old blanket will do just fine for most exercise purposes. If you need something that is more solid or provides more cushion, pin together two old towels and stitch together two long sides and one short side of the towels. Slip a piece of foam (from a fabric store) into the pocket formed. If you wish, sew Velcro to close the open side. Then you can take out the foam and wash your mat cover whenever you want.

get a grip Here's a tried-and-true trick: Squeeze an old tennis ball in your hand to strengthen your grip.

AEROBIC REPORT CARD

Aerobic exercise is basically sustained movement of the large muscle groups that works the heart, circulatory system, and lungs. To keep your heart in tiptop condition, you need to do some form of aerobic exercise regularly. This helps lower your blood pressure and reduce your risk of coronary disease. It also releases endorphins—which make you feel great! The chart below grades each exercise based on its aerobic benefit. The higher the grade, the better it is for your heart and body.

Exercise	Benefit Level	Calories per hour
Aerobic dancing	A	360–480
Bicycling (12 mph)	A	410–600
Golf (walking with clubs)	C	300–360
Jogging (5 mph)	A	600–700
Jumping rope	A	800
Skiing, cross-country	A	700–1,200
Skiing, downhill	C to B	500–600
Swimming (crawl)	A	275–750
Tennis (singles)	B	400–480
Walking	B to A	300–480

Home Sweet Home

- cleaning house

- laundry for less

- decorating on a dime

- frugal furniture facts

cleaning
House

ALTHOUGH FEW PEOPLE ENJOY
CLEANING, WE ALL NEED TO DO IT,
ESPECIALLY THOSE OF US WHO ARE PENNY PINCHERS.

caring for carpets and rugs

If you take care of a good carpet or rug, it will reward you with years of service.

- Turn area rugs periodically so that they wear evenly.
- Brush carpet edges and seams with a liquid resin (available at fabric and craft stores) to lock the yarns in place.
- Sew bias binding tape around the edge of a braided rug to protect the edge from wearing out.
- Remove the indentations in carpets caused by furniture by steaming them with an iron. Let the steam penetrate to dampen the fibers; then fluff them with your fingers.
- At least twice a year, vacuum the padding and floor beneath an area rug. Be sure to clean wall-to-wall surfaces frequently, as you can't vacuum carpet padding.
- Deep-clean your carpets twice a year, at the end of winter and summer. Hire a professional service or rent a carpet shampooer from your supermarket. If you have your carpets professionally cleaned, ask whether they will give you a discount if you move the furniture before they come. Some companies will discount up to 20 percent, because not having to deal with furniture will save them time and allow them to fit more jobs into that day.

carpet spills and stains

- Attack carpet stains as soon as possible. Use clean towels to soak up most of the spill. Then pour club soda over the stain and let it sit for a few minutes. Finally, blot the spot with a clean sponge. Repeat until the spot is gone.
- If a spill discolors your carpet, try a 50-50 solution of white vinegar and warm water. Dab the spot with a clean white towel and then blot it with a second clean white towel. Repeat until the spot is gone. Cover the area with a third clean white towel and let it dry completely.

● If chewing gum gets stuck on your carpet, rub an ice cube over it first until the gum hardens. Then use a blunt knife or spatula to scrape off the gum.

wall cleaning

If your walls look a bit grimy and dull, don't rush out to buy cans of fresh paint. Washing your walls costs only a fraction of the expense of painting them, and it can leave your walls looking bright and new. Use a clean sponge mop with a self-squeezing mechanism. Fill two buckets: one with cleaning solution and one with clean water. Clean a small section of the wall at a time, beginning at the bottom; if you begin at the top, the solution may drip down and permanently stain the paint below. Dry the clean sections with a cotton towel before moving on to the next area.

window-washing wisdom

Wash windows on a cloudy, dry day; windows washed in direct sunlight tend to streak, because the cleaning solution dries before you get a chance to wipe it off.

● Before washing windows, use the brush attachment with your vacuum cleaner to clean any dust, soot, cobwebs, or dead insects from the window frames and sills.

● Wash using the crosshatch pattern: Wipe the outside of each pane vertically and the inside horizontally (or vice versa). This method makes it easy for you to tell which side any streaks are on.

● Wash like the pros with clear water, changing it as soon as it becomes dirty. If windows are particularly dirty, add 2 to 3 tablespoons of white vinegar to 1 gallon of water.

● Rubbing alcohol makes an excellent (and cost-effective) window cleaner. Rubbing alcohol removes grease, evaporates quickly, does not freeze, and leaves no residue.

washable wallpaper

Most wall coverings can be simply vacuumed, except for delicate silk coverings, which require professional cleaning. If vacuuming doesn't get your wallpaper clean, here are some other wallpaper-cleaning tricks to try:

● To clean nonwashable wallpaper, rub it gently with an art gum eraser, a dough-type wallpaper cleaner (available from paint and hardware stores), or try using crustless slices of fresh bread.

- Beat a mixture of 1/4 cup liquid dishwashing detergent and 1 cup warm water to form stiff foam. Scoop up the dry foam and apply with a cloth or sponge to soiled, nonwashable wallpaper. Gently wipe off the foam with a clean cotton cloth.

- Clean a grease spot on wallpaper by blotting it with a clean paper towel. Hold a fresh paper towel over the spot and press with a warm (not hot) iron. Change the paper towel as it becomes greasy.

water-ring cures

A water ring on wood furniture can be devastating, especially if it is a good piece.

- Rub the ring with a rag dipped in denatured alcohol or turpentine. If this doesn't work, then use a soft cloth to rub lightly with a toothpaste (not a gel) that contains a gentle abrasive.

- If toothpaste doesn't work, sprinkle salt on the ring and rub it with a rag dipped first in lemon oil, then vinegar.

- If you have a new water stain on a wood table or counter, try rubbing it gently with a mixture of equal parts mayonnaise and fine fireplace ashes.

- Once the ring has been removed, polish the entire piece of furniture thoroughly.

candle wax conundrum

Candle wax drippings on dining tables are common, and some just seem to come off more easily than others. If you get a stubborn patch, try warming it with a hair dryer to soften the wax; then sponge it away with vinegar diluted with water. Rinse with clear water and dry well. Remember: Never scrape wax off with a knife! You'll only end up scratching the finish on the surface of the table. To get wax off a candlestick, try putting it in the freezer for a couple of hours. When you take it out, the frozen wax will come right off.

sofa shaver saver

Shaving cream can remove dirt and fresh stains from upholstery and rugs! Just spread it over the area to be cleaned, brush it lightly, and rinse off with warm water. If you're concerned about a delicate fabric, test an inconspicuous area.

soot and cinders!

Although it may seem like a chunk of money going up the chimney, if you use your fireplace at all, have it cleaned professionally once a year. A licensed sweep (look in your Yellow Pages) can remove the buildup of flammable creosote, which is the cause of most chimney fires. To save money, join with your neighbors to negotiate a lower group rate.

● Line the floor of your clean fireplace with a piece of heavy-duty aluminum foil before building a fire. After the fire is out, simply fold the foil over the mess and throw it out. (Or better still, use the ashes in your garden and recycle the aluminum.)

● Search antique or junk stores for a cast-iron fireback. When set against the back wall of your fireplace, this will both protect the brick and reflect heat into the room.

● Clean soot and smoke from fireplace bricks with a 50-50 solution of bleach and water. Spray the solution onto the bricks, scrub the bricks with a soft brush, and then rinse thoroughly with water. Wear vinyl gloves and be careful not to get the mixture in your eyes.

stinky sponges

Kitchen sponges sometimes develop a nasty odor that just permeates the kitchen. Before tossing out that stinky sponge, pop it into a mesh laundry bag and run it through your laundry with a load of white towels. (Use bleach.) Put the washed sponge in the sun to dry. (The sun kills certain bacteria.) Don't run sponges through the dryer, and never put them in a microwave, because sponges are flammable.

taking care of your range

Don't wait to care for your range until it is coated with grime.

● Wipe off cooking spills and grease spatters while the range top is still warm using warm, sudsy water and a cloth or sponge; clean the sponge frequently while you work.

● Wipe off the top of the hood—a real grease collector—whenever you wipe off the range top.

● Unless you have a continuous-cleaning oven, wipe out the oven with a soapy sponge after each use to prevent grease buildup; otherwise, the grease will burn and harden each time you use the oven.

- Place oven racks on an old bath towel in the bathtub and soak them in a solution of ammonia and hot water. Then scrub to clean them.

- Before using your oven's self-cleaning function, wipe off the frame and the part of the door liner that's outside the oven seal. These areas aren't reached during automatic cleaning, but they do get enough heat to bake on soil, making it harder to remove later.

- To clean under an electric range with a bottom drawer, remove the drawer so that it will be easier to get at the floor. For a gas range with a broiler below the oven, remove the broiler drawer.

defrosting

If you own a refrigerator-freezer that is not frost-free, be sure to defrost it as soon as the frost is about 1/4 inch thick; the thicker the layer of frost, the harder the unit has to work and the less efficient it will be. Letting too much frost build up also makes it more difficult to defrost.

- Turn off the unit, move everything out, and place pots of hot water in the freezer to speed the process. Never use metal utensils to try and "hurry" the ice out—you could cause serious (and costly) damage to the freezer. If you must scrape, use a dull plastic scraper and never scrape against metal parts.

- To further speed up the defrosting process, set your hair dryer on hot and blow away the ice.

SEVEN USES FOR BAKING SODA

① Carpets: Sprinkle baking soda over carpet, then vacuum.

② Drains: Pour 1/2 cup baking soda and 3/4 cup white vinegar in drain. After it stops bubbling, flush with very hot tap water.

③ Spills: Pour baking soda over spill. Let it absorb, then vacuum.

④ Fire extinguisher: Keep a box of baking soda next to your stovetop to quash grease fires.

⑤ Silver polisher: Dip half a raw potato in baking soda and rub. Wipe with a damp cloth, then a dry one.

⑥ Silverfish slayer: Sprinkle a 50-50 mixture of baking soda and sugar near baseboards.

⑦ Odor eater: Use a baking soda–water solution to deodorize a diaper pail and kitty litter box.

THE STAR FOR ENERGY SAVING

www.energystar.gov

The Energy Star, backed by the U.S. Environmental Protection Agency, is one of the most helpful appliance-shopping tools to come along in quite a while. Each appliance is tagged with a yellow energy rating card that tells you the estimated cost of running the appliance and whether it is in the high- or low-use category. The Energy Star is awarded to appliances that meet certain energy- or water-use standards. It makes sense to buy the most efficient appliance model possible. To read more about the program (and to find stores in your area that carry Energy Star products), check out this Web site.

⬤ When all the frost is gone, wipe out the freezer unit with soapy water and dry with clean cloths. Before turning it on again, dip a cloth in glycerin and wipe the freezer coils with it. This will help you remove the frost more easily the next time you defrost.

⬤ Stuck ice cube tray? Apply a dishtowel soaked in hot water to the tray's edges for a few seconds.

⬤ Frost in your frost-free? Check the defrost timer behind the grille. With the refrigerator running, use a screwdriver to turn the slotted knob slowly clockwise until you hear a click and the refrigerator goes off. Wait 5 minutes for defrost water to appear in the drain pan. If the frost doesn't melt or if the problem recurs, call for service.

cheap cleaning rags

Do not buy cloths for cleaning, ever! The best cleaning rags are made from old cloth diapers, T-shirts, and linen or terry-cloth dish towels. Although it is tempting to grab paper towels for cleaning, it's an expensive habit; save paper towels for microwaving and some other uses suggested later in this section.

⬤ To get into those hard-to-reach corners, slip an old sock over one end of a yardstick or broom handle and secure it with a rubber band.

quick cure for dingy dishwasher: Kool Aid

It is so discouraging to open your perfectly good dishwasher and be greeted by a stained, dingy interior. Don't snatch up one of those pricey cleaners—try a little Kool Aid! Yes, I know, sounds nuts, right? But just put one or two little packets of unsweetened, citrus-flavored Kool Aid in the soap dispenser and run your empty dishwasher through a normal cycle. The process will leave the interior sparkling. And at a cost of only about 10 cents a packet, this is a true penny pincher's miracle worker.

shining showers

When glass shower doors turn filmy, wipe them down with a soft cloth saturated with distilled white vinegar or a water softener solution. Shine with a dry cloth.

● The best time to clean a shower or bathtub is right after you've used it, when the steam has loosened the dirt. Just wipe off the damp surfaces with a clean cloth.

● Clean grungy grout with full-strength vinegar instead of with budget-busting bathroom cleaners.

● Wipe soap spots or film from tile with a solution of 1 part vinegar to 4 parts water. Rinse and dry with a soft cloth.

● Clean stained tub or sink surfaces with a paste made of equal parts cream of tartar and hydrogen peroxide. Spread the paste over the stain and scrub lightly with a brush. Let the paste dry and then wipe or rinse it off.

tile cleaning tricks

● Wipe off soapy film on ceramic tile walls or floors with a solution of 1 part vinegar to 4 parts water. Rinse thoroughly with clean water. Buff tiles to prevent streaking.

● For stained or mildewed grouting, apply a bleach solution (3/4 cup liquid chlorine bleach to 1 gallon water) with a cloth, sponge, or old toothbrush. Make sure to wear rubber gloves and rinse thoroughly.

clean shower curtains

Remove mildew from a plastic shower curtain by machine-washing it with regular laundry detergent. Add one or two towels to the washing load to act as buffers. Hang the curtain on its own rod to dry. If the curtain is stiff and unmanageable when you take it out of the washer, pop it (and the towels) into the dryer for a few minutes to soften, remove it promptly, and hang it while it is still warm.

EIGHT USES FOR VINEGAR

1. **Kettle cleaner:** Fill with equal parts vinegar and water; bring to boil. Let sit overnight.

2. **Window washer:** Put 2 tablespoons vinegar in 1 quart warm water.

3. **Reek wrecker:** For fish odor, fill pan with equal parts vinegar and water. Bring to boil, let simmer for three minutes. Wash.

4. **Plaster perker:** Mix 1 part white vinegar to 3 parts water to clean water-stained plaster walls.

5. **Crease crisper:** Mix equal parts vinegar and water in spray bottle; spritz on a little before pressing.

6. **Iron restorer:** Fill steam iron with 50-50 mix of white vinegar and water. Run iron on steam until dry. Repeat with clear water.

7. **Rust buster:** Soak rusty screws or nails in vinegar several days until rust dissolves. Scrub and rinse.

8. **Paintbrush reviver:** Soak in equal parts white vinegar and water until soft, then wash.

tidy bowls

Those fancy in-tank cleaners cost an arm and a leg. Yet they don't clean a bowl that is already soiled, and although they may slow down the accumulation of residue, they don't stop it. In other words, they don't really clean your toilet. So save your money and clean the old-fashioned way: Sprinkle the interior of the bowl with household cleanser and use a toilet brush to scrub around the inner rim and the bowl.

● For stubborn stains, use cleanser with bleach or add bleach to the bowl, let it soak for an hour, wipe gently with a brush, and then flush it all away.

● Flush a cup of baking soda down the toilet every week or so to help prevent the buildup of bacteria in the tank as well as to guard against clogging or backing up in the tank and drain field.

fresh air ideas

● Make your own air freshener: Mix 8 ounces of water with 10 or more drops of an essential oil—rosemary, eucalyptus, pine, lavender, or any of the citrus fruit oils—in a spray bottle. Add more drops of essential oil if you want a stronger scent. Essential oils are available at health food stores. They kill airborne bacteria and evaporate cleanly, leaving no sticky residue.

● Keep your closets smelling fresh and sweet by hanging pomanders in them. Insert whole cloves into an unpeeled orange, lemon, lime, or apple, covering most of the surface of the fruit with the cloves. To make it easier to insert the cloves, first make holes through the peel using a nail or pick. Tie a pretty ribbon around the finished pomanderfor hanging.

- Musty closet? Fill an old pan (from a store-bought pie or left over from a microwave meal) or an old margarine tub with charcoal briquettes and place it in the closet. The charcoal will absorb moisture and odors. Replace briquettes once a month (save the old briquettes for barbecuing).

- When you do your vacuuming, squeeze a few drops of lemon juice into the dust bag of your vacuum cleaner before you start it up. You'll find that your whole house will smell better.

- Buy bags of cedar shavings at discount pet supply stores. Stitch together small bags of cheesecloth or muslin, and tuck the bags in your linen closet and dresser drawers or hang them from your clothes closet rods.

NATURAL HOUSEHOLD AIDS

INSTEAD OF	USE
Ant killer	vinegar and water
Drain cleaner	boiling water, once a week
Furniture polish	3 parts olive oil and 1 part water
Aphid spray	pureed garlic, red pepper, liquid soap, and water
Black spot killer	baking soda, liquid soap, and warm water
Houseplant fertilizer	weak, tepid tea solution, weekly
Houseplant pest spray	mild soap-and-water solution, weekly
Mothballs	cedar chips
Oven cleaner	vinegar and baking soda
Brush cleaner	liquid detergent suds (for latex paint)
Paint softener	white vinegar and water
Roach repellent	bay leaves

- If you grow your own lavender (an easy-to-grow drought-tolerant plant), snip off the heads of the stalks and let them dry. Then make your own sachets using muslin, cheesecloth, or pretty scraps of any other fabric you have on hand.

the simplest air freshener of all?

Just cut a lemon or orange in half, set one half on a saucer and place wherever the air needs a bit of brightening (or odors need to be absorbed).

laundry for
Less

COST-CONSCIOUS WASH DAYS
SAVE ON ENERGY AND CLOTHING.

washers and dryers—cost and effect

Like most major appliances, a washing machine and a dryer are a big investment, and an important one (to which anyone who has had to lug laundry to a
Laundromat can attest). The two major points to consider are cost and effect.

COST Setting your sights either too upscale or too cheap will land you with an
appliance that is either much fancier than you need or one that doesn't work efficiently and thus costs dearly to use or repair.

EFFECT To determine the effect you need, make a list of the features most
important for your family and the key climate factors in the area you live in. If
you live in the arid Southwest, for example, a low-water-use washer makes good
sense. You'll be able to air-dry your laundry much of the year, so a fancy dryer is
not as important. If you live in the generally damper Midwest, efficient water use
is not quite as urgent, but an efficient dryer can be a time and money saver.

look for the energy star

The Energy Star program (see Resources box, page 82) is particularly helpful
when shopping for washers and dryers, since both water and energy efficiency
are included in the ratings. Energy-efficient washers come in both front- and top-
loading models. Front-loaders tumble laundry instead of agitating it, which uses
less water and is easier on your clothes. Some top-loader designs now use high-
pressure sprays to soak and rinse clothing instead of filling the tub with water
each cycle. A typical household does about 400 loads of laundry a year, using
about 40 gallons of water per load. The new, efficient washing machine models
use only 18 to 25 gallons per load—a substantial savings. In addition, the efficient models generally use 35 to 50 percent less energy! So though they will
probably cost a good bit more initially, an energy-efficient washer and dryer

could put money back in your pocket within a few years.

Much depends on how expensive power and water are in your area. If they are cheap, an efficient model's lower operating cost isn't likely to make up the purchase-price difference over a washer's typical 10- to 15-year life span.

keep your washer on an even keel

Use a carpenter's level to ensure that your washer and dryer are not installed off level, either front to back or side to side. If either machine is even slightly tilted, it can cause extra vibration and noise. Use a wrench to adjust the feet until your washer and dryer are in a perfectly level position.

save while washing

Set some clothes-washing ground rules for yourself, and you'll save water, electricity, and money over the years.

- Run only full loads. Running small loads wastes electricity and water. If necessary, toss in tablecloths, dishtowels, or seldom-washed items to fill up the load.
- Use cold-water rinses, because cold water uses less energy. Though laundry detergents clean your clothes better in warm water (at least 65° F), the rinses can always be cold. If you want to wash in cold water, liquid detergent may be your best bet, because it dissolves more quickly.
- Check with your energy and water utilities to find out whether they offer lower rates early in the morning or late at night, whether weekday rates are less than on weekends, and whether they have any tips on lowering your

Take a tip from our foremothers and put up a clothesline. The environment will thank you for it, your clothes will thank you for it, and your utility bill will thank you for years! Sunshine actually kills certain odor-causing bacteria so that your clothes will smell fabulous naturally. No more spending money on laundry products that claim to give clothes an "air-dried freshness." Another plus: Line-drying is easier on fabrics. In fact, most shrinkage occurs in the dryer, and fibers are worn down in the dryer. So line-drying will make your clothes last longer and look better, too. Sounds like a win-win situation to us.

SEVEN TERRIFIC STAIN FIGHTERS

① Alcohol (rubbing or denatured): Helps fight grass or dye stains.

② White vinegar: Safe for all fibers, but may affect some colors. Use 1 part to 3 parts water on food stains; saturate perspiration stains.

③ All-fabric (oxygen) bleach: Mild and safe on most fabrics; good for wine stains.

④ Petroleum jelly: Use to soften hardened paint, rubber cement, or tar before washing.

⑤ Club soda: Great for rinsing out stains on clothing, upholstery, rugs, and linens.

⑥ Nonacetone nail polish remover (banana oil): Removes glue or lacquer from clothing.

⑦ Hydrogen peroxide (3%): Use straight on wool or silk; mix with ammonia for a bleach. Great for bloodstains.

operating costs. Each region of the country is different with respect to energy and water resources, so it pays to find out how best to use the resources in your area.

don't overdo the detergent

If you find a lot of lint on your laundry, it's a sign that you are using too much detergent. Though it is tempting to add extra detergent when you have really dirty clothes, it actually doesn't clean any better. And excess detergent may not be fully washed away in the rinse cycle, so it can leave a film on fabrics that attracts dirt and causes garments to look dingy.

washer tricks

● Reduce the lint that can stick to dark-colored garments in the dryer by adding 1 cup of white distilled vinegar to each load of laundry during the final rinse.

● If you experience an "attack of the suds" (foaming over), just sprinkle salt on the foam to help settle it down.

● Prevent mineral buildup in your washing machine by filling the tank with water and adding 1 cup of white vinegar. Run the mixture through a complete wash cycle.

dryer dilemmas

If your dryer suddenly won't run, don't immediately call the repair service. First, be sure the door is completely closed. Second, check that the dryer is plugged in. **NO KIDDING!** The vibration from the dryer can eventually work a plug out, so it behooves you to take a look. Third, check the circuit breaker or fuse to make sure it hasn't tripped or blown. On a gas dryer, check that the pilot light is on. If all of the above failed, then it's time to call the repair service.

double-duty dryers

You can purchase a special accessory that allows you to vent moisture from the dryer indoors instead of outdoors during the winter when the air inside your house dries out from heat. A single dryer load can add more than a gallon of water to the air inside the house. Beats running a humidifier.

dry-clean in the dryer

A new weapon in the fight to keep clothes clean at less cost is the dryer dry-cleaner bag. Do they work? Yes! Follow the directions carefully, and you will be quite pleased by how great your clothes look—and the money you've saved.

HOMEMADE LAUNDRY AIDS

Brightener: Add lemon juice to the wash water.

Whitener: Soak yellowed linens in sour milk and then launder as usual.

Booster: Soak your whites in a mixture of 1 cup vinegar and 1 gallon warm water before washing to get rid of detergent residue and make the whites whiter.

Scrubber: Make a paste of vinegar and baking soda and rub it into stains before washing. Thoroughly soak perspiration stains with vinegar before laundering.

decorating on a
Dime

WITH DECORATING, AS WITH CLOTHING,
IT'S NOT SO MUCH WHAT YOU HAVE
AS WHAT YOU DO WITH IT.

use your imagination

The biggest secret of a fabulous decorator is imagination—the ability to see the possibilities in almost anything. The key certainly isn't spending the most money. And you'll be surprised at what you can do yourself at no cost at all.

assess potential Look at objects to see what they could become: An old milk can could be transformed into a lamp, the base for a small table, an umbrella stand, or a planter. Be creative as you see each object's potential.

express yourself Do you love music? Look for old sheet music with great covers whenever you're at an antique or junk store, garage sale or thrift store, or at a going-out-of-business sale at a music store. Hang the music on the wall above your piano, framed or unframed. Do you sew? Keep an eye open for antique (or just old) sewing equipment and display it on the walls and shelves of your sewing room.

or beds Quilts or beautiful afghans can be hung on a dowel on a wall or draped over the back of a chair or sofa to add color and warmth—and be handy for snuggling under.

make the most of color

Neutral walls have gone the way of the dodo. Color is in and is gloriously vibrant. Let your walls make as much of a statement as your furnishings (for a fraction of the price).

- To create a sense of flow from room to room, select a dominant color for your main room, then pick up different shades of the same color and use them in subtle ways throughout the house.

- It's no great surprise that desert colors—oranges, reds, browns, and yellows—are often used in decorating in the Southwest or that deep greens, earthy browns, and dark reds show up in mountain homes. Those are predominant colors in nature in those regions. The dominant natural colors of any part of the country can be used to subtly tie the interior of one's home to the world outside.

papering your walls

Although paint is the easiest way to add color to your walls, wallcoverings have come back into their own. Wallcoverings are easier to hang than ever before and come in a wide variety of styles. If you have walls that are in less than perfect condition, a wallcovering can disguise the flaws without the expense of replastering.

frugally fabulous floors

Don't make any decisions about new flooring until you've carefully considered whether you can revitalize the old flooring. Wood floors may need only a new coat of wax. Or you can rent a sander to redo seriously scuffed wood.

- Consider the wear and tear on a surface before you decide what to do with it. Wood floors enhance living rooms and more formal areas; rooms with heavier traffic, such as kitchens, bathrooms, and family rooms, need something that's tougher and won't require as much maintenance.

- If your wood floors are so badly worn that sanding, staining, or bleaching can't revive them, try rescuing them with paint, which can cover a multitude of sins, pits, and blemishes and can really brighten a room, to boot! Although the range of colors is small, deck paint is ideal for hard-use areas because it's durable and washable.

give an old floor a new look

If you have a clean, flat, structurally sound floor that needs covering, consider sheet vinyl. It is resilient, water resistant, easy to clean, and relatively inexpensive. Moreover, it comes in many patterns and colors, in 6- and 12-foot widths. You won't even need an adhesive; simply move the furniture, unroll the vinyl, and trim it to fit.

picture-perfect floors

Another increasingly popular flooring that is far less costly than hardwood is laminate. The surface of laminate flooring can be made to look like anything, from hardwood to tile to marble. Basically, a print of the desired surface look is laminated onto a fiberboard core backing. Laminate is easy to install (no adhesive is used; the flooring "floats," or lies unattached, on the subfloor), is extremely easy to care for, and is quite durable.

carpet costs

With carpeting, you generally get what you pay for. It pays to buy high quality because a good-quality carpet will last much longer and look much better after years of use than poor-quality carpeting will. It is also sound sense to purchase the right padding and have professionals install both. Because your floors really set the tone for your decor, carpeting is an area in which long-term savings should outweigh up-front costs. With carpet warehouses, home centers, and even department stores competing for your business, you should still be able to purchase high-quality carpeting for a reasonable price.

kitchen face-lifts for less

You may want a new kitchen, but do you really need new appliances or a new floor plan? If not, a kitchen face-lift might save you hundreds of dollars.

- Cabinet refacing: Even if you have this done professionally, you will pay much less than it would cost to have new cabinets installed. You can save even more, by doing the refacing yourself. This usually involves gluing new veneer over the old finish on all the vertical surfaces. You can get the veneer and instructions at home centers. You can also get new cabinet doors and drawer fronts to replace your old ones, refinishing the cabinet frame before installing the new doors and drawer fronts.

- If you don't want to go through the effort of a full refacing, take off all the cabinet doors and drawers and paint yourself a brand-new look. You can match the doors and the frames or, if you want some drama, paint them different colors. Paint the frames white and the doors and drawer fronts bright red, then look for a vintage '50s dinette set with a red tabletop and red-cushioned chairs. Or stencil a design of herbs on the doors and drawer fronts and paint the framework a pale green.

- Don't forget hardware! Knobs, handles, and drawer pulls come in an infinite variety these days; there's something for everyone's taste. If you've saved big money redoing your own cabinets, you can splurge a bit on hardware.

- Putting in your own tile backsplash can really change the look of the room. Like hardware, the variety of tiles available is staggering. You can go French country blue, Spanish-style bright, Southwestern saltillo, floral, or just about any other route you can think of.

- If you have a window that lets oodles of light into your kitchen, remove all curtains or coverings and install glass shelves to make a window herb garden.

You'll always have fresh seasonings for your cooking as well as a gorgeous window, especially if you use interesting containers.

mirror tricks

Mirrors, mirrors everywhere are a tremendous help in decorating. You can use them framed or unframed, as tiles, or as pieces of furniture.

- Add height to a small, low-ceilinged room (such as a powder room) by covering the ceiling with inexpensive, easy-to-install mirror tiles. Use the recommended adhesive.

- Place a large framed mirror in a small entryway to reflect light, increase the sense of space, and allow you to give yourself the once over before going out.

- Do you have a darkish room with only one window? Set a mirror on the wall opposite the window to give the illusion of another window and to increase the light.

- A series of small framed mirrors in varied shapes can be arranged down a darkish hallway or on the wall next to a staircase to catch light and add a bit of sparkle.

- For a recessed window, line the sides of the window recess with mirror tiles to reflect more light into the room.

- Look for attractive antique frames at flea markets, garage sales, and thrift stores. You may have to look beyond the so-called art in the frame. When you find a winner, remove the art and replace it with a mirror. Hang it above a dresser, a mantelpiece, or a powder room sink.

frugal furniture
Facts

WALL AND FLOOR TREATMENTS SET
THE SCENE, BUT FURNITURE PIECES
PLAY THE SUPPORTING AND STAR ROLES.

buying new furniture

department stores and furniture stores Both of these stores have a wide selection of furniture, from low-end pieces made with particleboard and veneer to high-end solid wood pieces. Both venues are worth checking out, especially when they are advertising sales.

price clubs These outlets usually have some furniture year-round, though the selection tends to reflect seasonal needs. The quality is generally high and the prices are often excellent: for instance, an oak double bookcase (48 inches wide by 84 inches high) for $199.99. You can find an even wider selection on their Web sites. On the Costco Web site, we spotted a mission-style Morris chair in solid oak with black Italian leather seat cushions and matching ottoman for $549.99, plus $121 for shipping!

discount superstores You won't find fine furniture at these stores, but they do offer a variety of everyday furnishings that make excellent fillers or supporting pieces. Dining-room chairs, computer desks, stools, side tables, and so on can be had for very reasonable prices.

thrift store bonanzas

Furniture is a category in which thrift stores shine. As you canvas thrift stores, you'll find that some stores carry more furniture than others and that some seem to acquire better pieces. If you are looking for a specific piece or style, tell the salespeople what you want; they may be willing to call you if it comes in.

great garage sale finds

Scouring garage (tag or yard) sales can also pay off handsomely. Look for ads or signs indicating that the sale will include furniture and go as early as possible.

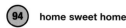

Make sure to check out sales in more affluent neighborhoods. Though you may pay a tad more, you also may find higher quality furniture. Tables, dining chairs, consoles, sofas, and end tables are among the pieces often sold at garage sales.

flea market facts

Although flea markets are a wonderful source of furniture, old and new, you have to work them like an expert to get the best merchandise at the best price.

go early Take your cue from crafty antiques hunters and arrive as the vendors are setting up their booths.

shun costly repairs Worn wicker may be selling for a song, but wicker costs an arm and a leg to reweave, so it's best to pass it by. Mildewed upholstery is almost impossible to freshen, so just leave it alone.

chat up the vendors Vendors are often collectors and tend to know who is selling what. They also frequently own shops or have some pieces at home that they might be willing to bring the next weekend.

comparison shop A number of vendors may have similar pieces. Check each piece carefully and bargain. Vendors will often come down 10 percent if you ask.

stay late Vendors don't want to have to repack wares, so they may be willing to lower their prices significantly toward the end of the day to make a sale. You can often score some excellent bargains this way.

auction patter

Like flea markets, auctions—if you know how to work them—can yield marvels.

arrive early Look over pieces that you're interested in during the presale period. Ask the attendant or auctioneer what the piece is likely to bring—that will usually give you a good estimate of the item's true worth.

avoid bidding wars Decide in advance what your top bid for an item will be and stick to it. Otherwise, you may go home with a really overpriced piece.

stay late Some of the best bargains can be snagged after most of the bidders have gone home.

other auction options

⦿ Moving and storage auctions often provide fabulous deals on furniture. Movers periodically auction off unclaimed goods out of their warehouses. Check newspaper classified ads or contact local movers for dates.

⦿ Business bankruptcies can yield bargains. For example, when a restaurant closes, it may auction off additional items, such as a car or a computer. Most bidders will be there for the tables, chairs, kitchen appliances, and supplies, so you may get the other stuff for pennies.

antique advice

If you decide to invest in an antique, make sure that you know what you are paying for. Consult collectors' guidebooks listing the prices of similar items sold at auction within the last year. (Most public libraries have such books.) Also check prices at other antique stores. If the item is very costly, consult an appraiser.

● If the piece has had alterations or repairs, you can often get the dealer to reduce the price. Check for such clues as legs made of a different wood, new screws, or machine-cut braces. Then bargain.

refinished to perfection

Another way to gussy up a piece of used furniture is to refinish it. If you haven't done much refinishing, practice on an inconspicuous part of the piece.

● Take apart a big piece of furniture before refinishing it. This will make working on any section a lot easier, and you're more likely to get the results you want.

● Take off the hardware and, for easier reassembling when you're finished, mark each handle, hinge, caster, and screw with tape and a pencil, noting its original position. Keep all the hardware in a labeled self-sealing bag so that you don't misplace anything.

● To check whether a liquid refinisher will work on your piece of furniture, soak a cotton ball in nail polish remover and press it against the surface. If the ball sticks, refinisher will do the job; if the ball doesn't stick, you will need to strip the piece with paint remover.

● Unlike paint remover, refinishing liquids (sold in home centers, hardware stores, and paint stores) just remove the top layers of old finishes, so you don't have to scrape or sand as much. You can't use refinishers on all finishes, however, so check the label carefully.

● Before you start applying stain, test the stain you want to use on a section that won't be seen, such as the bottoms of chair seats and the undersides of tabletops.

sofa, so good

Buy the highest quality sofa you can afford; it will last much, much longer than a cheaply made sofa and will look good far longer. The best-made sofas have a hardwood frame, joints secured with dowels or screws, and fitted blocks at the inside corners for added strength. Spring coils, eight to twelve per seat, offer greater comfort than horizontal steel springs.

- Take the fabric protection option. These guards are applied at the factory and come with a warranty. Do-it-yourself store-bought aerosols don't bond as well. Later, when water stops beading on the fabric, it's best to have new fabric guard professionally applied.
- If possible, get extra fabric when you buy an upholstered sofa or have an older sofa reupholstered. If you need to recover a cushion later, you will have a perfect match.
- Be sure to vacuum your sofa once a week and flip the cushions at the same time.
- If your sofa is starting to feel a bit softer than you like, buy a 1/2 inch-thick piece of plywood to fit under the cushions. Your old sofa will feel like new. You can also do this with armchairs that have started to sag.

bewitching beds

Although solid bedsteads are quite attractive, they can also be a significant investment, especially if you want real wood. To create the appearance of a headboard, try this fool-the-eye idea for a less-expensive option:

- Hang a new or heirloom quilt at the head of your bed. Use an inexpensive wooden dowel and add decorative finials for extra interest.

look aloft

One option to consider for furnishing a child's room or a guest room/office is a loft-style bed. To accommodate a loft, the ceiling should be at least 12 feet high. This height allows for a minimum of 6-1/2 feet of standing room below the loft and 4-1/2 feet above (enough to sit up in a bed or sit in a chair at a desk), plus 1 foot for the platform of the loft.

- The loft options are pretty amazing: You can have a single or double bed above, and under it an office setup, bookcases, bureau drawers, even a little fort for children. The prices of lofts vary considerably, so check around. Price clubs offer lofts occasionally; check their Web sites for options year-round. Unfinished-furniture stores can offer real wood at a decent price, and you can stain or paint the pieces to match your decor.

- You can also construct a loft yourself pretty easily, especially if you have some woodworking skills and the right tools. Plans are available in furniture-making books (check the library), or you may be able to download instructions off the Web.

- Be sure to take into account the ventilation needs of someone sleeping near a ceiling. The loft area will be warmer in the winter (heat rises), but also warmer in the summer. If the room doesn't have air-conditioning, remember that fans can make a big difference in airflow.

mattress matters

Few things affect a good night's sleep more than a mattress, so buying a well-made mattress can be a real investment in good health. Once you've found and purchased a good-quality mattress, take care of it, and it will last much longer.

- Count the number of coils. Full-size mattresses should have at least 300 coils inside; queen-size, at least 375; king-size, a minimum of 450 coils. In choosing between two mattresses that have the same coil count, check the thickness of the steel of the coils. The lower the number, the thicker the wire and the longer the mattress will keep its support firm.

- Turn your mattress frequently to maintain even support. Switch the mattress end to end as well as turning it over. Some manufacturers recommend turning every two weeks for the first three months, then turning every two months for the life of the mattress. To keep track, put a bit of masking tape with the date last changed somewhere on the mattress.

- If you have an older good-quality mattress that has become a bit softer than you like, don't rush out to a store, unless it's a lumber store! A sheet of plywood, 1/2- to 3/4-inch thick, can be slipped between the mattress and the box spring to make a fine bed support. You'll get extra years from your mattress at a fraction of the cost of a new one.

wonderful wicker

You can find wicker furniture at garage or yard sales and thrift stores for a song. As long as the weaving is sturdy, don't pass a piece by because it is saggy or a bit scuffed. It is easy to bring wicker back to radiant life. And don't just look for wicker patio furniture. You can also find headboards, side tables, dining tables and chairs (perfect for a breakfast nook), bookcases, towers (for storing towels in the bathroom), love seats, rocking chairs, and so on.

- To tighten a saggy wicker chair seat, turn the piece upside down. Using a damp sponge, wet the underside of the seat (except for the chair's rim). Let the chair dry for 24 hours or overnight; the cane probably will have shrunk back into shape.

- Give a new look (and longer life) to wicker with latex paint. Be daring with your color selection: Match the decor of a particular room, go primary for fun, use forest green for a woodsy effect, or chill out with classic white.

- Create an antique look by using a deep-color latex paint and diluting it. Use a ratio of 1 part water to 2 parts paint. Apply the paint solution with a brush and, before it has dried completely, wipe the raised surfaces with a cloth to remove some of the paint.

- If you want to change the look of wicker fast, spray-paint it with latex-based paint. Set the piece in a large cardboard box with one side cut off. Work in a well-ventilated space, preferably outdoors, on a dry, calm day.

bookcase bonuses

Unless you have to fit an exact space, it's usually easier to buy bookcases than to build them. Try unfinished furniture stores, used office furniture outlets, and thrift shops for solid cases that only need a quick coat or two of paint. If you do need a custom fit, building a bookcase is one of the easiest types of furniture projects to do, even for those with minimal carpentry skills. If building isn't for you, an unfinished furniture store will often custom-craft bookcases for a bit more than their normal price for ready-made pieces.

- If you have a bunch of mismatched old bookcases acquired during various prior lifetimes, you can often pull them together into one harmonious whole by grouping them and then painting all of them the same color—usually white or the color of your walls.

- Whether you are buying bookcases or building them, make sure the shelves are at least 8 inches deep and 9 inches high to accommodate books of average

or small size, such as standard novels and paperbacks. This also is a good size for videotapes and DVDs. For larger books, such as art and reference books, the shelves should be 12 inches deep with 13 inches of clearance. The small plastic storage units that hold CDs also fit nicely on this size.

● Transform a plain wall with ordinary windows into an attractive architectural feature by constructing bookshelves above, below, and on either side of the windows. Fill some of the shelves with books, but leave space to display cherished objects or collections.

● Block out noise in apartments and townhouses. If you share one or more walls with neighbors, install floor-to-ceiling bookshelves along the walls separating the apartments to help muffle noise. You'll find that books are great sound absorbers.

● Make mini-libraries in unexpected places—on a wide landing, under a staircase, above a doorway, or in the corner of a room, and build a custom-shaped bookcase.

fabric matters

When you're choosing an upholstered piece, such as a sofa or armchair, it's important to examine the quality of the fabric. A piece may look great, but you want it to wear well, too.

cotton Quite versatile, strong, and comfortable. If untreated, it's less stain resistant than some synthetic fibers.

wool Very strong, long-lasting, naturally water-resistant, and generally soft to the touch; some people are sensitive to wool.

linen High-end and pricey, linen is strong and durable, and keeps its crisp look.

silk Also high-end; extremely strong, resilient, and luxurious.

rayon Comfortable, smooth, and soft synthetic fiber, but tends to wrinkle when used alone. Best in a blended fabric.

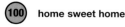

nylon Strong, long-lasting, resistant to rot, mildew, and abrasions; it doesn't absorb liquids well.

acrylic Manufactured fabric that offers many qualities of wool, it's fade-resistant but tends to pill.

olefin Manufactured fiber that resists soil and abrasions, it is often used in blends.

polyester The new generations of polyester are still extremely strong and resilient, but don't have as many drawbacks (comfort, for example) as their predecessors. Great in blends.

purchasing options

Obviously, the best way to buy a piece of new furniture is to go into the store and pay cash. But there are times in our lives when we need something to sit (or sleep) on and we simply don't have the whole price in our pocket. What to do?

- Don't fall into the "rent-to-own" trap. Like leasing a car, the agreements are often fuzzy and you could end up paying almost twice what the piece is worth.

- Furniture stores are some of the only stores left that offer lay-away plans. This is where you put down honest money, then pay over time until you own the piece. Then the piece is yours to take. This means paying for something you don't get to use, but there is no interest charged as there would be if you bought on credit—a great piece should be worth waiting for, right?

- If you have to wait for delivery, don't lend the store your money. Put down as small a deposit as you can, then save for the next six to eight weeks so that when the piece is ready for delivery, you can pay the rest without strain.

Bonus Tip!

THREE-STEP SCRATCH REPAIR

1. Buy a wax pencil at a hardware store or home center in the same color as the damaged piece (or slightly darker). Trace along the scratch with the wax pencil, working from top to bottom and making sure that the wax fills the scratch completely.

2. While the wax sets, cover a small wood block (a child's toy block is ideal) with a soft rag. Using the edge of the block, rub across the filled scratch with the wood grain to remove excess wax and flatten the filling.

3. Buff with a soft rag. The scratch should be barely noticeable.

CHAPTER 5

Penny-Smart Parenting

- bargain-basement babies

- lower cost kids

- free-time fun

bargain-basement
Babies

ONE OF THE MOST LIFE-CHANGING
EVENTS YOU CAN EXPERIENCE
CAN ALSO BE ONE OF THE MOST COSTLY.

baby super-duper stores

The enormous stores that cater to babies and toddlers with row upon row of cribs, changing tables, strollers, and so on are unquestionably convenient, since you can pick up anything under the sun for your baby. But are they cheaper than baby departments at traditional stores? As usual, that depends. In a comparison of Babies"R"Us, Target, Sears, and Burlington Coat Factory, we found a decent range of cribs, changing tables, strollers, playards (playpens), bassinets, car seats, diaper disposal systems, and clothing at very similar prices for comparable items. Make a list of **"must haves"** and then check the stores near your home to determine which ones have the best prices that day on the items you need.

price clubs for babies

If you're shopping for baby furniture, strollers, car seats, and so on, price clubs may have one or two models to choose from, but such stores don't stock the same baby items consistently. That being said, on a recent visit to Costco, we saw a Cosco Alpha Omega convertible car seat (for children weighing 5 to 80 pounds) for $99.99—a price competitive with that at discount superstores. Costco was selling a 128-count pack of Huggies disposable diapers for $29.99, while Target was advertising jumbo packs (30 to 42 per pack) for $10.88. Clearly, on that day, Costco was offering a lower price per unit. You can also find fairly high-quality baby clothing at good prices in price clubs.

resale heaven

A popular penny-pinching destination that makes loads of sense is the children's resale shop. These stores, which have sprung up all across the country, buy used clothing, furniture, and other baby items and then resell them. Clothing for infants and toddlers tends to be worn for a very short time, so you can pick up

like-new clothes—even high-end clothes from Baby Gap and Gymboree—for a few dollars.

garage sale chic

The one clothing area in which garage (or tag) sales can be fabulous is baby stuff. Babies outgrow clothes so fast, their clothes tend to stay in better shape than those for older children. Be sure to go through boxes of baby stuff; they can be treasure troves of barely used, high-quality items. You can also pick up infant swings, chairs, bedding, mobiles, and just about anything else your baby needs at garage sales.

go to the back of the store

Specialty children's stores, such as Gymboree and Baby Gap, have darling, well-made baby clothes but at budget-breaking prices. Don't despair. Specialty stores also have sensational sales, particularly at the end of a season, when they're trying to clear out stock. Walk on by the new stock and head to the back racks, where the clearance items hang. You can pick up things for 50 percent to 75 percent off. If you make a point of shopping for your child a year in advance, you may pick up some fabulous pieces at penny-pinching prices.

zero need for 0-3 months

Although those itsy-bitsy onesies are too cute, avoid buying many newborn clothes. Instead, go for the 3–6 month sizes for newborns; they grow amazingly fast.

baby shoe scam

Babies don't need shoes, so the only reason they're sold is because adults think they look cute. In fact, most pediatricians recommend going barefoot as much as possible well into early childhood to allow a baby's feet to develop. When toddlers do need shoes, choose soft, flexible ones with soles that won't slip but will move with the child. And buy cheap, because children go through shoes like water through a sieve.

diapers

Ah, the endless debate pitting the environment against convenience. So how do you decide which is more economical for your family? Do the math.

cloth diapers These last forever (practically), first as diapers and later as the best cleaning cloths you'll ever find. Though the initial investment is higher for cloth diapers, plastic pants, and pins, than for a big package of disposables, it's a one-shot expense. A set of cloth diapers will keep a baby supplied from birth through potty training, depending on how you fold them, and will produce no landfill waste. On the other hand, there's a utility cost: You must use water to wash them and electricity or gas to dry them. If you live in an area where water is plentiful for washing and sunshine for drying, cloth diapers make more sense, both economically and environmentally.

disposable diapers These diapers are not reusable, but they offer great convenience and are more absorbent than cloth, so you don't have to change them as often (good for you, but not so good for the baby). Moreover, the cost of disposables has come down over the years, and you can buy them in bulk for a good price at discount stores or price clubs. Disposable diapers don't use water resources, but they do produce waste (unless you want to spend more and buy

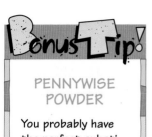

biodegradable disposables). If you live in an area where water is at a premium and you can't count on drying clothes outside, disposable diapers may be a more economical and environmentally sound choice.

prudent diaper pails

If you decide to go with cloth diapers, you will need a diaper pail. Any large bucket with a tight-fitting lid will do, but be sure little fingers can't open the pail. (Even a few inches of water in any pail or tub poses a drowning hazard to children.) Buy or make a mesh bag with a drawstring opening that fits the diaper pail. Fill the pail about two-thirds full with water and add a cup of white vinegar. The vinegar, which kills bacteria, will keep the pail from smelling and will also help whiten your diapers when you wash them. When the diapers reach the top of the water line, just pull the mesh bag out and dump it (and the diapers) into your washing machine.

wipe out extra costs

You do not need to buy wipes for your baby. You can make them yourself instead:

- Buy a bundle of discount washcloths at a price club or discount store (or buy a few at a time when you see them at garage sales and thrift stores). Keep them in the bathroom near your baby's changing area. When it's time to change the baby, dampen a washcloth in the sink (if the baby has a really dirty diaper, dampen one washcloth and rub a little soap over it, then dampen a second to rinse) and use that to clean the baby's bottom. Toss the dirty washcloths in your diaper pail to wash with the diapers.

- To make your own disposable wipes, cut a roll of paper towels in half cross-wise. Put a half roll in a plastic container with a tight lid. Combine 1–1/2 cups of water with 1 tablespoon of liquid baby bath soap. Pour the mixture over the towels to saturate them and cover the container. When you need a wipe, tear off a sheet from the roll.

creative cradles

When babies are tiny, you don't have to spend money on fancy bassinets:

- Line a large wicker basket with a folded baby quilt to make a nest for your baby.

- An old dresser drawer makes a secure bassinet.

- A Moses basket (available at some import stores and on several Web sites) is a wicker basket with a handle on each side. It's made to carry a small, sleeping baby and can easily be carried from room to room with you.

beddy-buys

Buying a crib can be a big investment, but it doesn't have to break the bank.

- A used crib can be a great bargain—just check out the classifieds. But don't buy one unless it meets all current standards for crib safety (see Getting a Good Crib, page 110).

- Check out sales at baby superstores, discount superstores, and even department stores. Ask about floor models, because they tend to be discounted.

- Transitional cribs that turn into toddler beds are more expensive than a regular crib, and their usefulness is debatable.

- Toddler beds are not necessary. Once your child can climb out of a crib (or starts trying), switch him or her to a regular bed. If you are uncomfortable with the height of a regular bed, buy an inexpensive side rail or put the mattress on the floor until the child is older.

BYOB (build your own bibs)

Purchased bibs are an unnecessary expense when you can make them or improvise:

- Stitch two ties—cut from grosgrain ribbon, seam binding, or twill tape—to a short end of a dish towel or hand towel to make an easy-to-wash bib.

- Cut an old T-shirt up the back and hem the cut edges. Add a Velcro or snap closure at the hemmed ends of the neck band to make a bib that amply covers your baby's clothes.

pads for pennies

You can make your own changing pad for very little: Pin together two bath-size towels and trim them to fit the top of your dresser or table. Stitch together the two long sides and one short side of the towels to form a pocket. Buy a piece of inex-

pensive foam (available at fabric stores) to fit into the pocket. Now you have a changing pad you can wash as needed; for convenience, make two or three pads, so you always have a clean cover on hand.

● Another easy cover for a changing pad is made of old pillowcases—either those you have on hand or picked up at garage sales or thrift stores or at a discount store.

budget blankets

A child can become mighty attached to a "blankie," which can lead to scenes of tragedy when the blanket falls apart from all that love. A trip to your local fabric store can provide a solution to the cost of a good blanket and the tears when it disintegrates. Polar fleece fabric is soft and fluffy, can be thrown into the washing machine innumerable times, and is practically indestructible. And if you buy remnant pieces in late winter or early spring, you can get a square yard for $3 to $5 (or less)! You can add satin binding around the edges or make a simple rolled hem, and you have a blanket that will last! If you're really smart, you'll buy 2 yards and make two identical blankets so that when one is being washed, your baby will have the spare.

bathing babies

You don't need to buy a special baby bathtub. Those are more for the comfort of Mom and Dad than for the baby. For years babies were bathed in the sink, and that still works pretty well. Line the sink (preferably a large kitchen sink) with an old towel to prevent slipping.

papering with memories

Save the paper from your baby-shower gifts to use to line the drawers of your baby's dresser. You'll save on liner paper and relive precious memories each time you open a drawer.

extending the juice

Although most babies love juice, they don't require it full strength. So, don't waste your money on "baby" juices. Buy plain juice concentrates (the least expensive, but be sure they are marked 100 percent juice with no added sugar) and reconstitute as per the package directions. When you are filling a bottle or sipping cup, fill the container about one-third to half full, then top it off with plain water. Your juice will last longer, and your baby will consume less fruit sugar, which can contribute to early tooth decay.

frugal baby food

Once your baby is given the go-ahead to start solid food, don't spend your money on those cute little jars of baby food. Using a food mill, food processor, or blender, simply purée cooked carrots or peas or canned fruit in water (not syrup). As the child grows older, just purée whatever you are having for dinner.

- To make it easier on yourself, search garage sales or thrift stores for an electric coffee grinder. Take it home and wash it well with hot, soapy water. Then use that to grind up your own baby food. The cup is a terrific size for babies.
- If you want more convenience, pick up some small plastic cups that have tight-fitting lids at garage sales or thrift stores. Then make large batches of food and store the leftovers in the cups, ready to use in a moment.

baby-sitting co-ops

If you have a group of friends with children, try setting up a baby-sitting co-op to save money and your sanity. Draw up a schedule of times that each set of parents can sit. Each time parents baby-sit for the co-op, they earn points. Then when they want to go out, they use points to have another set of parents watch their children. Once the co-op is running smoothly, you can expand it to include other parental needs, such as chauffeuring and toy swapping.

AU NATURAL

The fewer chemicals a baby's skin comes in contact with, the better. At your local health food store or natural grocery (and even at some discount superstores or chain drugstores), you can find baby care products that are made with natural ingredients, as opposed to strong chemicals. You can also find loads of books with instructions for making your own baby care items. But a general rule is the gentler, the better.

baby teeth bargains

For a long time it was thought that the health of baby teeth didn't matter; only healthy permanent teeth mattered. **WRONG!** Putting a baby to bed with a bottle of milk or formula or, even worse, juice can lead to tooth decay in infants! That practice can affect the way the child learns to eat or can lead to later dental problems. If a baby must have a bottle while in bed, give him or her water.

● Gently clean your baby's gums and early teeth with a damp washcloth. As your child grows, buy a soft-bristled toothbrush and child-safe toothpaste and teach your youngster how to use the brush properly.

● At about age 3, your child can start flossing and brushing alone. (You may have to help for a while.)

● Start taking your child to a dentist at about age 2. Look for someone with a family practice or see a pediatric dentist so that the experience is pleasant. The habits you instill in your tiny children will, hopefully, stay with them for the rest of their lives.

GETTING A GOOD CRIB

Here is a list of musts to check out before you purchase or use a crib:

● The crib has not been recalled by the U.S. Consumer Product Safety Commission (**www.cpsc.gov/kids/kidsafety**)

● The slats are no more than 2–3/8 inches (60 mm) apart.

● Slats are not missing, loose, cracked, or splintered.

● The crib has no sharp or jagged edges.

● The mattress fits tightly into the crib: No more than two fingers fit between the edge of the mattress and the crib side.

● The mattress support is securely attached to the crib headboard and footboard.

● The screws/bolts holding the crib parts together are tight and none are missing.

● The corner posts are 1/16 inch (1–1/2 mm) high or less.

● The crib has no cutouts in the headboard or footboard.

● The drop-side latches are too difficult to be released by a young child.

● The mattress is covered with a well-fitting crib sheet. Never use adult sheets.

● Never put pillows, comforters, stuffed animals, or other soft items in the crib.

● Always remember: Never lay an infant on his or her tummy to sleep.

lower cost
Kids

CAN YOU RAISE CHILDREN IN THIS DAY
AND AGE WITHOUT GOING BROKE?

junk the juice boxes

Juice boxes may be handy, but they are high in cost per unit, and they create a lot of waste. Instead, pick up a reusable plastic bottle (sports bottles work well) and fill that with the juice of choice (made from frozen concentrate and cut with water to reduce costs even further). For a treat, once in a while use half juice and half seltzer or sparkling water.

buy in bulk; dole out in dribs 'n' drabs

Food producers love to offer small sizes of a product to entice parents (and children) with portions that are "just right." Don't be fooled by cute packaging. You're paying for it big time. Instead, buy the largest size container of raisins, crackers, cookies, and so on, and transfer them to small plastic containers or bags that can be washed and used again.

food size matters

Small children like small food, but prepackaged bite-size foods cost more. Luckily, you can feed your children portions that match their size and still hold down food costs: Blocks of cheese are less expensive than slices per unit, but your children will enjoy it more if you cut the cheese into sticks or cubes. Baby carrots, bought in big bags for economy, are friendlier than big carrots. For no-cost fun, cut kids' sandwich bread with cookie cutters.

brown-bagging it

Get back in the habit of making lunches for children to take to school: It's cheaper, and you'll have better control of what your children are eating. Be sensitive to what is cool to carry lunch in (lunch boxes or brown bags), but don't let that dictate your youngsters' diet. Start tucking a cloth napkin (a bandana makes a fun one) in and remind your children to bring back any reusable packaging. You'll create less waste and won't be spending your money on disposable objects, which is money down the drain. As your children grow older, you can turn over the job of making lunch to them (with a little supervision, of course).

kids' clothing

Buying clothing for children is not very different from buying clothing for yourself, with one notable exception: Kids go through a lot of clothes quickly. For children's clothing, here are some smart shopping destinations:

department stores As with adult clothing, you can often find excellent buys in children's wear during sales and on the clearance racks at both high-end and mid-range department stores. But you'll frequently pay more at these stores than at cheaper alternatives, despite a sale.

discount department stores Ross, Marshall's, T.J. Maxx, and other discount stores can offer fabulous prices on name-brand clothing for the younger set. As is always true with discount stores, you won't know for sure what they have until you get there. To get the best selections, ask the store manager to tell you what days shipments arrive.

specialty stores As with baby clothes, stores such as Gap Kids and Gymboree have well-made clothes for older children that are truly adorable, but they're equally budget boggling. Luckily, these stores have some excellent sales. Always give the clearance racks a quick once over: You never know when you may find a steal!

outlet malls You can do some serious shopping during back-to-school or holiday sales events, but make sure you know the cost of basic kids clothing before you go, or you might not get the most from an outlet.

discount superstores Wal-Mart, Kmart, Target, and other discount superstores can really save you money, especially if you look for sales and check all the clearance racks on a regular basis. T-shirts, jeans, leggings, sweatshirts or sweaters, dresses, shorts and skirts, pants, and underwear are all available in styles that children like, that wear reasonably well, and that are budget-friendly.

secondhand when you can

Resale, consignment, and thrift stores, so fabulous for babies' and toddlers' clothing, lose a bit of their usefulness when children outgrow those sizes, because older children tend to wear out their clothes before the togs can make it to a resale store. However, a few exceptions to this rule make a trip to your favorite secondhand store well worth your while:

- Kids' coats and jackets—these are usually pretty well made, so they last a bit longer.
- Seasonal specialty clothing—ski pants and snowsuits are often outgrown in one season of wear, so they are more likely to be resold.
- Dressy dresses and jackets—these are worn so seldom, they generally still look good enough for resale once they're outgrown.
- Teens sometimes find bygone styles are retro and hip. Encourage your teen's penchant for fashions of the past; they're cheaper than buying new name-brand clothes.

extending elements

Sometimes kids seem to just grow straight up, not out. So their pants or skirts or dresses still fit in the waist and hips but are too short. Letting out the hem is sometimes a solution but doesn't always work and is impossible with jeans. Luckily, at least for girls, something old can be new again:

for pants Buy some trim, braid, or ribbon at a fabric store and sew several strips of different material along the hem of the pants to extend them.

for skirts or dresses Consider buying lace or other trim and adding it to the bottom hem. If you sew, you might buy a remnant of fabric that matches or contrasts with the dress fabric and stitch a bottom tier to the hem.

shoes for fast-growing feet

There is something positively uncanny in the way children's feet grow—often much faster than the rest of their bodies. So spending lots of money on shoes for kids is usually foolish. The most important factor is room to grow, so as soon as your child

AT RISK

www.nfpa.org/riskwatch.com

As a parent (or grandparent), your biggest concern is the safety of your children. And though we all try hard to anticipate and prevent injuries, it is hard to foresee some of the things that can hurt children. The National Fire Protection Association Web site, offers an injury prevention program focused on children ages 14 and younger. The program provides safety information about cars, burns, poisons, water recreation, bikes, choking, and more. Though the program is designed for use in schools, parents and other caregivers, as well as kids, can use the information. This Web site is well worth a visit.

When a child was no longer a toddler or baby, they graduated to adult furniture. Though it's tempting to indulge in cute but costly children's furniture, it's a waste of money. If you buy good quality wood furniture in a natural tone, you can soften the look of a child's room with pastel walls, child-geared wallpaper, bed-clothes, and curtains in bright fabrics, and collections of stuffed toys or dolls. The furniture will grow with the child and serve him or her into adulthood. The soft furnishings can be changed over time to reflect the child's changing age and interests.

complains of lack of toe room (or you notice that your youngster is walking on the sides of his or her feet or doesn't want to wear a particular pair of shoes), buy new shoes. But never spend a lot. Search discount superstores, department stores, shoe stores and price clubs for good deals instead.

double-duty beds

When it's time to buy a big bed for your child, consider a captain's bed, which consists of a mattress set on a frame that has drawers under the bed. If space is limited or you have children sharing a room, this is a real space saver, providing storage and a sleep space in one piece.

● For older children or teens, a loft bed, with a storage or study area below, is also a space saver and can be made if you have some woodworking skills or if you can find a local carpenter or handyman to build one for you. If you have to purchase one, you'll find a wide variety of prices and styles available. Ikea and other stores carry them; usually they come as kits that you bolt together.

have a ball with baskets

You can find cheap baskets at garage sales, flea markets, thrift stores, and craft or fabric stores. When you see a basket for a good price, snap it up; they're amazingly useful. If using baskets in a child's room, you can spray-paint them in a color to match the room or to spiff them up.

● Keep a basket for kids' bath toys in the bathroom, tucked in a corner. Make a rule that after baths, all the toys must go into the basket; your bathroom will stay neater, the toys won't get lost, and if you're entertaining, you can hide the basket in a closet.

- Assign each family member a basket (painting each to identify which basket is whose). Place the baskets near the most-used outside door, on a shelf or in a closet, to serve as a handy mitten, hat, and scarf storage spot.
- Toy boxes are really unnecessary and can be dangerous to little fingers. Instead, purchase plastic laundry baskets or big plastic tubs (wait for a Dollar Day sale at your local superstore or drugstore) to hold toys. You can assign a different color tub to each child, which helps keep the toys straight and makes toy pickup faster and easier for the kids, too. If several young children or teens are sharing one bathroom, storing all their toiletries (especially as they get older) can be a logistical nightmare. Give the kids a basket apiece to store their own toiletries in, and have them keep the baskets in their closets or on a dresser.

pillow power

Instead of spending money on child-size chairs that are soon outgrown, try some penny-wise pillow ideas:

- Buy a large foam pillow form at a fabric store and make a simple cover for it. Floor pillows allow a child freedom to cuddle up wherever they wish, and they are safe and easy for children to move.
- Create a pile of old decorative pillows you have on hand or pick up at garage sales. Let your child make his or her own little nest for reading or listening to music.

sitting pretty

Don't spend money on booster seats for those youngsters who have outgrown their high chairs

WHAT A SITE

Here are some great Web sites for children. Go online with your kids and check them out.

www.kidfu.com
Five monitored chat rooms

....

www.kidscom.com
Lots of games along with monitored chat rooms for preteens

....

http://kidswriting.about.com /mpchat.htm
The Creative Writing for Teens site offers a monitored chat room for sharing writing ideas plus information about the mechanics of writing, genres, and more

....

www.ala.org/parentspage /greatsites
The American Librarian Association's search engine has links to more than 700 sites, all reviewed and recommended by children's librarians

....

www.kidscastle.si.edu
Smithsonian Magazine's interactive site

....

www.kids.gov
The Federal Consumer Information Center's site for kids includes lots of links

....

http://disney.go.com /disneyinteractive
Games and activities for various age groups

(continued on next page)

www.niehs.nih.gov/kids
The National Institute of Environmental Health Sciences site

www.school.discovery.com
The Discovery Channel's site for teachers and students includes a section providing students with study tools

www.kidsmoney.org
The site provides sections with questions and answers about allowances and kids' money

www.nationalgeographic.com/kids
The National Geographic Society site for kids

http://dir.yahoo.com/education
Yahoo!'s huge education site

www.bigidea.com
VeggieTales info., games, music, etc.

www.pbskids.org
All the Public Broadcasting System favorites, from Sesame Street and Barney to Zoom, Zoboomafoo, Sagwa, Dragon Tales, Arthur, and more

www.scholastic.com
Great kids' publishing site, with areas for parents, kids, and teachers and featuring activities based on favorites such as Harry Potter, Clifford, the Magic School Bus, and more

but can't quite reach the tabletop without a little added height. Take your old phone book (just the right height!) and wrap it in an old pillowcase. This trick is also great to remember when you're visiting friends or relatives who are not set up for small children.

● You don't actually need a high chair at all. An infant can be fed in a portable car seat set in its upright position or simply held in your lap. When the child can sit upright (about the same time you begin introducing solid foods), you can buy an inexpensive three-in-one booster seat ($15 to $20 at discount superstores). This seat, which has a seat belt and removable tray, can be strapped onto a sturdy kitchen or dining-room chair. The tray has a high position and a lower position to accommodate the child's size as he or she grows. When the child no longer needs the tray, it can be removed altogether, and the seat can be used as a booster seat. A bonus is that these seats usually fold up so they can be taken along on car trips with ease.

a case for books

One simple piece of furniture is absolutely essential to a child's room: a good sturdy bookcase. And it's not just for storing books! A bookcase is so versatile that it can accommodate your child's needs from toddlerhood through the high-school and college years. When you put a bookcase in a toddler's room, be sure to secure it to the wall so adventurous little ones who decide to climb it won't pull it down on top of themselves.

free-time Fun

KEEPING KIDS HAPPY AND
ENTERTAINED REQUIRES A LITTLE
INGENUITY BUT NOT A LOT OF MONEY.

dining in

Once in a while (not just on a significant occasion, such as a birthday), set your table as if company were coming and treat your children like honored guests. Serve their milk in special glasses, light candles, have music playing in the background, and encourage the family to dress up. That doesn't have to mean putting on uncomfortable fancy clothing: Everyone might wear dress-up clothes, pajamas and bathrobes, or Halloween costumes for fun. The whole occasion won't cost you a cent more than a regular meal.

penny-wise picnics

Impromptu picnic meals, out of doors or in, can make a simple meal much more fun and save you money in the bargain. Your kids will enjoy it, too.

- When you are spending the day with your kids at a park or an amusement center, avoid the added expense of buying food there; pack a lunch instead. Include a treat or two so your children will feel that the lunch is special.
- On a rainy or snowy day (or a real scorcher) when you're stuck inside, surprise your child with an indoor picnic. Spread a tablecloth or old bedspread on the floor, serve picnic foods on picnic plates, and, for added atmosphere, set houseplants around the cloth to create an outdoorsy atmosphere.

at the movies

Unfortunately, taking the whole family out to the local quadraplex for the latest hot movie can really break the bank, even if you look for bargain matinees. (The cost of popcorn alone can top the cost of matinee tickets!) Thankfully, with videos and DVDs, movie night can be enjoyed in the comfort of your own home. Movie rental stores usually have a "cheapie" night or two during the week, and libraries loan videos and DVDs free. Make loads of popcorn, turn out the lights, and curl up with a film that the whole family can enjoy.

cultural expression

You don't have to spend tons of money to introduce your children to art, music, dance, and theater. Just learn to use a few of these tricks:

museums Most museums have a free day, and many have free or extremely inexpensive programs for children.

theaters Legitimate theaters often charge a significantly reduced price for tickets during previews, which function as rehearsals before an audience. Some have free matinees, aimed at introducing children to live theater, or one performance during a run for which you pay what you can. The same is true for dance companies, symphony orchestras, and even opera companies. Call the performing arts companies in your area to ask for details.

college performances If you live in a town with a college or university, take advantage of student performances. College choirs, symphonies, theaters, dance troupes, and art galleries usually charge very little, and you'll have the thrill of seeing stars in the making. And older children often respond strongly to performers close to their age.

take me out to the ball game

Most kids love going to sporting events. But with the ever-growing price of tickets, taking the family out to a professional sports event can cost almost as much as going to the theater—more if you want to sit anywhere close to the action. Check for promotional days or nights to lower the cost somewhat. Or try the minor leagues or become a fan of your local college teams. The tickets are usually less expensive, the games are scrappier, the fans are more loyal, and the players aren't doing it for the paycheck—yet. Don't just try the men's teams; women's softball, basketball, and soccer are hot right now, as are women's volleyball, lacrosse, and swimming and diving events.

the cost of memberships

Children's museums, science centers, and nature centers generally offer family memberships and are usually a bargain. Though the initial outlay may make you pause, if you live in an area where most of a season (very cold winters or very hot summers) must be spent primarily indoors, a membership in a top-notch museum or center will quickly pay for itself. Furthermore, members usually receive advance notice of special events, discounts on those events, and some special benefits including food or gift discounts. And if that's not enough, many museums and centers have reciprocal relationships with centers in other cities across the country, so you will have free access to those when on vacation.

class distinctions

Classes for enrichment or fun are terrific for kids. You can find excellent classes through most parks and recreation departments for all ages, and the cost is minimal. (The YMCA and YWCA also offer excellent classes, but the membership fees tend to be heftier.) Take a class in a foreign language, modern dance, pottery, step aerobics, basketball, improvisation, Chinese cooking, tumbling, feng shui, or anything else you or your children care to try. Even better, take a class with your child and get to know them better, too.

making music

It's wonderful when a child expresses an interest in taking music lessons, and it is definitely something to encourage, but you shouldn't invest in a musical instrument until you know this isn't just a passing fancy. Most music stores rent instruments, so call around for the best deal.

secondhand sounds

Buying a musical instrument secondhand can offer great savings, but be sure to ask a music teacher or someone who actually plays the instrument to check it out before you buy. And be wary of used guitars for sale on the cheap; they are often warped so badly that the strings are as much as an inch from the frets, making them nearly impossible to play.

ART SUPPLIES IN BULK

Many art supply companies sell paints, canvas, brushes, and other supplies by volume. Big craft store chains (Ben Franklin, Frank's, Michael's) also offer good prices, especially when they have sales. You can even find crafting supplies at fabric stores. And don't forget bags of scraps, ribbons, fake leaves and flowers, empty spools, buttons, and so on. Also look online, if time is of the essence or you don't have a good outlet nearby. Try these three Web sites:

www.dickblic.com

www.discountart.com

www.createforless.com

bowled over

Kids love to bowl, and bowling can be done inside or outside. You can make your own bowling set for practically nothing!

● For bowling pins, save 2-liter plastic soda bottles (or ask friends and family to save them for you) and wash them out. Use any sort of soft ball as the bowling ball. For very small children, leave the bottles empty and use large balls. As the children get older, fill the bottles with sand (to make them tougher to knock over) and use a smaller, heavier ball. If you want to make an impromptu bowling alley in your driveway, garage, or basement, just prop two long two-by-fours (or two-by-eights, if you have them) about 3 feet apart, with a board across one short end to stop the ball.

stacking up savings

stacking cups These are still one of the most popular early toys for tots. But you don't have to buy them. Look through your cupboards for old plastic cups to make your own set. Or check out garage sales for a set of measuring cups.

building blocks Another simple toy you can make is building blocks. Cut small pieces of wood from two-by-fours or four-by-fours (or ask a local lumber store to save them for you). Sand off any rough edges. Either stain to bring out the wood tones or paint in bright colors. (Make sure the stain or paint is safe for children; check the label, and if in doubt, ask for help at the paint counter.)

FINGER PAINTS

A rainy day (or scorcher) sanity saver!

| 1-1/4 cups all-purpose flour | 1 cup water |
| 3 tablespoons glycerin | assorted food colorings |

● Combine the flour and water in a medium-size bowl. Divide the mixture equally among three small bowls.

● Stirring constantly, add 1 tablespoon of glycerin to each batch, along with the desired amount of food coloring. Make fresh as needed.

long live board games

If you want to extend the life of your favorite family board games (particularly those played often and with enthusiasm by the youngest members of your household), coat the boards on both sides with shellac or polyurethane varnish right after you buy them. The games will last longer, and you can clean the boards easily with a damp cloth. Store the game pieces in plastic self-sealing bags.

chalk talk

- Wrap masking tape around the middle of chalk to keep it from breaking (and to keep hands cleaner).
- Coat chalk or charcoal drawings with hair spray to keep them from smudging.

revive that marker

Give new life to a dried-out marker by dipping the tip in an acetone-based nail polish remover. Replace the cap and let the marker sit for a couple of hours before using.

postcards

Kids love getting mail, and they especially love receiving picture postcards, which cost little to buy and mail. Ask relatives or friends who live out of town (it doesn't matter where the cards come from) to send a postcard for a child's special day (birthday, first tooth out, graduation from preschool, end of baseball season, dance recital). Then designate an area of the child's room as the card wall. Install inexpensive corkboard (to prevent tape or pin marks in the wall) on which the cards can be displayed.

be constructive: don't throw it out

Save every paper towel roll, toilet paper roll, margarine tub, yogurt cup, plastic bottle cap, soda pop bottle, plastic jar, oatmeal or cornmeal container, coffee can (with plastic lid), and sturdy paper box. Let your kids build castles, forts, mountain ranges, and more with all these free construction materials.

animal cracker race

This is an ideal game for two to four younger children: Use an old checkerboard (or even better make your own). Each child gets one animal cracker. Designate one corner square as the Start position and place hurdles (a chocolate kiss or a marshmallow) on random squares around the edge of the board. Each child rolls a die once, then moves his or her cracker the number of squares indicated by the die. If a player's animal cracker lands on a hurdle, the player must go back two squares—but gets to eat the hurdle! The first animal cracker to make it all around the edge of the board wins. And the winner eats his or her cracker!

story sack

On days when the weather keeps you inside, when you're on a long car trip, or during evenings in hotels, this can be a fun pastime for everyone in the family: Fill a bag with pictures cut from old magazines. Take turns with your children picking out images and making up stories about them. Write out or tape-record the tales you create.

stir crazy

Kids love to help in the kitchen, especially if they get to eat what they make. Assign fun activities they can tackle with their bare hands, such as kneading bread dough or cutting out cookies. Decorating a sheet cake or a batch of sugar cookies is another favorite: Supply the youngsters with an array of sprinkles, chocolate bits, jelly beans, nuts, or fresh berries, and tell them to be creative. Let them eat their masterpieces when they are done.

PAPIER-MÂCHÉ

An old-fashioned favorite for making piñatas or gifts.

    1 cup flour   2/3 cup water
    newspaper strips (about 1-1/2 inches wide)

- Combine the flour and water in a medium-size bowl. Stir until it is the consistency of thick glue. If a thicker mixture is desired, add more flour.

- Dip each strip separately in the paste and gently pull it through your fingers to remove any excess paste. Then apply the strip to the surface you want to cover. (Clay, cartons, bottles, or other disposable containers make a good base; if you want to make a piñata, cover a blown-up balloon.) Repeat until the object is completely covered. Let dry.

- When the surface is dry, decorate with poster paint. For a longer-lasting and harder surface, coat with shellac after the paint dries.

---

 penny-smart parenting

stickers savings

Everyone gets more junk mail than they'd like to, and most of it goes right into the trash. But before you throw away the ads, look through the envelopes. You may find free stickers (showing thumbnail-size magazine or CD covers, for example) that your kids will enjoy pasting on their creations.

greening of the thumbs

Another activity children usually like to help with, if encouraged, is gardening. If you have the space, give your children their own plots on which to grow whatever they fancy: tomatoes, watermelons, sunflowers. Teach them how to prepare the soil, plant the seeds, and care for their plants. If space is limited, buy a window box planter or several small pots and let them learn container gardening.

PLAY CLAY

A good modeling dough for children, this can also be used to make holiday ornaments.

1/2 cup table salt (do not use rock or sea salt) 1/2 cup hot water
1/2 cup cold water   1/2 cup cornstarch
2 drops food coloring (optional)

● Combine the salt and hot water in a large saucepan and bring the mixture to a boil over high heat.

● Meanwhile, stir the cornstarch into the cold water until it is well mixed. Add the food coloring if desired.

● Pour the cornstarch mixture into the boiling salted water, stirring constantly and vigorously to keep the mixture from lumping up. Reduce the heat to low and cook, stirring constantly, until the mixture is stiff.

● Remove the pan from the heat and, using a large spoon, carefully turn the mixture onto a breadboard. Let cool, then knead until smooth.

● Use immediately or wrap in plastic wrap and store in an airtight container. If desired, clay models can be preserved by air-drying at room temperature for three days or by baking at 200° F for two hours.

CHAPTER 6

Cent-sational Special Occasions

○ penny-wise parties

○ the well-planned wedding

○ happy homemade holidays

○ all good gifts

penny-wise
Parties

AS ANY SUCCESSFUL HOSTESS
WILL TELL YOU, THROWING A MEMORABLE PARTY
ISN'T ABOUT SPENDING GOBS OF MONEY.

cost-effective entertaining

One way to keep a lid on costs is to think of parties as either theme- or event-based. Your theme can be very simple—such as a TGIF (Thank God It's Friday) or board-game night—or as elaborate as an ethnic feast or karaoke sing-along. Event-based parties are built around a special occasion, from the Superbowl or Kentucky Derby to an anniversary or birthday. Building your menu and decorations around a theme or specific event will help you make a big splash for less money. Why? Because the choices of food and décor will be clearer, allowing you to tailor the party for effect, not expense.

where to shop?

Big party stores are all over the place and you can find great stuff there for a good price. But we have found that buying party supplies is less costly if you purchase them over a period of time whenever you see a sale. Having a stock of party stuff on hand will spare you from last-minute shopping—which tends to add up. Also, don't assume that big party stores have the best selection or the best prices. Sometimes little mom-and-pop stores offer more variety and cheaper prices in order to keep your business.

- Check out drugstores for paper plates, cups, balloons and party favors.
- Craft and fabric stores often have all sorts of party favor ideas. They also can have terrific sales, especially if you hit them around the holiday season.

candles in the night

Buy candles whenever you see them on sale and keep them handy for entertaining. A good selection of taper-style and column candles can be used to create a warm or elegant party atmosphere with a minimum of fuss. Don't forget votive candles. They are also a beautiful and versatile party accent.

○ Greet your guests in style with luminaria lining your front walkway. You can make these traditional Mexican Christmas candles yourself. Simply pour a thick layer of sand inside white lunch-size paper bags and place a tea lights or votive candles in the sand of each bag. When lighted from within, the lunch-bag candles produce a warm and beautiful glow. Instead of bags, you can recycle 16-ounce cans and use a tin punch to make designs on the sides for the light to shine through.

○ Place small scented votive candles in holders in each powder room. This will make the room smell nice and the light will make it easier for your guests to find the bathroom.

○ For an eye-catching, informal look use single candlestick holders of different shapes and sizes set in groups.

○ Clean out your fireplace and place a collection of different-sized column candles during warmer months to produce a warm inviting look without the heat.

frugal flowers

Of course, serious penny pinchers grow their own cutting flowers so that they never have to spend money on them. But even those of us who depend on store-bought blossoms can find ways to keep costs down.

○ Only buy flowers in season—the more exotic the bloom, the higher the cost.

○ Buy flowers in bunches; pre-made flower arrangements tend to cost more and limit your options.

○ Buy just a few flowers and fill in with greens, preferably from your own garden (herbs such as rosemary or lavender are lovely to use in arrangements).

○ Fresh fruit and vegetables, especially different varieties of hard squash and nuts, can be pulled together for a distinctive and unique centerpiece.

hold it!

Your don't have to use a standard vase to hold flowers. If you use your imagination, you can liven up your flower arrangements. Here are some suggestions:

○ If you're throwing a baby shower, have friends who already have babies save their old baby-food jars for you. Put one jar at each place setting with a tiny bouquet of violets, sweet william, lily of the valley, and, of course, baby's breath.

○ Pick up small and unusual old bottles at junk or antique stores, flea markets, garage sales, or thrift stores—they make eye-catching vases. Set them at each place at a sit-down dinner. Place a blossom or two in each bottle, plus a place card. Or use them to tuck mini-bouquets throughout the house, including the bathroom.

○ Sunflowers are easy to grow and make a dramatic statement when used in arrangements—the only problem can be finding a vase to accommodate them. Try using an old milk pail, umbrella stand, or wrap a plastic waste can with burlap and tie the burlap in place with some raffia.

○ Hunt through thrift stores, junk shops or flea markets for old cookie, mason, canning, or apothecary jars—all make wonderful containers for flowers.

balloon bouquets

Few things say "party" quite so definitively as balloons. Buy latex balloons in bulk and rent a helium tank from a party store. Filling your own balloons is usually less expensive than buying an already filled bouquet. Buy a big roll of curling ribbon and cut it into long pieces. Tie them to each balloon and slightly curl the ribbon. Then just let them float around the room—instant party!

food for a frugal feast

This is where a price club can save your budget! They offer excellent selections of meat, poultry, fish, vegetables, fruit, wine, beer, hard liquor, breads, crackers, chips, juices, and sodas. Plus, you'll find big boxes of frozen appetizers if time is short, and even fresh dips, sauces, sushi, cheese, and enormous desserts (including sheet cakes for special occasions that can be decorated to order). Depending on your budget, you can pick up everything for a gourmet spread or a low-cost blowout and still come out on top financially.

○ If you want to prepare a formal, sit-down meal, select one course as the star and spend extra time and money on that. Many gourmet dishes actually don't require expensive ingredients—you just have to be able to cook well.

○ A big piece of meat, such as a turkey, boneless ham, or roast can feed a crowd easily and fairly economically. Add rice or pasta, vegetables, salad, bread, and dessert (cookies, a sheet cake, fresh fruit with chocolate dipping sauce) for a delicious menu.

eat, drink, and be merry

Planning a party around a particular food or beverage is another easy and low-cost party idea.

wine and dine If you have friends who really appreciate wine, plan a menu, then ask each guest to bring a bottle of wine for each course. Make sure they bring a description of the wine's characteristics. Set a limit on the amount spent on each bottle—wine doesn't need to be expensive to be good.

bring on the brew With the explosion of microbreweries, the variety of beer available today is both delicious and exciting. Host a beer-tasting party and invite your friends to bring a six-pack of their favorite stout, pale ale, amber ale, or bitter. Mexican, Indian, and Chinese food are all enhanced by beer. A selection of appetizers from any or all of these cuisines would be fabulous and relatively cheap to make or buy.

easy, inexpensive party ideas

All you need is a little imagination to throw a party that's a lot of fun without costing an arm and a leg. Try these ideas:

movie night Let a movie shape the menu: serve fried chicken, collard greens, grits, and iced tea with *Gone With the Wind*; deep-dish Chicago-style pizza with *The Untouchables*; a selection of German or Austrian pastries with *The Sound of Music*; or a vat of Texas-style chili, buttermilk biscuits, and beer with *My Darling Clementine*. Ask your guests to come dressed in costumes for fun.

game night Have a selection of board games that your guests can play in teams. Serve a selection of finger foods, such as mini pizzas, chicken satay, empanadas, stuffed mushrooms, and pot stickers.

so you wanna be a star Rent a karaoke machine and let your friends do their best Elvis Presley, Aretha Franklin, or Frank Sinatra impersonation (the sky's the limit in terms of music). Just warn your neighbors first, or invite them.

Serve champagne punch and canapés, and ask everyone to dress in their best "star" duds.

ethnic potluck Ask each guest to bring a dish from a particular country or region such as Greece, Denmark, New England, or the Florida Keys. The host and hostess provide beverages, tableware and linens. Check out CDs of appropriate music and ask a travel agency or the tourist board for posters or brochures to use in decorating.

tgif pajama party Invite your friends to wear PJs or their favorite lounging outfit. Serve fun comfort food, like roast chicken and mashed potatoes, tomato soup, grilled cheese sandwiches, or big messy tacos. And make sure to set a "no talk about work" rule.

kid-friendly party ideas

Here's some approaches to try for children's parties:

wild west Have children play pin the tail on the donkey, toss clothespins in a cowboy hat, and try to rope the rocking horse. Introduce children to "partner, may I?" and send them on a "steer hunt" with a cow-shaped piñata. Play classic cowboy music to set the mood. Serve wagon-wheel macaroni and cheese, lil' doggies (cocktail franks), and prairie grass salad (shredded iceberg lettuce). Party favors could be plastic cowboys and farm animals tied up in a red bandana.

desert island Fill a small wading pool with sand and bury "treasures" there for children to find. Let them dive for "pearls" (small white rocks), enjoy a round of coconut "bowling," and send them on a "shark hunt" (shark piñata). Play calypso music, hang bunches of bananas in your trees for the kids to pick, quench thirst with a tropical punch, and serve mini kabobs of pineapple and ham. Party favors could be a small bag of chocolate gold foil coins (treasure) in a cardboard box (treasure chest) the children decorate themselves.

camp birthday If you're planning a party for older children, set up tents in your backyard for an outdoor sleep over. Have the children go on a scavenger nature hunt, toss rope rings over cans of beans, and play "black bear scare" (one person is the bear, the rest hide and the bear tries to catch them). Then set up an outdoor fire pit and tell scary stories. Roast hot dogs and have the whole crew work together to make a s'more "cake." Instead of making each s'more sandwich separately, layer graham crackers, chocolate bars, and melted marshmallows into the shape of a cake. For party favors consider getting an inexpensive paperback book about a camping mystery or adventure suitable for their age level.

the well-planned
Wedding

AH, WEDDINGS«THE ROMANCE
THE EXCITEMENT, THE COST!

a basic budget

There was a time when the bride's parents were expected to pay for the entire wedding bill. Not anymore. These days, the bride's family, groom's family, and the couple often do a three-way split. Sometimes each family will pay for a particular aspect of the wedding. If the couple is fairly established financially, they may decide to pay for the entire wedding themselves. However you decide to manage your wedding costs, plan for the following:

- About half of the entire budget ends up going toward the reception, including location rental, food, and drink.
- Roughly 10 percent will be spent on clothing for the bride and groom, including rentals.
- About 10 percent will go toward invitations, special transportation to and from the reception for the bridal party, and various fees, such as those for the clergy.
- The final 30 percent is divided between music and entertainment, photography (or videography), flowers, and other decorations.
- Happily, there are ways to save in each of these areas and still have a glorious wedding.

prudent prioritization

- First, decide how much you want to spend on the entire wedding. If the families are splitting the costs, get together and discuss how much each feels comfortable with.
- Next, make a list of the things you'd like to include in the wedding from the biggest to smallest detail.
- Now, the hard part: Prioritize the list, from most important to least. This will help keep you on budget. Lower priority items that don't fit the budget can be

adapted or approached more creatively. For example, if superb food is important to the bride and groom, finding a great caterer should be given the highest consideration. To offset food costs, you can economize on transportation to and from the reception by decorating cars instead of renting limousines. It's crucial for the bride and groom to agree on a list of priorities. If each family supports the couple's choices, the wedding will be a happier event.

the guest list

The one thing that will determine how costly your wedding will be is the guest list. It is not necessary to invite everyone you or your family has ever known. A bigger crowd doesn't make the day any more memorable. In fact, the more people that come, the harder it will be for the bride and groom to visit them all. First, the couple should decide on how many people they want at their wedding. Then they should ask family members to submit lists of people they would like to invite. There will have to be some bargaining with family members, if the lists go over the preferred number of guests. Deciding whom to invite may not be easy at times. But if you stick to a set number, you'll keep costs down and may even have a more memorable wedding.

religious considerations

Generally, members of a religious group are permitted to hold a wedding in the place of worship for free or at a minimal cost. Along with the place of worship, you'll likely have access to staff musicians and even a wedding coordinator for the ceremony. If you are a nonmember, but wish to be married in a place of worship, the fee will be larger.

◉ Often a house of worship has an adjoining hall of some kind, which is usually available for a reception at a modest fee. Many halls have full-service kitchens, but often there are restrictions about serving alcohol.

comforts of home

Until the last century, wedding receptions were almost always held at home. The concept is both sensible and lovely. If the bride or groom have access to a special residence belonging to a member of the family, the wedding and reception can take place there free of cost. The money saved on a location rental can be spent on catering and décor instead.

◉ In cooler weather, have the wedding indoors in front of a fireplace or a

window with a beautiful view. The reception can move from room to room.

- In good weather, a backyard gazebo, a pool, a particularly exquisite area of a garden, or even a tent or canopy can make an eye-catching wedding site.

special places for cents

If you want to save money and have something special, throw away your idea of a conventional wedding site and open up your imagination. Get out the tour book of the area in which you are to be married—you may find some terrific ideas for locations there.

city or county parks A well-landscaped park with a community hall can often be rented for a very modest fee. Or you could have a "picnic" wedding at a park shelter beautified by flower garlands, white and silver balloons, and so on.

public beaches and parks If you are nature lovers, these venues, and others, like mountain areas, can provide spectacular scenery for a one-of-a-kind wedding. You may have to be creative when it comes to the food. A big old barbecue is great fun and a cold buffet can travel just about anywhere.

historic buildings Historic houses or public buildings are also a good bargain. They have often been renovated so that they can accommodate functions and add a truly unique feel to the celebration.

museums Many art, history, or nature museums are available for functions in their off hours. They tend to have large kitchens and provide truly memorable surroundings. Ask about member discounts for functions.

botanical gardens You can't ask for a more naturally lush location. They frequently have facilities for functions. Plus, the landscaping is always in top form, regardless of the season. Ask about member discounts for functions.

college chapels These and other buildings at colleges and universities offer a particularly cost-effective and meaningful choice if the bride and groom attended the same college. Many colleges have lovely chapels and halls that can be used for receptions. Alumni often receive substantial discounts.

investing in invitations

This is a great opportunity to trim the budget and express yourself. Instead of traditional engraved invitations, stop by your favorite stationery store to consider different options. You can find exquisite stationery and even do-it-yourself invitation kits. A hand-written invitation on a card that really reflects who you are is much more intimate and evocative than a printed one.

○ If you can't hand-write your invitations, have them printed rather than engraved. Good printing looks wonderful and costs about half as much.

○ If you've chosen simple, elegant paper, you can still dress up the invitations by adding wax seals, foil, ribbon, and so on. Sprinkle a little confetti or potpourri inside the envelope before you seal it.

○ Chose your stamps with care. The post office is usually very helpful in offering a variety of appropriate stamps. Bring a sample of the invitation with you so they can weigh it and determine the correct postage.

getting the dress for less

Spending hundreds to thousands of dollars for a dress you wear once just doesn't make sense to us. Invest that money or save it for a down payment on a house, don't spend it on a dress—even if it is for your wedding.

check the closets If it's still in good condition, the gown that was worn by your mother, mother-in-law, aunt, or grandmother might be a fine choice. You'll honor them by wearing it and get a dress for free. Pay a good seamstress to alter the gown to fit you perfectly and splurge a little on lingerie, shoes, or other accessories. If the dress is extremely dated, have it slightly altered to reflect both the past and the present.

gently used Check antique stores, thrift stores, and consignment shops. You may be surprised at what you find and the price you'll pay.

get dramatic If you really want a one-of-a-kind dress, call the costume shops of your community theater or try the drama department of a nearby college or university. You may be able to hire a costume designer to create a dress for you. Ask to see a portfolio of designs and some garments he or she has created. A school of fashion design may also have graduate students eager to establish themselves by creating a truly unique dress.

buck tradition An elegant ivory suit, a simple white slip dress, a pretty tea-length gown in antique lace, or just a dressy dress that looks great on you can all be wonderful wedding attire. And don't limit yourself to white—it has only been traditional since the time of Queen Victoria. Many cultures use other colors for wedding dresses.

rent it If you really want a traditional designer gown, a less-expensive route is to rent it. Check the Yellow Pages under "Gown Rentals and Sales."

beautiful budget blooms

The rule here is the same for any entertaining: Buy only flowers in season and, if possible, arrange them yourself (or ask a friend or relative who's good at arrangements to do it).

○ For simple charm, use flowering potted plants on tables at the reception, lining the aisle, or tucked in various places for color. Tie ribbons or raffia around the pots and encourage guests to take them home. Potted plants cost much less than cut flowers and won't wither and die.

○ Go for the greenery! Use pine boughs in winter or luxurious ferns in summer to add texture, color, and elegance to an arrangement for very little outlay. Use ribbons or carefully tuck candles among the greenery.

○ Fill glass bowls with fresh fruit and tuck a few flowers among them for maximum effect with minimal cost.

fabulously frugal food

For many, the formal sit-down dinner seems to be a must for a wedding reception. But it isn't really necessary and may actually detract from the event. Weddings often provide people with a chance to catch up with each other. If guests are seated at a table and required to sit there for a few hours while food is brought to them, they may not enjoy themselves nearly as much as if they had the freedom to eat when they want, what they want, and with whom they want.

○ A sit-down meal requires a number of servers and you pay for each and every one.

○ A buffet can allow you to spend more on the food itself, offer more

variety to please many different tastes, is flexible, and requires only those attending the serving tables.

○ Don't limit yourself to dinner! A morning wedding lends itself to a sparkling champagne brunch or a light and luscious lunch. An early afternoon ceremony could be followed by an elegant high tea with finger sandwiches and strawberries and cream. A late afternoon service would lend itself to a fabulous cocktail party with delectable finger foods. All of these options can be truly delicious at less than the cost of a formal dinner—and a lot more fun, too.

○ Because you will be serving cake, don't feel you must offer other desserts. A platter of fresh fruit is refreshing to the eye, a nice finish to a meal, and a godsend to those who are watching calories. If you want to dress the fruit up, offer chocolate dipping sauce on the side.

WEDDING WEB SITES

www.discount-invitations.com or 1-888-969-9394

www.discountbridalservice.com or 1-800-874-8794

There are so many Web sites devoted to weddings—from help with planning to saving on everything from invitations to dresses—it would be impossible to note them all here. To access these sites just type the words "discount" and "wedding" in your search engine. The two sites above are worth checking out.

the cake caper

You want your wedding cake to look beautiful but you also want it to taste good. It's a good idea to sample a cake first to make sure you like it before serving it at your wedding.

○ Rather than go to a private bakery, ask around to find someone who bakes specialty cakes at home. They usually charge less and the cake is often better.

○ Check out the bakery department in your local grocery store. Unlikely as it may seem, some of these produce dazzling cakes at an easy-on-you price.

○ The least expensive route is to ask a family member who's a great baker to do you the honor of making your cake as his or her wedding gift. To dress the cake up, have your florist make a miniature version of your wedding bouquet as a cake topper.

○ For ease of serving, have the actual wedding cake made smaller, and keep a second large sheet wedding cake ready to be served out of sight.

a budget for beverages

Although there are folks who hail an open bar as a sign of a good party, do you really want them at your wedding? Wine, beer, and a good selection of nonalcoholic beverages, plus champagne for the toasts, is a less pricey and ultimately more satisfying approach.

bring your own bottles The markup on any kind of alcoholic beverage is pretty steep so you'll save money just by shopping and buying your own. Call around to see which stores offer the best prices and buy in bulk. And don't forget keg beer, if you're having an informal outdoor reception.

regional references If you live in or close to an area that produces wine, you may want to call some of the vineyards. You may be able to get a great price on a high-caliber wine or champagne by purchasing cases directly from a vineyard. This is also a way to share something special about your home region with your guests. (Some vineyards also offer outstanding wedding facilities!)

microbrewing The same philosophy of regional pride can be adapted to your choice of beer. The proliferation of microbreweries has been astonishing, and you should be able to find one close to home. Again, by purchasing directly, you may get a break on the price of really special brews.

sparkling sips Champagne or another sparkling wine really makes the toasting special, but few people want to drink it throughout a party (unless you buy the highest quality, bubblies tend to promote headaches). Save the sparklers for the toasts—it will set them off as special, and you can then invest in a better quality sparkling wine.

time (and other) factors If you're having a morning wedding, mimosas can be festive; afternoons can call for a tea- or juice-based punch. A winter wedding with a Renaissance feeling could lend itself to mulled wine or spiced cider; the heat of summer in the Southwest could inspire big pitchers of white and traditional Sangria. Let the time, the season, the place, and personal taste dictate your beverage offerings.

options, options Make sure you have lots of nonalcoholic beverages on hand, too. Sparkling water, iced tea, lemonade, fruit juices, or punch—even big pitchers of iced coffee if the bride and groom are known to love their java.

thrifty notes

Music is an important part of just about any wedding. Personal taste, venue, and budget will dictate the music you choose. If you're getting married in a mountain park or on a beach, a guitarist, flutist, or other portable instrumentalist is appropriate. If you're hiring a hall for dancing, a band or disc jockey will be needed.

○ If you are having the ceremony in a house of worship, they probably have a pianist or organist on staff. You may be required to use this person or pay them a fee if you don't (this is how they make their living). Unless they're terrible (not likely), hiring the staff musician is generally the most cost-effective option.

○ If you are planning to have the reception in the same place that you're being married, hiring someone who can play at both may be less expensive.

○ Check local schools of music, colleges or universities to hire excellent musicians at a much lower cost. You can also ask about vocalists and student dance bands that might meet your needs.

○ DJ's don't all wear disco suits! A disc jockey can be a very economical alternative to live music at your reception. Shop around. You should be able to find someone who understands the mood you are trying to create and can work with you to select the perfect music.

frugal photos

You don't want to break the budget, but you do want to hire a good photographer. His or her pictures, after all, will become your wedding memories. Ask friends and family members for recommendations on good photographers. You may even want to call your local newspaper or photo supply store for leads. Look at portfolios and interview each candidate to find the best match in personality and approach. Talk about your budget honestly and see what he or she has to offer. Often, a package can save you money.

○ Ask the prospective photographer if they would be willing to just shoot pictures and deliver you the negatives and proofs instead of a formal package. You'll save tons of money if you can reprint the photos and create a wedding album yourself.

○ For great informal shots, put a cheap disposable camera on each guest table.

○ If you will be married in a house of worship, make sure that you check with them first about rules for photographers and videographers. They are frequently stricter than you might imagine.

○ Ask your photographer to give you digital copies of the pictures on a CD, so that you can e-mail pictures to all.

do everyone a favor

Giving a small gift to each wedding guest is a charming custom that can quickly get out of hand. How many of us have little gewgaws sitting in drawers somewhere? We hate to just throw them away, but usually they are useless. Why not take a different approach?

light of love Small scented candles with ribbons in your wedding colors tied around them.

gift of green Packets of seeds, either a flower that was featured in the wedding, or an herb with significance, such as rosemary (remembrance and friendship).

native foods If you're being married in the Southwest, a packet of salsa spice; northeasterners could give tiny bottles of maple syrup.

picture perfect Make copies of your engagement photo or other snapshot that captures the relationship; purchase inexpensive frames and give those as a lasting memento.

pamper your guests Packets of bubble bath, tubes of peppermint foot lotion (relief after all that dancing), and other small indulgences.

share a toast Small bottles of wine or champagne as a toast to family and friends who have gathered to celebrate.

happy endings

The wedding is over, you're off on your honeymoon! Or are you? Don't feel you must rush directly from your wedding to your honeymoon. For one thing, you'll be exhausted after *the* big day. You may want a quiet night at a hotel, or even at home before taking off. By taking the time to relax, even for a day or two, you'll enjoy the trip more. And you'll frequently have to take off days from work around your wedding; if you want a longer trip, waiting may be the answer. We know a couple who waited an entire year after their wedding so they could save up money and vacation days to splurge on a long honeymoon trip to the British Isles.

If you've never planned a wedding before, here's a quick course. As always, careful planning pays, saving you not only money but a lot of last-minute hassles.

6–12 MONTHS AHEAD

- Set budget.
- Choose date and time for wedding and reception.
- Book locations.
- Rough out guest list between families.
- Select caterer and begin choosing menu.
- Meet with person who will officiate and discuss ceremony.
- Select and invite wedding attendants.
- Select wedding dress, bridal attendant dresses, and accessories.
- Register for gifts.
- Order invitations or begin writing your own
- Select wedding rings.
- Contract with photographer, videographer, and musicians.

3 MONTHS BEFORE

- Order flowers.
- Plan and book honeymoon.
- Select attire for groom, best man and usher.
- Check requirements for a wedding license with state agency.

2 MONTHS BEFORE

- Determine seating arrangements.
- Finalize menu, beverage service, and decor.
- Mail invitations (at least 6 weeks before date).
- Make arrangements for rehearsal dinner.
- Book transportation for wedding party.
- Select gifts for wedding party.

1 MONTH BEFORE

- Arrange lodging for out-of-town guests.
- Final fitting for wedding attire.
- Order wedding cake.

2 WEEKS BEFORE

- Arrange for hair and make-up, if being done professionally.
- Call invitees who haven't responded to determine final guest list.
- Give caterer the final number of guests.
- Schedule wedding rehearsal.
- Confirm honeymoon bookings.
- Have blood tests, get marriage license.

THE WEDDING DAY

- Best man gives officiant the fee.
- Eat a light meal before the wedding.
- RELAX AND ENJOY!

happy homemade
Holidays

IT'S HARD TO KEEP A LID ON
SPENDING AROUND THE HOLIDAYS. IT'S
A TIME OF JOY, OF SHARING, OF SHOPPING.

garage sale decorating

Looking for holiday items (or those that can be adapted) on the cheap? Get thee to some garage sales! We've walked away with exquisite unused table linens, a bevy of candle holders, strings of lights, ornaments, holiday tins (which you can reuse for food gifts or for decorating), artificial trees—and much more. Plus you can look for bowls, cookie jars, and baskets of every size and shape to adapt for any holiday. All for mere pennies! Drop by sales throughout the year and keep your eyes open—you never know when someone is going to clean out their garage, basement, or attic. Chances are, you'll walk away with some sensational seasonal stuff.

fun at the fabric store

Most fabric stores double as craft stores these days. Visiting one of these stores can make holiday decorating fun and easy. Keep an eye out for sales, usually just before and after a holiday. You'll be able to pick up decorations and holiday-themed fabrics for a song, anywhere from 50 percent to 75 percent off the full price. And don't forget to poke through the remnant bins before leaving. You never know what you might find: a piece of lace to use on a small side table, a piece of velvet to wrap around a pillow, or a bright floral fabric to line a spring basket.

quick, easy (and inexpensive) decorations

Most of the decorating ideas below can be adapted to fit Christmas, Chanukah, or Kwanzaa, depending on the colors you choose. Even if you don't celebrate a holiday at this time, these decorations are a wonderful way to celebrate winter. For inventive ideas on gift giving, see pages 146 to 149.

- Pile old or inexpensive glass ball ornaments in a pretty bowl or basket.
- Place a mirror flat in the center of a table. Arrange several candlesticks (they don't have to match) on top of the mirror. Add some greenery, maybe a wire-edged ribbon or strand of curling ribbon wound around the candlesticks, and a glass ball or two.
- Old holiday tins, especially reproductions of antique tins, can be set on kitchen shelves and filled with real or artificial flowers or greens, glass ball ornaments, pine cones, or nuts. They can also be used as holders for large column candles (just make sure they are solidly seated by using melted wax to hold them upright).
- Pick up antique toys at garage sales and flea markets and tuck them everywhere; add bows for more color.

natural beauty

Many of the most inviting decorations can be picked up on a walk through the woods or even in your backyard.

- Pick up pine cones, nuts, interesting-looking twigs and leaves around your house, your neighborhood, or on a nature walk. You can spray paint them gold, silver, white, or leave them in their natural state. Arrange them in glass, metallic, or wooden bowls, tuck them along the mantel or on bookshelves and windowsills. You can also attach thin strings to them and then hang them as ornaments on a Christmas tree.
- During fall pruning, set aside any shapely branches or twigs that you cut off. Spray paint them gold, silver, white, or leave them natural and set them in a large container (milk pail, umbrella stand, even a pretty metal waste can). Add a bow and little lights strung through the branches for a truly eye-catching decoration.
- If you are a seashell collector, you can use some of your favorites for holiday decorating. Large open shells, such as clam or abalone, can be used to hold candles. Starfish can be strung as ornaments or set upright on a mantel. Sand dollars make wonderful ornaments, too.
- Don't forget the fruit: A large glass bowl or distressed wooden bowl heaped high with bright red and green apples, golden oranges, or pomegranates makes a charming accent anywhere. If you want, tuck sprigs of holly or pine, and nuts between some of the fruit.

o, christmas tree

A Christmas tree is a veritable must-have for people who celebrate Christmas. However, a traditional pre-cut tree in a stand isn't the only choice available.

cut your own If you really want a fresh tree, your best bet is a tree farm. Usually the prices are good, plus you'll know the tree is fresh and thus will last longer and look better. Selecting and chopping your tree can be a fabulous time for the family. Many tree farms offer hot chocolate or cider to warm you up while you chop and shop. They also sell handcrafted ornaments, decorations, and gifts.

last minute bargain Start a family tradition of buying and decorating a tree on Christmas Eve, and you'll be surprised at the bargain-basement price you can get for a tree.

again and again The most economical approach is to invest in an artificial tree. Some of these trees are so realistic you practically have to touch them to realize they are not real. Though the better-looking trees cost more, this is a one-time investment that should pay for itself in a few years. Just think, you'll never have to water or worry about your tree drying out during long holiday trips again. Also, an artificial tree is fireproof, unlike a dried-out real tree.

mini-trees If you live in an apartment or have reached the point where putting up a full tree is more trouble than it's worth, consider a miniature artificial Christmas tree. You can buy them plain, with lights, or completely decorated. They go up in minutes, will serve you well for years, and are relatively inexpensive. They are positively cheap if you buy them at post-holiday sales.

deeply rooted The most expensive, but environmentally friendly option is to buy a tree from a nursery that you can plant in the yard later on. If you have the acreage, you'll be beautifying your property and helping the environment, too. Planting trees helps reduce global warming!

If you'd like to shop online for discount Christmas decorations, try www.christmasdepot.com (or call 1-877-353-5263). They offer a wide selection of everything from artificial trees to music, at fairly good prices. You'll also find decorations for Halloween.

thanksgiving

Make this an incredibly fun day—a real celebration of family and friends. And don't let it wear out your nerves or your pocketbook.

the pleasures of potluck If you're not planning a traditional family dinner, host a potluck feast where each guest brings their favorite side dish or dessert. The host provides the turkey and tableware. This can be great fun, especially if your guests bring a favorite family recipe. Because it's potluck, you'll end up with a fabulous meal without the stress of preparing it all alone.

one-man band If you really love cooking all the holiday dishes yourself, you're in luck. Traditional Thanksgiving meals celebrate the foods of the season, so they are usually a bargain. Not only are fall vegetables and fruits, such as sweet potatoes, pumpkins, brussels sprouts, oranges, and apples, at their freshest and cheapest, but many supermarkets will give you a turkey if you buy a certain amount of goods—like $80 or $100's worth—within a certain period of time. (If you don't have enough food purchases, stock up on staples.)

turkey table talk

The classic cornucopia always looks beautiful as the table centerpiece during Thanksgiving dinner. If your table is cramped, you may want to put it on the mantel or a side table instead. Here are some other decorative ideas:

○ If you don't have a cornucopia, substitute a rustic basket overflowing with miniature pumpkins, squash, gourds, Indian corn, nuts, pomegranates, apples, or oranges. Tie a big raffia bow around the sides of the basket or the handle, and trail the ends through the autumn bounty.

○ Use miniature pumpkins or small gourds for rustic candleholders. Just cut a hole in the top large enough to fit the end of a candlestick.

○ Collect and press autumn leaves throughout the fall. Arrange pressed leaves down the center of the dining room table, tuck a few into grapevine wreaths, or tape some to the windows. Also dry some leaves without pressing them flat and gather them in big wooden bowls.

○ Pots of mums are usually on sale around this time of year. They last longer than cut flowers and the colors are perfect for Thanksgiving. Buy several small pots, set them in baskets, tin buckets, or wooden bowls, tie ribbons or raffia around them, and place them separately or in groups throughout the house. Later, you can plant them in your garden for year-round beauty.

halloween

Halloween appeals to people of all ages as a time to dress up and pretend, play with friends, and have fun. It's no wonder that it's become one of the most popular holidays. Practically every store you walk into has tons of Halloween decorations for sale. Because you can make them easily yourself, however, why spend the money? You'll find some do-it-yourself Halloween ideas below.

scary stuff

ghosts in the night There are three relatively easy and cheap ways to make ghosts. White plastic garbage bags can be opened, a ball of wadded up newspaper stuffed into the head area, then a rubber band used to secure the neck. You can draw a face on the head with indelible black marker and hang these plastic ghosts from trees, the eaves of your house, and just about anywhere else. They are waterproof, too—a distinct advantage. You can also pick up white sheets at garage sales throughout the year, make a solid wad of newspaper for the head, and secure the neck with string. Another fabric that makes great ghosts is cheesecloth; use a white or clear balloon for the head and these ghosts will really float.

scarecrow fashion Scarecrow clothes are a cinch to find at garage sales (ratty jeans, plaid shirts, old gloves or mittens, hats, etc.). Because straw can be a bit hard to find, use wadded up newspaper to stuff the clothes. Make the head out of plain muslin (usually less than two dollars a yard at fabric stores), and draw on the face with markers.

ghoulish graveyard Cut headstones out of stiff cardboard or plywood (if you have access to power tools). Attach a garden stake to the back of each headstone, then pound into the ground. Paint the stones white and add goofy epitaphs.

pumpkin patch Pumpkins are easy to grow, so why not grow your own for carving or using in arrangements? The kids will love watching the patch as it develops. If you have to buy pumpkins, you can usually pick them up cheaply—check out farmer's markets for specials.

costumes on the cheap

Years ago people never thought of buying a Halloween costume—part of the fun was making your own. This art can easily be revived with a bit of creativity.

Garage sales and thrift stores can be treasure troves for costume pieces.

- To make a wig, glue Easter "grass," raffia, or yarn to a stocking cap, old swimming cap, or old pantyhose with the legs knotted and cut off.

- Clean out old makeup and let the kids use it as face paint.

- To make white makeup for a clown face, combine two tablespoons of cornstarch with one tablespoon of solid vegetable shortening. Add a few drops of green food coloring to get monster decay, a few drops of red food coloring to add a dash of the devil, blue coloring for corpses and ghouls, and yellow for a lion face.

- For extra bulk and padding, wear a large size of pantyhose under the costume and stuff with rags, wadded newspaper, or small pillows.

easter

This is a time to celebrate the return of spring. The holiday is about renewal, rebirth and hope—and usually comes laden with lots of candy eggs and bunnies, too.

- Don't buy a new basket year after year. Choose one sturdy basket with a wide mouth and a broad shallow base and store it with your other Easter items. The night before Easter, have your child set it somewhere (on the back porch, under a special tree or bush, or at the foot of their bed). Then use raffia for grass and fill the basket with toys, books, and goodies.

- Take advantage of sales after Easter to stock up on refillable plastic eggs. You can fill them with small candies, stickers, trinkets, and toys, and reuse them year after year.

Christmas is the season for cookies of all kinds, but most people don't have enough time to make as many as they might like. One option is to host an old-fashioned cookie exchange: Invite six friends and ask each to bake six dozen of the same cookie. At the party, each person takes home one dozen of each type of cookie or six dozen assorted cookies! For an added touch, ask each participant to make six copies of their recipe, so you each get six dozen cookies and five new recipes!

all good Gifts

MOST PEOPLE CHERISH GIVING
A GIFT TO A LOVED ONE. WHAT THEY
DON'T CHERISH IS SPENDING A FORTUNE.

shopping smart

Ever thought you could find someone the perfect Christmas gift in the middle of July? What about scoring a divine birthday present three weeks after a person's birthday? Shopping smart means buying things you think a person will like when you spot them and when the price is right. It also means never buying anything in a hurry. If you do, you're likely to spend more than you want to and maybe even settle for a less than ideal gift. A smart shopper is always looking for gifts throughout the year. If you go to a craft fair, don't just think in the short term. If you see a hand-painted vase that would delight Aunt Mary and it's a steal, buy it. Vacation trips, country fairs, flea markets, auctions, gift shops at museums and botanical gardens, are all excellent sources of one-of-a-kind presents anytime of the year. Establish a drawer, closet shelf, or trunk in your home as the gift store. Then when a birthday, special occasion, or holiday approaches, you'll be able to reach in and pull out the ideal present for anyone on your list.

personal gift certificates

One of the nicest and most personal presents you can give is an offer of time or service during the year.

- New parents or parents of small children can always use the gift of babysitting, not just for a much-needed evening out, but for doctor or dentist appointments, to get their hair cut, or just to grocery shop without distractions.
- Seniors may need help with big tasks such as cleaning out an attic or garage, mowing a big lawn, spring cleaning, or fall pruning and weeding.
- Someone who doesn't drive would love a book of trip coupons. Each coupon could be redeemable for a run to the grocery store, the eye doctor, and perhaps a "surprise" trip to somewhere they don't get a chance to go to often.

- Offer dinner on a night of their choosing to someone you know is constantly overwhelmed by work or family needs. Cook up a lasagna, casserole, or stew, add a loaf of bread, salad, brownies and a bottle of wine. Put it all in a pretty wicker basket. They will be eternally grateful.
- If someone loves to garden, give him or her a gift of gardening time. He or she will appreciate a willing helper to dig, weed, plant, and water. Add a picnic to celebrate your gardening achievements.
- If your spouse loves to be pampered, wrap a bottle of massage oil with a promise to give him or her a back rub. Add a touch of romance with a book of "date night" coupons that includes dinner for two (out or at home), dancing, a movie, or a long walk together.

flower power

Cut flowers are always a lovely gift, but live plants that bloom last longer and continue to give pleasure for years.
- Buy inexpensive terra-cotta pots and paint them to suit the occasion or the taste of the person. Transplant a seasonal plant or a personal favorite of the recipient into the pot. Include care instructions on a hand-decorated tag.
- Small tin pails, old cookie tins and jars, old pottery bowls or pitchers, and cheese crocks make eye-catching planters. Use them for a plant and give to a friend who likes these collectibles. They'll be thrilled!
- Create a window herb garden for a friend who's an avid cook. Plant a variety of herbs in a long planter or a group of little pots arranged in a shallow basket or tin tray.

gifts from the kitchen

You don't have to be a gourmet to make a delicious gift to eat, as you will learn from these simple and easy ideas.
- Cookies are welcome just about anytime, especially around holidays. A basic sugar cookie dough is easy to make, and you can buy or make icing to decorate them.
- Sweet breads such as banana, nut, cinnamon raisin, carrot, and poppy seed make lovely gifts. Wrap them in aluminum foil with a beautiful ribbon to dress them up.
- Do you have a secret family recipe for chili, pasta sauce, or a dessert topping? Make it and pour it into decorative bottles. Include directions for use and storage.

GIFT GIVING GUIDE

Each wedding anniversary has a symbolic motif, which can be a gift-giving guide.

ANNIVERSARY MOTIF

ANNIVERSARY	MOTIF
1st	Paper
2nd	Cotton
3rd	Leather
4th	Linen
5th	Wood
6th	Iron
7th	Copper
8th	Bronze
9th	Pottery
10th	Tin
11th	Steel
12th	Silk
13th	Lace
14th	Ivory
15th	Crystal
20th	China
25th	Silver
30th	Pearl
35th	Coral or Jade
40th	Ruby
45th	Sapphire
50th	Gold
55th	Emerald
60th	Diamond

○ Buy a bag of pretzel sticks and whip up some honey mustard dipping sauce to go with it.

○ If you are a canner, homemade jams and jellies are among the most prized gifts you can give.

○ Do you have lavender growing in your garden? Harvest it for making potpourri, sachets, or drying in bunches. Dried rose petals, marigolds, and geraniums also make lovely potpourri.

○ Does your garden overflow with herbs? Make pesto with excess basil or dry extra rosemary, thyme, and other herbs as gifts. Present your gift in pretty antique bottles (found at garage sales, flea markets and junk stores).

wrap it up

Want a fun project for the kids? Make your own gift-wrap. It's a great way to add a personal touch to giving. You'll need butcher paper or thin brown paper. Then have the kids sponge paint, make potato prints, stencil, finger-paint, or paint designs to create one-of-a-kind wrapping paper.

○ Fabric is excellent wrap, especially for awkward shapes.

○ Aluminum foil or gold foil paper are simple to mold around unusually shaped items, such as a hammer, tennis racket, or football.

○ Use a section of the newspaper that reflects the gift, the giver, or the person receiving the gift. Use the sports section the athlete (active or armchair), book review section for the bookworm, and food section for the cook. The funnies are amusing for just about anyone.

● Decorate white or brown paper bags with paint, markers, stickers, stamps, and ribbons for personal gift bags.

ten blue-ribbon gift baskets

anniversary Do a little research and recreate dishes served at the couple's wedding. Add a bottle of champagne and toasting flutes. Line the basket in the wedding colors.

baby shower Fill with practical items the new parents will need: sleepwear, undershirts, bottles, bibs, diaper cloths, rattles, pacifiers, booties or socks, and so on.

birthday Create a basket based on the person's favorite pastime. If he or she loves tennis, line the basket with a sweat towel, visor, sports drinks, wrist and head bands, tennis balls, fancy tennis shoe laces, and a note promising a game.

bridal shower Line several baskets with pretty tablecloths. Tuck in a recipe box, napkins, candles, and candlesticks. Ask each guest to bring a favorite recipe on a card plus a utensil used in the recipe and add them to the baskets. Distribute so each guest gets a basket with a new recipe and utensil.

graduation Welcome the graduate to the next phase of life by filling a basket with a cookbook of simple recipes, boxes of instant food, a bag of subway tokens, a commuter coffee mug, and other items for a young, newly independent person.

new job Line the basket with a map showing the route to work, add a big coffee mug, gourmet coffee or tea bags, trail mix, a small potted plant, a family picture, and an emergency office grooming kit.

new neighbors Create a welcome basket lined with a map of the area, add a chamber of commerce guide to local businesses and attractions, a contact sheet with neighbors numbers and names, a plant for their yard, or a ready-to-go meal.

starting school For a new kindergarten student, line the basket with a fun T-shirt, add bundles of graphite and colored pencils, a box of crayons, safety scissors, and packs of favorite snacks. Tailor the idea for each level of school.

thank you Line the basket with a picnic cloth and fill it with gourmet foods such as canned oysters, Greek olives, caviar, paté, spreads, crackers, and a bottle of sparkling cider.

wedding Create a honeymoon basket by lining it with fabric used in the wedding or in the wedding colors. Include champagne with two glasses, peppermint foot lotion, massage oil, a box of fancy chocolates, a scented candle (with matches), and tuck loving notes from family and friends.

CHAPTER 7

Going Out and Spending Wisely

- discount fine dining
- bargain culture
- sporty savings
- cheap thrills

discount fine
Dining

AS A REWARD FOR YOUR FRUGALITY,
YOU DESERVE A NICE MEAL OUT,
BUT DON'T LET IT BUST YOUR BUDGET.

early birds get more than worms

One way to enjoy a great restaurant meal for less is the early bird special. This is basically the same food, served at a time when the restaurant traditionally experiences low volume. It's good business for the restaurant, and for you. You get a great meal and they don't have empty tables. A variation on this is a pre-theater menu. Often, these offers are set menus with a choice between two to three items for a fixed price (excluding beverage).

off-season specials

In some parts of the country, tourism falls off during certain times of the year. In many coastal resort areas, for instance, there are fewer tourists in the winter. The same applies to many ski resort areas in the summer. Off-season is an ideal time to take advantage of some great travel and dining opportunities. Many will offer terrific room rates and two-for-one entrees, free appetizer with purchase of entree, or other culinary deals. If you live in an area that has a high season for tourism, call and ask about specials during the off-season.

coupons de cuisine

You can find discount coupons for top-notch restaurants many different ways. And you can save a significant amount.

entertainment book This is that thick book of coupons sold by scouting troops, church youth groups, and schools. The coupon book costs from $30 to $50 and contains page after page of coupons. In the dining section, you'll find a number of coupons dedicated to fast-food restaurants, but you will also find a surprising number of excellent restaurants with two-for-one coupons. You buy one entree and get a second one of equal or lesser value for free.

valpak These are mailed all over the country, usually in a blue envelope. Many

RESTAURANT WEB SITE
www.restaurants.com

This site lists fine eateries in the U.S. and internationally. You enter a city or region and the site offers restaurants with ratings and personal reviews, plus costs for an average dinner. You can download a map to the restaurant, often book a table online, and even give your own input. Plus, they have a link to tell you which restaurants have coupons available.

people toss them—and other similar coupon packages—out as soon as they see them. Don't! Along with coupons for oil changes and dry cleaning, you'll find a number of dining coupons, often to high-quality restaurants. Sometimes the coupons will offer a two-for-one deal; sometimes it will be a fixed-price meal or a special selection of entrees at a discount. Again, the savings can add up quickly.

newspapers Scan your local newspaper (or if you're on a trip, the local paper of the city you are visiting) for restaurant ads. Sometimes they double as coupons for a two-for-one meal or a percentage off the bill. You should check every day, but especially the day the entertainment section comes out (usually Friday). Keep a close eye on the newspaper when the weather has been nasty for a period of time—even the best restaurants may run a special to lure folks back.

chamber of commerce In order to encourage tourists to visit local restaurants, the chamber of commerce may offer a selection of coupons. Call them to find out if any are available. If you're flying to a different destination, don't forget to stop at the airport tourist desk. You'll find flyers for lots of local attractions, sometimes with discounts, and you may find restaurant coupons as well. It's worth a look.

back to school

Another venue for fine dining at an easier-on-you price is a culinary institute. These are schools where students learn to be chefs. Often, you can have extraordinary meals there. Even better, you can sometimes watch the food being prepared—entertainment included with the cost of the meal! But be warned: If you go to one of the top academies, you might pay more. The trade-off is that you will be getting a truly gourmet meal for much less than you would at the restaurant these talented chefs will eventually cook at or start themselves.

do the split

Most restaurants serve far more food than just about anyone can consume easily at one sitting. Of course, penny pinchers never leave food behind (doggie bags are hip, you know). One way to expand your taste horizons without blowing the budget is to share either the appetizer or the dessert (or both). As long as you are each purchasing an entree, most restaurants don't have a problem with this.

let's do lunch

If there is a divine restaurant that you've been longing to try but the prices for dinner take away your appetite, consider dining there for lunch instead. The prices on lunch menus can be 25 percent cheaper than the same items on a dinner menu. What's more, many such restaurants have "business specials" at lunchtime that run even less. Also consider trying that restaurant for a less costly weekend brunch.

i dine, you dine

Do you like discount dining but can't remember to bring the coupons? Try **www.idine.com**. This elder statesman of dining clubs has some 7,000 participating restaurants nationwide, and the discounts are given via credit card. To join, you register up to three of your credit cards online. The membership fee (about $49) is deducted from your savings when you begin using the program. Once the fee is paid, you'll start to see the savings on your credit card bill—and most restaurants offer from 10 to 20 percent off on your entire bill, including tips, taxes, and yes, even alcohol! Naturally, there are restrictions: Many restaurants limit the times the discount applies (not on peak hours and sometimes not on weekends), some require online booking, some only give you the discount on one visit per month, and there is a cap on how much you can spend to get the savings (not usually a problem for a penny pincher). All that being said, this is a good program if you like to eat out relatively frequently.

a family affair

It's nice to take the whole family out once in a while, but the final tally can cast quite a pall on the evening. Before making reservations, call around and check the papers for restaurants that offer a "kid's night" where children (usually under 12) either eat free when an adult meal is purchased or receives a significant discount. This will make the dining experience a pleasure from beginning to bill.

bargain
Culture

DO YOU ENJOY CULTURAL EVENTS,
SUCH AS THE SYMPHONY, THEATER,
DANCE, AND MUSEUM SHOWS?

dramatic discounts

Taking a family of four to a Broadway show has gotten to the point where the cost could underwrite the domestic budget of a small nation. Individual ticket prices for major shows have soared to an absurd point. Luckily, there are less-expensive alternatives.

half-price ticket booths In New York City, there is the world-famous TKTS booth, selling tickets to Broadway, Off-Broadway, dance and music events on the day of the show for up to 50 percent off the regular price (plus a $3 per ticket service charge). This is a terrific deal that is well worth the effort, but there is some risk involved. You may end up spending several hours waiting in line. When you get to the counter, you may not get tickets to the exact show you want (so have several in mind that you'd be willing to see). You also may end up with tickets in the nosebleed section. Usually, however, you can score tickets for fabulous seats. Besides New York, many major metropolitan cities now offer half-price ticket booths. Call the city's chamber of commerce to find out if they have one or if there is another way to get discount tickets for a show.

two-fers These are vouchers that you can use to buy two tickets for the price of one. You'll find these ticket-shaped two-fers everywhere if you just look—at the desk in hotels or near the cash register in restaurants and newsstands. Often they are for new shows that need to build an audience or older shows that have been running a while. The hot-ticket shows rarely have vouchers, but you can find them occasionally. The benefit of vouchers is that you don't have to stand in line at a central booth. Instead, you go directly to the box office to purchase the tickets.

previews and matinees Generally speaking, a preview is a dress rehearsal in front of an audience. You may witness some glitches that are still being ironed out, but most often a preview is just like a normal performance—except you pay a little less to see it. You'll also pay less to see a matinee performance because they tend to be less well attended than evening shows. To take advantage of these options, buy the tickets in advance directly from the box office.

student and senior discounts Many theaters all over the country offer lower rates to students with valid ID cards and seniors who have proof of their age.

theater thrift

If you love theater, you should consider purchasing a subscription. While a subscription requires a big chunk of cash, the savings are significant when compared to buying individual tickets to shows—as much as 50 percent cheaper! As a subscriber you will also be given other benefits: the best seats, the ability to change seats or performance dates easily and without penalty, discounts on tickets for friends, invitations to special events, advance notice of sponsored extras, discounts at nearby restaurants and shops, lost ticket insurance, and more. Since you'll know the dates of the shows well in advance, you can plan for babysitters or dinner out if you want to make a real evening of it.

● Some professional theater companies, in an effort to serve lower-income people, offer one "pay what you can" performance per run. Ask the box office for details.

operatic notes

While opera by and large is not a bargain to attend, you can still see some of the greatest performers and companies for less than full price. Try the same techniques used to procure theater or symphony tickets on the cheap, but if they don't yield enough savings, consider the standing room option. You definitely will need comfortable shoes and a good attitude. But if you're willing to stand, you can see performances at the Metropolitan Opera in New York City for a pittance—and this is true of many opera companies. We caught opera diva Kiri Te Kanawa in Mozart's Cosi fan Tutte for a mere $15 per person. Halfway through the performance, a nice man who had to leave gave us his orchestra tickets for free. We had incredible seats for the second half of the performance!

miserly museum moments

Every museum we've encountered has one day or one evening a week—or sometimes one day a month—that is free to all. For some reason, most museums offer their weekly free day on Tuesdays. Whenever a museum offers these days, take advantage of them. You can see the best art in the world, from masterpieces by the classic masters to cutting-edge modern works, all for free.

- If you are a member of a museum where you live and are visiting a museum while on vacation, ask about reciprocity before paying the entrance fee. Many museums will let you in free if you are a member of a sister institution.

community cultural costs

The main difference between professional and amateur theater is that professionals are paid. If you love drama, consider your local community theaters—they often produce professional-quality shows for considerably less. Plus, the theaters may be closer to where you live, making getting there cheaper and easier.

- Community symphonies, chamber music ensembles, and other music venues are also a great deal. Often, you can hear amazing performances by talented amateurs. Some groups will sponsor a professional guest performer at a few concerts, adding even better value to a ticket.

- Local dance companies are frequently associated with a training program or dance school. The ticket cost is minimal and the performances can be superb.

- Check out your local museum scene, too. In one community we know, a tiny storefront museum dedicated to wildlife in the area has grown over the past 20 years to become a major educational facility with a state-of-the-art campus. Even so, you can still purchase a ticket at bargain-basement prices thanks to community support.

back-to-school savings

Colleges and universities have some of the best deals going for performing and visual arts.

- College theater can be very exciting. You'll often see talented actors developing their skills. Good theater departments usually employ several artists-in-residence—professional directors, performers, or designers who are training the department's students for a specific performance. With works ranging from classics to experimental shows, college theater can be a stimulating and cost-effective way to see live performances.

- Schools with music departments offers all kinds of performances throughout the year, from symphony to solos, jazz ensembles to a cappella singing-groups—all for a bargain price and sometimes free.

- Dance programs at universities and colleges can be just as varied as the music and theater programs, with ballet, jazz, and modern dance all represented. These are truly exciting to witness and you'll be able to afford several performances rather than blow your budget on just one.

- Art departments usually have their own galleries where works by students and often by professors are displayed. If they charge a fee at all, it is usually minimal.

membership matters

Do you belong to **AAA** (American Automobile Association) or a union of some kind? Check your membership benefits—you may be entitled to discounts at all sorts of entertainment venues. The money you save at theme parks, performance arenas, and sporting events may be worth the cost of your membership!

booking entertainment

Those Entertainment Books have more than restaurant vouchers in them—you'll also find coupons for theater, symphony, opera, and other musical or dance performances. Usually, the coupons offer a two-for-one discount. Occasionally, they will be for specific performances, but mostly they are only limited by availability.

summer freebies

Think summer, and images of warm summer nights, fireflies, and brilliant sunsets come to mind. But what about free shows and music? Most communities offer free performances throughout the summer, usually in a park where you can hear the symphony or see theater, dance, and other types of performances. Bring a picnic and your family will enjoy some wonderful evening performances under the stars. Granted the quality may vary, but for the price, you just can't beat it.

see a show for free

One way to get into theater and music performances absolutely free is to volunteer to work as an usher for a local theater group or symphony. The work is not strenuous nor terribly time consuming, and you will be providing a real service to the theater itself. Your reward: great shows for no cost.

Savings
sporty

ENJOY THE THRILL OF LIVE
SPORTS WITHOUT PAYING
THROUGH THE NOSE.

professional prices

If you're going to pay professional athletes a gazillion dollars a year, you have to charge sports fans more to see them. Unfortunately, there are not many ways to save on buying tickets to professional sporting events. But we do have a few ideas that you may want to try:

group power Many arenas will offer a discount for a group sale. If you have a group from work, church, synagogue, or other organization, buying in bulk can save you a modest amount per ticket.

sharing the savings You and a friend or a group of friends can purchase a subscription and divide the season's tickets. Subscriptions are slightly less expensive than individual tickets so this approach will reduce your cost. The downside is that you can only go to the games that you and your friends agreed upon before purchasing the tickets.

promo discounts Take advantage of any and all promotional discounts. You'll have to keep a close eye to find and take advantage of these when they're available, but the effort might be worth your while.

get cheap seats Modern stadiums and arenas are designed so well that even the nosebleed seats have good sight lines—you're just farther away. Be sure to bring your binoculars so that you can get a closer look at the action. You can still experience the fun of a live game at the lowest stadium prices that are available.

the finances of food

Even if you score discounted tickets to a professional game, another place where they still try to get you is in the price-gouging food concessions. Avoid them like the plague. Instead, tuck some sandwiches and popcorn into a backpack and drink water. It's healthier and a whole lot cheaper than overpriced hot dogs and sodas.

● More and more stadiums are starting to offer picnic areas where you can watch the game while you eat. This is a real boon to a family—you're still out the cost of the tickets, but you can pack yourself a delicious home-cooked meal, and save on food costs.

minor miracles

As people become more disenchanted with professional teams, they are rediscovering the joys of the minor leagues. Many professional teams have farm teams where they train up and coming talent. Check to see if any of these teams are in your local area. At minor league games everyone gets a great seat because the stadiums are much smaller. These games tend to be more family friendly, and the ticket prices are vastly lower.

spirited school savings

Athletic teams at colleges and universities can inspire tremendous fan loyalty. You can find terrific variety, too—literally a sport for everyone. The only drawback is that it can be hard to get tickets to college or university events because the students and alumni are so very loyal. But these competitions are well worth seeking out if you want to watch some memorable games.

beginner's bargains

Do you have a standout high school team nearby? What about youth football, soccer, or Little League? If you have young children in your family, it especially makes sense to check out some of these games. Because they're usually free, you'll never find a better bargain for spectator sports and the games can be really fun to watch. For adults, community basketball and baseball leagues can be a great deal and a good time, too, whether you play or watch.

outside of the box: think different

For many years, the most popular American sports were baseball, basketball, and football (with hockey not far behind). Not anymore. Nowadays, the field, so to speak, is wide open and there are a lot more venues for spectator athletics than ever before.

women's team sports In Tucson, Arizona, home of the University of Arizona, the passion for women's softball is beginning to rival that for any of the men's teams. And this is not an isolated phenomenon. Around the country, women's

SPORTS FUN ON SITE
www.sportsfansofamerica.com

This is a must-visit Web site for sports fans. It covers everything from local teams to professionals. There are links to buy tickets, information about events, and more.

college athletics are rapidly gaining ground, including women's basketball, softball, lacrosse, and soccer. At the professional level, there's the Women's National Basketball Association league (WNBA) during late spring and summer. Most cities that have an NBA team also have a WNBA team. Whether college or pro sports, women's athletics is amazing and there are usually seats available on game day.

soccer This sport, long a favorite in nearly all the rest of the world, has exploded in popularity in the U.S., both in participants and spectators. The games are fast and exciting; the skills breathtaking. See if there's a youth or adult league to check out in your local area.

swimming and diving There are folks who wait for the summer Olympics just to watch the water sports. If you have a college or university nearby (or even a high school) with a ranked swim team, these are extremely exciting events to attend.

gymnastics Another favorite of the Olympics, both men's and women's gymnastic events, are full of heart-stopping moments, graceful routines, and supreme athleticism. Check with high school coaches, college athletic departments, or gymnastic schools to find out about competitions in the area.

martial arts Martial arts schools frequently offer demonstrations and there are competitions between schools. These are exciting to watch and cost little or nothing.

horse shows and dog shows It can be thrilling to watch riders negotiate their horses over huge fences or observe trainers as they make their dogs complete a series of paces. Usually, the cost of attending these events is very low or free. If you have never been to a horse or a dog show, give it a try. Check area stables for event information and local dog trainers for up-and-coming shows.

working it out

If you really want to have a good time with sports, join a team or get involved in a sport yourself. Although finding a team once you've left school can be more challenging, there are a few places you can check out.

the ymca A local Y will offer teams for every age in just about every sport. Of course, each Y has different facilities, so you may have to search around for one that fits your needs. All in all, they are a good source for team sports.

city or community recreation centers The parks and recreation department in just about every city or community usually sponsors lots of sports teams, from elementary age through seniors. Golf, tennis, swimming, dancing, gymnastics, basketball, baseball, softball, and more are offered for a minimal fee (usually just to cover costs). Call the parks and recreation department nearest you and ask for a brochure of sponsored events.

alumni associations Many alumni associations try to coordinate events to bring fellow alumni together. Some even sponsor sports teams. If your chapter doesn't currently sponsor sports teams, give them a call and suggest it.

religious groups If you attend a house of worship, you probably already know if a team exists. If one doesn't, there may be people who might very well want to form a team or two. Some houses of worship have basketball courts or surrounding fields that can be used for sports.

work Many places of employment have softball and other company teams. If yours doesn't, why not put up a notice asking if folks are interested in starting a team of some sort?

snow-bunny savings

Skiing, especially cross-country, can be a terrific exercise, but it can be very a costly pastime. One way to lower the costs is watch what you spend on equipment.

● At the end of the season (around Easter), search ski shops for last year's model of skis, poles, boots, and clothing. The difference in design from year to year is negligible, and you'll pay considerably less buying skis on sale.

● If possible, visit a ski area at the very end of the season to take advantage of their sales. Most ski resort stores, even posh ones, want to get rid of as much of this year's merchandise as possible and offer outstanding discounts.

● Seek out lesser known or less popular ski areas to lower the cost of a day of skiing. Use the Internet, word-of-mouth, the AAA guides, and a good map to look for places that are off the beaten path and are more likely to want to woo skiers to their resorts.

cheap
Thrills

IF YOU JUST LOOK,
INEXPENSIVE ENTERTAINING
EVENTS ARE ALL AROUND.

getting to know you

Even if you've grown up in a town, you probably don't know about all the sites of interest to visit there. If you are a member of the American Automobile Association (AAA), go to the nearest office and pick up a free tour book for your area. You can also try to find one at a secondhand bookstore or your local library. All the pertinent information about these events is in the guide, including their prices and any free days or times. Plus, if you are a member of AAA or other type of club, you may be entitled to discounted tickets for many attractions.

botanical garden bargains

Like museums, most botanical gardens sponsor a day each week where people can come and visit free of cost. These gardens are usually extraordinary to stroll through and have much more than trees and flowers to look at.

you won't snooze at the zoo

Although zoo entrance fees have gotten a bit pricier in recent years, spending a day at the zoo is still an excellent deal. Most zoos today have a lot more to offer than just looking at animals in a cage. Some have imaginative play areas for kids, including sprinkler fountain plazas for cooling off. There are also train rides and the occasional merry-go-round. Usually there are lots of picnic tables scattered about. You'll want to pack a lunch; the food sold at zoos is rarely cheap.

pick-your-own frugal farms

If you grew up in a rural area, going to a farm and picking your own fruit may not seem that wonderful an idea to you. But for those of us who were raised in cities or suburbs the thought of being able to pick apples, for example, is downright exciting. At pick-your-own farms, there is rarely an entrance fee. You usually get to ride on a wagon to the picking area. Many farms have places for children to play made from hay bales and corn stalks. Often there is a petting zoo where your children or grandchildren can meet goats, sheep, donkeys, and chickens up close and personal. Best of all, most farms offer a large variety of fruit you can pick—from strawberries to pumpkins.

theme park thrift

Yeah, these places can be a lot of fun, but they can really set you back—if you're foolish enough to pay full price and then eat at one of their overpriced concessions. But you don't do that, right? Just about every theme park has off-season specials, which offer discounts on tickets, a two-for-one voucher, or some other kind of coupon to reduce the cost.

frugal fun parks

Although smaller than your major theme parks, these local places can offer hours of fun—usually for a lot less. And they sponsor discount days during off-peak times to further lower your costs. You can often find coupons—in newspapers and flyers—for go-carts, laser tag, bumper cars, mini roller coasters, merry-go-rounds, and even one free game of miniature golf with the purchase of one game. One water fun park we visited discounted the entry fee by 30 percent after 3 p.m. to attract more business before the park closed at 7 p.m.

Good Old Ways

One of our favorite special events is a relatively old-fashioned, but surprisingly heart-stirring one: the air show put on at our local Air Force base. If you have any kind of military base nearby, call the public affairs office and ask about events that nonmilitary folk can attend. The air shows are particularly thrilling, but you may find naval bases with open houses on aircraft carriers, marine bases that allow you to watch drills (really inspiring), or even Army band concerts. Show your support for the men and women in uniform and have a good time to boot.

let's go to the fair!

Fairs and festivals offer an excellent opportunity to go out and spend little to nothing, while having a wonderful time. Whether the focus is crafts, music, art,

GET INTO NATURE

www.sierraclub.com

The Sierra Club is dedicated to protecting and preserving the natural world. They want people to explore nature, enjoy it, and appreciate it so that they'll protect it for future generations. On their Web site, you'll find information on trips sponsored by the club and great parks all over the country just waiting for you and your family to explore.

dance, or a specific ethnic heritage, there's a fair or festival to tickle your fancy. Sometimes there will be a small entrance fee, but usually there's not, especially if the fair or festival is held on public land like a park, street, municipal parking lot or campus. The food can be pricey so eat first and carry snacks. If you're shopping for gifts, you may spot some well-priced, unique items. But even if you just walk around and look, fairs and festivals can be big fun for small bucks.

national and state parks

State and national parks all charge a fee for day use and for camping or other recreational use. When you consider how little you pay for what you get, you'll come to appreciate that these parks offer an amazing deal. From the Cape Cod National Seashore in Massachusetts to the Grand Canyon in Arizona, we have some of the most breathtaking national parks in the world. Luckily, forward-thinking naturalists and statesmen like John Muir and Theodore Roosevelt have ensured that scenic treasures like these will be preserved for future generations. Whether you pack a picnic and just go for the day, or load up your tents and camp for a week or two, visiting a state or national park will be a guaranteed adventure and good time at a reasonable cost. You will be able to walk, hike, climb mountains, swim in lakes, tube down rivers, drive through the most incredible scenery, spot wildlife, and savor the beauty that belongs to all of us.

speaking of books

Big chain bookstores, like Barnes & Noble and Borders, as well as privately owned hometown stores, have blossomed into dynamic meeting places these days. To draw potential customers into the store, they often host a variety of events throughout the year. Programs include author readings and signings, book discussion groups of all kinds, and kids programs with storytelling and crafts. We recently saw ads for a swing dance exhibition (followed by a lesson), a Shakespeare performance by a local theater company, and music ranging from bluegrass to classical guitar—all for free!

the library: beyond the books

Your public library is much more than just a place to take out books, videos, and CDs for free. Libraries have become community centers that offer computers, book clubs, and fabulous children's programs including story times, craft programs, visits from "celebrities" (like Clifford the Big Red Dog), and much more. Next time you go in for a book, ask your librarian for a schedule of activities.

more store savings

Bookstores are not alone in their effort to lure folks in with special events. You can find all sorts of unusual entertainment at any number of stores.

sporting goods stores These range from the small, sport-specific store to the mega-complexes. The smaller stores will have smaller events, sometimes in their parking lots and often tied in with a sale. The mega-complexes have rock-climbing walls, simulators, and all sorts of interesting hands-on, try-it-out areas for any number of sports.

music stores As you might imagine, these specialize in musical events that sell CDs, but they can offer wonderful opportunities to hear some terrific local artists (or the occasional guest star) performing for free.

toy stores Many of these kiddie entertainment emporiums, especially the smaller ones, are taking a page from the bookstores and planning events for children of all ages. We've seen Harry Potter events, American Girl teas, storytelling, singalongs, pajama parties, and oodles of arts and crafts mornings, afternoons, or evenings.

food stores Wanting to appeal to more than just the main shopper in the family, you can find health fairs offering flu shots, blood pressure and cholesterol screening, "farmer's markets" with seasonal crafts, foods, music, and more.

CHAPTER 8

Thrifty Travel

- up in the air
- discount detours
- savings at sea
- frugal family fun

up in the Air

be your own travel agent

For years, working with a skilled travel agent was one of the most effective ways to save money. Travel agents still can be effective, but today they have competition: the home computer. These days anyone can search the Web for the best fares, hotels, or tours, and make their own arrangements.

○ To make your research faster and easier, bookmark your favorite sites for bargain travel, hotels, and cars on your computer. This step makes comparison shopping much quicker and simpler every time you want to use the computer to make reservations.

○ What if you don't happen to have a computer to use for your research? Don't despair. You can still find travel information by phone, but it definitely will be slower; getting through to a customer service representative can take time and lots of patience.

sites for savings

There are dozens of travel sites now on the Internet. Some of the most popular are Travelocity, Expedia, Cheap Tickets, and Orbitz (see Resources box, page 171).

○ Club costs: AAA and other auto clubs, price clubs, and membership organizations frequently offer full travel services, including airfares. Though we have not had luck getting the absolute cheapest fares with these clubs and organizations, they are worth checking out.

○ Dirt cheap? We found a pretty cool Web site, which is called traveldirt.com. It had links to actual reservation sites, but was also full of information on strategies for finding cheap airfares, saving on parking at airports, credit card mileage programs, and more. They also had pages devoted to travel safety, health away from home, maps, family travel tips, cruises, discounts on hotels, and auto travel. The site is interesting, valuable, and well worth a visit.

going to the source

After you've checked the availability of flights and price of tickets with several of the travel sites, go directly to the airline's Web site or call the airline itself. When we've done this, we've gotten a slightly better deal on the flights we really wanted than was shown on the travel site. It doesn't always work that way, but it's worth trying. Most airline Web site addresses are almost always www.airlinename.com (for example, www.americawest.com).

the southwest story

One carrier to always check is Southwest Airlines. Southwest doesn't allow its flights or fares to be advertised on any other Web site than its own (with the exception of Sabre, which can be difficult to access unless you're a travel agent). You will often find the cheapest flights through Southwest—the company that pioneered no-frills flying. Southwest has always kept its fares very low by eliminating food service and viewing air travel as a get-there-fast-and-cheap proposition.

cost-effective charm

If you decide to call the phone reservation numbers instead of booking online, learn these tricks to make the most of your phone time:

○ Do your homework first. Check newspapers or online sources to get a sense of what the best fares are at the time you want to travel, and which airlines are offering specials. You can use this information to spur the agent into topping the deals you've already found.

○ Call very early or very late. If you catch a ticket agent at a time when they're having fewer phone calls, you're more likely to get their full attention and help finding the best fares. What if American is offering a great deal, but you prefer to fly United? Ask the United agent if he or she can match the rival offer.

○ Most important (and this is true of anyone you call wanting a favor), use every ounce of charm in your stock. We've found the greatest strategy is making the agent laugh by being a happy, verbally entertaining, presence in the midst of their shift. By nudging the client-salesperson relationship in a more sympathetically human direction, we've found that we both got a better deal and enjoyed the interaction much more. A win-win situation, wouldn't you agree?

budget airports

One of the reasons Southwest can offer lower fares is because most of their flights originate and land at less-popular airports. This helps the airline keep their costs down and it may work as a bargain fare strategy for other airlines, such as JetBlue, as well. Many airline Web sites have a "check nearby airports" feature that can automatically zip you to a smaller, usually cheaper, destination.

go small for big bargains

Although everyone knows about major airlines, there are many smaller airlines well worth checking out.

more for less A greater number of seats on the smaller airlines are sold at a bargain rate, and the difference between the highest and lowest fares isn't as big as on major carriers.

small feels good After September 11, widespread panic wreaked havoc with the major airlines, causing personnel and service cuts in an effort to lower fares. However, the smaller airlines haven't been as affected and in some cases their business has actually improved. Smaller can feel more secure to nervous travelers.

constant savings Great fares on major carriers tend to be short-lived and often hard to get. The fares on smaller carriers change less over the course of the year and are consistently lower.

timing is everything

In many travel guide's tips about saving money, the virtues of making reservations early to save money are extolled over and over. The travel guides are right. You'll usually get a decent price if you make reservations several weeks in advance, and you're more likely to get the flights and seats you want if you book early. But booking too early has burned us. Most airlines don't offer a supersaver fare until close to the departure date. It's a gamble: Do you wait and hope the airlines drop their fares, or do you take the safe route and buy tickets way in advance? It depends on the trip and your nerves. The smart approach is to keep an eye on normal low fares to destinations you travel to regularly. Get to know the range of reasonable prices to that destination. Then, if you really need to travel at a certain time, on a specific date, start checking fares about six weeks before your trip. When you see one that you know is reasonable and meets your needs, go ahead and book it. If you wait until the last minute, you may get a further discount, but you'll often have to be flexible about things such as nonstop flights, departure dates, and seats.

off-peak perks

It is still usually cheaper to fly off-peak, departing on a Tuesday, Wednesday, or Thursday. Flying at odd times—very late at night, for example—may also save you some cash. Check carefully and see how much you can save by adjusting your dates and times (if possible), and then determine whether it is worth the inconvenience.

carefree couriers

If you really want to save money on airfare, consider traveling as a courier. To take advantage of this option, you'll need to travel alone, have a very flexible schedule, and travel really light (carry-on bags only). That's because you'll be traveling with a package (frequently documents) to deliver to a legitimate company. To find ads seeking freelance couriers, check newspapers and magazines, or go online. The Web site run by the International Association of Air Travel Couriers (www.courier.org) contains all the information you need about becoming a courier. Furthermore, you can join the association for $45, fill out the application online, and start checking for flights. You'll get the best bargain on airfares closest to the package delivery date. This is an increasingly popular way to travel cheap and is becoming more competitive, especially for favorite destinations or times of the year, so research your options carefully before committing yourself.

fly for free: get bumped

If you have a really flexible schedule and like to gamble a bit, try to get a ticket on an extremely popular flight—one that tends to be overbooked. If there are too many passengers, airline representatives will often ask for volunteers willing to give up their seat in exchange for a $100 to $200 travel coupon or a free ticket good for any destination in the United States. If the later flight keeps you at the airport overnight, the airline will sometimes throw in free accommodations, too.

parking pluses

Unless you have great public transportation or someone willing to get you to and from the airport, you will probably end up leaving your car in a parking lot for a period of time. The closer the lot is to the airport, the higher the parking fees tend to be. Unless you want to pay a ton of money, never leave your car in short-term parking for more than an hour or two. The long-term parking options at most airports are relatively decent, and shuttle buses run frequently between the lots and the departure gates. But the cheapest option is a satellite parking lot on the airport outskirts. They charge up to half what long-term airport lots cost, offer frequent shuttle bus service, and are usually fenced in and guarded.

bargain buses?

Many cities have privately owned shuttle buses that will pick you up at one of several central locations (or even at your home) and take you to the airport. If you are traveling alone, that could be a less expensive option than parking at the airport. If you're traveling with a family or a group of friends, private shuttle bus costs can become more expensive than driving and parking at the airport. If you live in an area with good public transportation, that will probably be the cheapest option of all—unless you can get a friend or family member to drive you.

SITES FOR SORE POCKETS

Try one of these Web sites for discount travel, whether you just want to book a flight or a room or buy an entire package.

www.travelocity.com

www.expedia.com

www.orbitz.com

www.cheaptickets.com

www.travelnow.com

www.onetravel.com

www.travelzoo.com

O If you are going to a city where you don't need to rent a car to get around (such as Chicago, New York, or San Francisco), don't just jump into a cab or an airport bus to get into the city. With your return to the airport, you can easily end up adding another $40 or $60 to the cost of the trip. Most metropolitan areas have excellent cheap public transportation that will take you to the heart of the city. You can get from O'Hare to downtown Chicago, for example, on the Blue Line rapid transit train in 40 minutes for $1.50, and it often beats cars stuck in traffic.

O If you are not renting a car at your destination, don't forget to check to see if your hotel offers free (except for a tip) airport transportation service for guests.

discount
Detours

IT'S NO VACATION IF YOU HAVE
TO BE CONSTANTLY CHECKING YOUR
WALLET AND WORRYING ABOUT MONEY.

touring for savings

Packaged tours can be a godsend to those traveling on a budget. If you're exploring an out-of-the-way destination, they can also be the safest way to travel. On a
package tour, the dates and times are preset, and the cost usually includes lodgings, some meals, sightseeing, and transportation to the places in the tour. Airfare
is usually extra, though it also may be included. Tours take the hassle out of planning a trip because all the arrangements and details are handled by the tour operators. Tour operators usually take care of any problems during the tour, as well.

join the club for thrifty travel

Almost every club you can think of offers some sort of travel service, often
with some terrific discounts on tour packages. Of course, auto clubs, like AAA
have built their reputation on rating hotels and getting member discounts, but
they also offer tours by bus and rail. Price clubs, such as Costco and Sam's
Club, have pretty extensive travel services and you can locate a good deal
through them.

travel agent to tour guide

You've already become your own travel agent to save money. Have you ever considered becoming a tour guide to save even more? All you need to do is contact
several tour operators and offer to put together a group for a specific tour.
Usually, if you get enough people to sign up, your travel costs will be covered
completely; if you sign up more than the minimum needed for a tour, you may
garner considerable reductions for a companion. To organize a tour, you'll need
to gather friends or acquaintances that share a specific interest:

○ Wine tasting tour of France, Spain, or Germany

- Literary tour of the British Isles, visiting all the homes or areas written about by literary giants
- Asian art tours of China, Japan, Korea, and/or any other Asian country
- "In the footsteps of the Raj" tour of India, exploring Indian royalty and the influence of British occupation

sightseeing specials: 50 percent off

When you travel to a city, pay a visit to their tourist bureau to find out about city-sponsored tours. You'll find that many places have inexpensive walking tours with excellent guides that charge far less than big tour operators do. If you do a little research, you may find several tours for free — our favorite price!

discount dreaming

Regardless of where you're traveling, one of the biggest expenses is often lodging. Although we feel that cleanliness and quiet are the top priorities, you have to determine your own "musts" and how much you're willing to pay for them. Try these tips to get a good hotel room at a traveler-friendly rate.

- First search the travel sites on your computer — Travelocity, Expedia, Cheap Tickets, and more — they all have hotel connections to find you deals in the city you're visiting. Check several sites to see which comes up with the best deal. If you belong to an auto club, check their Web site too. But before you book, call the hotel directly. You may land an even cheaper rate by phone.

- Don't just call the national toll-free number for hotel reservations; spend a quarter or two and call the hotel itself. Nationwide reservation desks don't always net you the best rate because they aren't aware of special promotions at individual hotels.

- Check your Entertainment Book — they have a discount hotel number that provides discounts of up to 50 percent on lodging around the world.

- Open that blue envelope from ValPak. We found a coupon for 50 percent off every second night at participating Holiday Inns.

- If you belong to Costco or Sam's Club, check their travel services — Costco was recently offering up to 15 percent off on reservations at Best Western hotels.

- Ask about corporate rates. Even if you own a small business or work as a freelancer, you may qualify for a discount of as much as 20 percent.

- Ask about discounts for seniors, special offers for members of clubs (like AAA), promotional rebates, or anything else that could lower the cost of a room.

A SITE FOR
HOTEL SPECIALS

www.hoteldiscount.com
or 1-800-715-7666

While looking for discounts on hotels, we found www.hoteldiscount.com and were impressed with what the site had to offer. They list themselves as getting you "rates up to 70 percent off — rooms for sold-out dates." We don't know about sold-out dates, but the rates were terrific.

O Try a discount hotel broker by contacting the tourist bureau in the city you want to visit. They can lower room prices by as much as 50 percent.

O Don't forget to haggle, especially if it is off season. Empty rooms cost the hotel money, so see if you can talk them down a bit on the room rate.

sleeping for quarters

For some people, a luxury hotel is the only way to travel, but the wise penny-pincher traveler knows that a place to sleep need only be clean and preferably cheap so that you can spend your money on food, sightseeing, cultural events, sports, shopping, and other enjoyable activities.

college dormitories Many schools have made it a business to rent dorm rooms to travelers during the summer when there are few students around. And they charge very modest fees. Of course, you might have a bathroom down the hall, but the savings will more than make up for that. The University of London, for example, will rent a dorm room for about $35 a day, including breakfast.

hostels Not just for youth, there are hostels for senior citizens, families, couples — you name it! A good source to explore is www.hostels.com, produced by an independent group, not an international hosteling organization.

religious retreats You can often book a room at a retreat run by a religious organization. Because most people are there for religious reasons, there will be more rules to follow. The facilities are usually very well maintained.

bed and breakfasts Also known as B & B's, these establishments have long been a way to get a room at a bargain rate, especially outside of the U.S. For some reason, American B & B's have evolved into high-end inns — not always at bargain prices. In other countries, however, you can still save money at a B & B. Typically, this is a private home that has set aside one or more bedrooms for paid guests with breakfast included. Sometimes you'll have a private bath; most often, you'll share. The breakfast can be a simple continental affair of bread, rolls, pastry, fruit, juice, and coffee or tea, but in some cases, you might be presented with a hearty home-cooked feast. Ask about the meals when you make your reservation.

other alternatives There are other, off-the-beaten track, places to lay your head. To find out about them, contact the tourist bureau in the city or area you want to visit and ask about alternative lodging ideas.

swapping for savings

Another way to lower the cost of lodging is to consider swapping your home or apartment with someone in another city, state, or country. There are many books written about home-exchange clubs, so check your library or bookstore. Usually, there is a fee to join the club, and then your name will be added to a list of people interested in exchanges.

○ When you write up your listing, be sure to include any and all amenities that would make your home particularly appealing: access to public transportation, historic sites nearby, parks, mountains, lakes, rivers, natural areas or wildlife refuges, theaters, sporting venues, amusement parks, museums, shopping, and so on.

○ If you have regular access to a health club, swimming pool, tennis courts, beach, special parking or the like, include this information in your listing, too.

○ Get it in writing: the home exchange networks have standard contracts available and you should use them. The contract should include a guarantee that swappers will pay replacement value for any damage.

cars on the cheap

You can find some great deals on rental cars, but you'll have to look for them. This is an area in which a little time spent surfing the Net can yield you great savings. Check all the major travel sites, auto club sites, and the home page of each the major rental car companies for specials offered only over the Internet.

coupons, coupons, coupons Next time you get your credit card bill, don't just toss the glossy inserts—you may be throwing away discount coupons for car rentals. Check fliers in the mail, the magazine or newsletter from your auto club or price club, look up your frequent flier Web site, and see if they offer coupons or discounts. Also scan airline inflight magazines on your next trip for clippable coupons.

size cents Always book the cheapest car going, which is usually also the smallest (though not necessarily). Because these cars are limited in numbers, the rental agency will generally offer you an upgrade for the same price. In fact, if they don't have the car you ordered and want you to upgrade, don't let them trick you into

THE ELDERHOSTEL EQUATION

**www.elderhostel.org
or 1-877-426-8056**

Founded in 1975, Elderhostel is a nonprofit organization that offers education and travel opportunities for people 55 and older. Their motto is: The world is our classroom. Elderhostel offers unique package tours to destinations all over the world. In some cases, the lodgings are at a university or college; more often they are at good hotels. Classes and tours are included in the cost, as are many meals. These trips are for seniors who never tire of learning about other cultures, crafts, geography, art, music, natural history, and more. Contact them at the Web site or toll-free phone number above for information or a free catalog.

paying more for it, especially if you reserved ahead with a credit card. On the other hand, if you get to the car rental desk and they actually have that mini you don't really want to drive for a week, they are always happy to let you upgrade—and may still give you a good deal on it.

rental rip-offs Though each and every car rental office will try its hardest to sell you insurance while you're driving their car, it's almost always a waste of money. Check with your own car insurance agent, your auto club, or your credit card company. You'll probably find the coverage offered by the rental company is simply duplicating coverage you are already paying for. However, this may not be true overseas.

fill 'er up In the past, the car you rented would always have a full tank and it would save you money to return the car full of gas, preferably from a cheapie gas station. The times have changed, however, and now you'll often be getting a car with only a half tank. Since the rental company simply requires you to return the car with the same amount of gas as at the time of rental (or they'll refill at high rates), it makes no sense to put in more gas than necessary. Ask for details before you rent, then follow the cheapest option.

riding the rails for less

Train trips can be lots of fun. Amtrak (www.amtrak.com) has a number of special deals, including discounts for senior citizens, students, families, special packages, and more. But you can also find coupons from other sources:

○ The Entertainment Book has coupons for special trips, such as two-for-one coupons for the Grand Canyon Railroad, which goes from the town of Williams, Arizona, to the rim of the Grand Canyon—with lots of Wild West entertainment thrown in.

○ Clubs and organizations, such as AAA (www.aaa.com) and Costco and Sam's Club travel services, also offer discounts or packages on rail trips.

foreign exchange

Exchanging currency can cost a bundle if you don't know how to do it right. Never exchange large amounts of currency where it is most convenient. For example, if you exchange dollars for foreign currency at the airport, you'll pay an absurd service fee. Your best bet will be banks and foreign exchange companies before you leave or in the country you are visiting. Like anything else, you'll want to shop around to get the best rate.

tips on tipping: when not to tip

More travelers squander money with excessive tips than anything else. We're not advocating squeezing people when they provide you with good service, but tipping practices vary widely from culture to culture. For instance, many European restaurants include a "seating" or service fee in their final bill. Make sure you check closely to see how much of a tip you're being charged already before you decide to tack on an additional tip. If you want to give something extra, five or ten percent is more than generous. Before you travel, check with a guidebook or travel agent to find out local tipping customs. Leaving the tandard of 15 to 20 percent without a thought is not the penny-pinching way.

HOME EXCHANGE THE EASY WAY

....

www.exchangehome.com
or 1-800-848-7927

....

Out of curiosity, we went online and input "home exchange" into our search engine. We couldn't believe how many entries popped up, and they seemed to cover just about anyone! There were listings for home exchanges for seniors and the disabled. One major site we found was for Exchange Homes. Founded in 1986, this large company offers a yearlong membership for $30. Members can list their homes and can browse possible exchanges online. The company protects the privacy of their members and bars nonmembers from accessing the exchange lists. They have a useful frequently asked questions area that can give you a thorough overview of how exchanges work.

savings at
Sea

surfing for sales

Using your computer to check out specials can save you big bucks, even if you end up having to use a travel agent or booking directly through the company. Surfing several sites can give you a good overview of the cost of a cruise and how to save a few hundred bucks.

onetravel This site, for example, was showing a seven-night Eastern Caribbean cruise on the Disney Magic (without airfare) for $940.35; a Western Caribbean cruise was $972.77.

travelocity This site had a seven-night Eastern Caribbean Thanksgiving Cruise for $679 on Carnival, a four-night Western Caribbean holiday on Norwegian for $159, and a seven-night Mexican Riviera on Royal Caribbean for $599.

AAA The AAA site showed a three-night Pacific Northwest cruise from Seattle on Royal Caribbean from $299, and a 12-night Alaska Glacier Cruise from Vancouver to San Diego on Celebrity from $900.

costco The online travel services here offered a seven-day, smoke-free Eastern Caribbean cruise on Carnival from $589, and a Disney Wonder cruise for four nights from $629.

consolidated savings

Consolidators are the middlemen between the cruise lines and the consumer. Each line will usually provide a consolidator with a number of cabins for each cruise. These consolidators will sometimes offer deals that are the lowest around with the advantage of one-stop comparison shopping. You can find ads in the travel section of most major newspapers under either "consolidators" or "discounters." And there are several Web sites now available, too.

- GalaxSea Cruises of San Diego offers specials at www.galaxsea.com (1-800-923-7245).
- Spur of the Moment Cruises has a site that specializes in last-minute bookings (www.spurof.com) that can save you 50 percent or more on a cruise.

spontaneous savings

Although with most cruises, you're best off booking at least one month prior to sailing to garner a good fair, if you can travel at the drop of a hat, you may find a great deal by waiting until literally the last minute. And there are now Web sites that can help you find those last-minute marvels:

www.site59.com This young site was bought out by Travelocity recently so you will find some packages that appear on both sites. Site59 specializes in last-minute deals —any time from two weeks to three hours before leaving, and they guarantee a savings of up to 60 percent. When you go on the Web site, you'll see a "cruise quick-shop" button to the right of the screen that will take you right to the listing of sailing-soon packages at a deep discount.

www.11thhourvacations.com A few years senior to Site59, this site can offer savings from 35 to 70 percent on cruises and travel packages, as well as airfare and hotel rate discounts. The site also has a frequent-user rewards program, plus two-for-one vacation specials.

www.lastminutetravel.com This site actually has offerings from many different carriers and operators, including JetBlue and Spirit. As its name indicates, the site specializes in last-minute deals, but you can also book in advance here.

saving cents on cruises

A few before-you-embark tips to keep extra costs from spoiling your cruise experience:

SAVINGS AT THE SOURCE

Check the web sites of the major cruise ships to take advantage of special offers.

Carnival Cruise Lines
www.carnival.com

··································

Celebrity Cruise Lines
www.celebritycruises.com

··································

Disney Cruise Lines
www.disneycruise.com

··································

Norwegian Cruise Line
www.ncl.com

··································

Princess Cruises
www.princesscruises.com

··································

Royal Caribbean International
www.rccl.com

··································

Windstar Cruise Line
www.windstarcruises.com

GREAT RATES FOR FREIGHTS

If you want to check into freighter cruises, try the outfits listed here.

www.freighterworld.com
or 1-800-531-7774

. . . .

www.freightercruises.com
or 1-800-996-2747

○ Even though all the major things are included on a cruise, tips are not—and they can add up significantly. Drinks (other than coffee and tea) are not included, nor are many shore excursions. Check what is and is not included carefully before you sign on the dotted line.

○ Don't limit yourself to the planned excursions from the ship—contact the tourist bureau of the port you'll be visiting ahead of time and see what they can offer you. Doing your own land tour can be more fun, tailored to your interests, and a lot cheaper. Just be sure to get back on time so the ship doesn't leave without you.

○ Inside cabins are just as large as the outside ones and generally cost a lot less. The only thing you'll miss out on is the view from your room, but if you plan to be out and about most of the cruise, this shouldn't be a problem. Spend the money you'll save on the cabin on a shipboard massage or extra excursion.

frugal freighting

If you are the adventurous type, you may want to look into freighter cruises. If you have a flexible schedule and a taste for something a little unusual, freighter travel can be a great way to go.

○ Freighters carry a lot fewer passengers than a cruise ship, generally no more than 12.

○ Freighters don't usually allow children under 13 or seniors over a certain age.

○ Freighters have fewer amenities, but they often have a small pool, a library with books and videos, a lounge, deck chairs, and even a shop.

○ Freighters have an itinerary, but they are subject to change depending on the cargo. The trips are generally longer and they go to more unusual ports of call than a normal cruise ship.

○ Freighters are much more casual; there are no big formal dinners, casinos, glitzy shows, or organized activities.

○ Traveling on a freighter costs half as much as traveling on a regular cruise line; the fee covers everything on the ship except alcohol. If you're looking for an inexpensive offbeat adventure—a no-frills trip with a small group of like-minded travelers—a freighter cruise might be a terrific option for you.

frugal Family Fun

TRAVELING WITH CHILDREN
CAN BE WONDERFUL AND DOESN'T
HAVE TO COST A LOT, IF YOU DO IT RIGHT.

natural thrift

One of the best family vacations is also the cheapest: camping. If you own equipment, the only major outlay will be food and gas. If you don't own any gear, try to rent or borrow some from friends for the first outing or two, that way you'll be sure everyone likes it before investing any money. Campgrounds can range from those that require you to backpack to a remote wilderness site to KOAs (Kampgrounds of America) or other privately owned campgrounds that have sites with showers, stores, entertainment rooms, or swimming pools nearby. You can really pick and choose the type of camping experience that you and your family want. Campground fees will vary considerably too. Some state parks offer a site where you can pitch a tent for as little as $5 a night. Private campgrounds can charge up to $20 or $30 for a site.

beyond tents

If you don't like sleeping in a tent but still want to have a camping experience, try locating a cabin. Cabins are available in state and national parks as well as private campgrounds such as KOA. Cabins are popular, so be sure to book in advance. Usually they are one-room structures, with wooden bunks, a table and benches, and a wood-burning stove. Some are more rustic than others; all provide you with four walls and a roof to sleep under.

national treasures

The United States is full of extraordinary national parks. Many of these have lodges or some type of hotel, if camping is not for you. The most popular parks tend to fill up during peak times so you should reserve campsites or other lodgings well in advance. (For information, try www.nps.gov or 1-800-365-2267.)

GOLDEN AGE PASSPORT
···
www.nps.gov
or 1-800-GO-PARKS
···

If you are 62 or older, get a Golden Age Passport from the National Park Service. It gives you free entrance for life to any national park, monument, historic site, recreation area, or wildlife refuge run by the NPS. If a park has a car fee, the passport admits you plus all your passengers. If there is a per person fee, it admits you, your spouse, and children. It even offers the passport holder a 50 percent discount on federal use charges for facilities and services, such as camping, swimming, parking, boat launching, and tours. To apply, you must show proof of age (driver's license or birth certificate) and must prove you are a U.S. citizen or permanent resident. There is a one-time $10 charge.

If you plan to visit several national parks in a short time, consider getting a Golden Eagle Passport. For a set price, the passport permits you to visit any National Park or monument as often as you like for one year. Passports are available at any national park.

state sites

Many people skip over state parks in the rush to secure a campsite in a national park. But these state gems shouldn't be overlooked. Campgrounds, cabins, and even lodges found in state parks provide wonderful opportunities for family vacations. Among other activities, many offer hiking, fishing, boating, and swimming in just about any natural setting from desert to alpine meadow.

home away from home

Rather than stay at a hotel, you may find renting a house or condo to be a cheaper, more family-friendly option, especially if you have young children. You'll have the most luck renting a house in popular tourist destinations. We found a home on the island of Eleuthera in the Bahamas during peak season starting at $60 per night. In Maine, houses or "house-keeping" cottages are available for rent during the summer starting at less than $500 a week. Check with a local real estate office or try typing the name of your destination plus "vacation rentals" in your search engine.

culture convergence

One of the most remarkable things about the United States is the wide diversity of cultures within our borders. You don't need to travel abroad to meet an astonishing variety of people—or feel as if you've experienced something wonderfully different from your daily life. Since you can probably find such an enclave within driving distance, you can make this a family trip to remember without breaking the bank.

native american reservations One example is the Navajo Nation spanning the Four Corners of Arizona, New Mexico, Utah, and Colorado. There, you'll find Navajo, Zuni, and Hopi communities, each with its distinctive fascinating culture, extraordinary handcrafts and artworks as well as stunning scenery. Check within your own state— you may be amazed at the areas of interest to visit where your children can be exposed to (and learn respect for) the ancient cultures of our continent's First Peoples.

amish country The most well-known enclave of the Amish is probably in Pennsylvania, but it is by no means the only one. A visit to Amish Country will transport you to another time— when life was much simpler—and introduce you to a culture that thrives in a setting that is centuries apart from most modern communities.

border crossings

If you want to introduce your children to life in a different country, you are in luck. Folks in the Northern states can usually drive up to Canada, and those in the Southwest can drive down to Mexico. Both countries are easy to visit from the States and offer many attractions, including good packages for families.

- ◎ In Canada, experience the British culture of Victoria, the old-world French charm of Montreal, the glorious scenery of Banff, or the cosmopolitan delight found in Toronto.

- ◎ Mexico offers the sun-drenched excitement of the Mexican Riviera, the awe-inspiring Mayan ruins of the Yucatan peninsula, the splendor of the Copper Canyon, and the thriving metropolis of Mexico City.

FAMILY ADVENTURES
www.familyadventuretravel.com

There are a host of publications and Web sites devoted to family vacations, but one we particularly like is sponsored by Family Adventure Magazine. This bi-yearly magazine not only provides information on family adventure travel, it also lists companies around the country that specialize in adventure travel throughout the world. You can find the magazine at bookstores, newsstands, and some specialty shops or you can order it from:

The Family Adventure Magazine
P.O. Box 469
Woodstock, NY 12498

CHAPTER 9

Thrifty Home Improvements

- cost-saving home care

- do-it-yourself damage control

- reduce, reuse, recycle

cost-saving
Home care

WHEN IT COMES TO HOME MAINTENANCE,
THERE IS NO QUESTION THAT A STITCH
OR NAIL IN TIME SAVES NINE.

up on the roof—with care

A leak in your roof can mean much more than trouble up top; it can lead to damaged walls, floors, and belongings. A well-sealed roof requires regular care to do its job properly, but it will pay off in the long run. If your roof is steeply pitched, it's best to hire a professional roofer to do repairs.

- If you have an unfinished attic, start your inspection there. Use a strong flashlight and look for signs of water along the rafters and framing or in the insulation.
- Next, choose a sunny day to do an outdoor examination of your roof. Check carefully for any bare spots on asphalt surfaces, broken shingles or tiles, lumpy or wavy areas indicating buckling, or asphalt shingles starting to curl up or curl down (clawing). Use binoculars to get a close look without having to climb up on your roof.
- Check the flashing around chimneys, vents, and anywhere there's a joint in the roof, because leaks frequently begin around flashing. Small holes can be temporarily repaired with roofing cement, but if the flashing is wearing out, it should be eventually replaced.
- Do repairs to asphalt shingles on a dry, sunny day when the temperature is between 65° F and 80° F so that the shingles will be flexible but not hot.

straightening the curls

You can fix curling asphalt shingles yourself. Choose a day that is dry and warm so the shingles will be flexible. Gently lift up the curled section of the shingle and apply roofing cement beneath it, following the manufacturer's directions. Press the shingle back in place and weight it (a brick works well) to hold the shingle flat while the cement dries, about 30 minutes.

replacing a worn asphalt shingle

- Lift the shingle above the damaged one and insert a pry bar to remove the nails holding the damaged shingle in place. Carefully pull out the damaged shingle.
- Brush away any debris and slide in a new shingle. If necessary, gently pry up the surrounding shingles slightly to insert the new one fully.
- Use roofing nails to attach the new shingle, being careful not to damage the shingle above the new one. Using a putty knife, apply roofing cement under both the new shingle and the one above; then press each in place.
- If you don't have a replacement shingle, you can often repair a damaged shingle by cutting a piece of sheet-metal flashing to fit under the shingle. Coat the bottom of the metal patch with roofing cement and slip it into place; then coat the top of the patch with roof cement and press the shingle to it.

replacing a wood shingle or shake

- Using a hammer and a chisel, carefully split the damaged wood shingle along the grain. Gently pull the pieces out. If needed, insert small wedges under the upper shingles to hold them in place while you work.
- Instead of removing the old nails, use a hacksaw to cut them flush to the surface.
- Using a caulking gun, run a bead of roofing cement over the back of the new shingle and over the top of the shingles underneath. Slide the shingle into place; if necessary, place a piece of scrap wood at the base of the shingle and use a hammer to gently tap it fully into place.

great gutters, houseman!

One of the best and easiest ways to protect your house from water damage is by installing good quality gutters and then maintaining them. Gutters keep water from rotting your siding and help prevent seepage into your basement and possible erosion of your house's foundation. Four times a year, look for and remove any blockages in the gutters and the downspouts. Examine seams for leaks and look carefully for spots of rust.

- Wearing heavy-duty gloves, scoop out any leaves or other debris from the gutters. Begin at the downspout end and work your way up the gutter. As you work, mark any sections that may need maintenance or repair so that you can see them as you walk around the house.
- When the debris is all gone, flush the gutters using a hose and starting at the highest point.

- Many people use mesh screens to keep leaves out of gutters, but this hampers cleaning them. Putting a leaf strainer in the top of each downspout is more practical.

siding lines

- Once a year, give your siding a bath to preserve its finish. For painted wood siding and aluminum siding, use a solution of 1 cup extra-strength detergent (sold at paint or hardware stores or home centers) and 1 quart chlorine bleach in 3 gallons of water. Apply with a brush or sponge, and wear rubber gloves, safety goggles, and protective garments. Rinse thoroughly.
- To spruce up vinyl siding, just hose it down and sponge-wash it with a mild liquid detergent. Rinse with spray from your hose.
- Always begin washing your siding from the bottom and work your way up — the siding soaks up less detergent that way and is less likely to streak.

masonry musts

- Use a power washer (you can rent one) on a low-power setting to spray masonry walls clean.
- To kill mold and mildew, add 1 cup of bleach to each gallon of water. Rinse the masonry with plenty of clean water afterward to flush away the bleach solution.

everlasting decks

Composite lumber, which is made from waste wood products, requires no staining or sealing, is weather- and insect-resistant, can take years of strong sunlight without problem, will not rot or deteriorate, and is splinter free. There are several products available now (Trex is one brand name) for beautiful, maintenance-free decks, and though they cost more than real wood does, the long-term benefits far outweigh the initial costs. Plus you'll be helping the environment by using composite lumber rather than regular lumber!

windows on the world

- If a double-hung window — the most common type of window — moves but doesn't slide easily, clean out the sash channels with steel wool. Then vacuum the area until no dust remains and lubricate the channels by rubbing them with bar soap or paraffin, or use a silicone spray.

● Old paint can often be the culprit if windows are sticking to the point that you can't open them at all. After checking to make sure that the window isn't nailed or screwed shut, use a utility knife to cut around the sash, breaking the paint seal evenly. Gently tap the sash with a rubber mallet (not a hammer!) to loosen it.

before the storm

● If the frames of your aluminum storm windows have oxidation deposits, use a lightly abrasive household cleaner, a mild detergent, or fine steel wool to rub the deposits away. After cleaning, apply automobile paste wax to the frames. Reapply the wax annually.

● On a wooden storm window, pry out any loose and crumbling glazing compound and apply fresh compound.

● Check and tighten any hanger hardware and unclog weep holes at the bottom of the sash.

● If you will be repainting wood-framed storm windows, be sure to check the fit first; extra layers of paint can make the windows too big to reinstall.

● If the corner joints of wooden storm windows have become loose, use small mending plates on the inside corners to reinforce the joints and strengthen the corners. Drill pilot holes first to avoid splitting the wood.

fixing a hole

● To mend a larger hole, cut a piece of screening 1/2 inch larger than the hole and unravel its edges to leave points all around. Bend the points at right angles to the patch. Slip the points through the screen and bend them back flat to hold the patch to the screen. Affix the patch by coating its edges with clear glue or nail polish.

- To repair a small hole or tear in a plastic or fiberglass screen, use a No. 18 tapestry needle and very fine nylon fishing line. Zigzag-stitch over the hole or tear; do not pull the line taut or you may pucker the screen. Paint over the stitching with clear glue or nail polish.

drive on!

Do repairs on your driveway when the weather is 60° F or above; the asphalt will be softer and easier to use and will set more quickly and form a better bond.

- Every few years, coat the entire driveway with an emulsified asphalt or coal-tar sealer. Read the directions before you begin; different manufacturer's recommend different approaches. The sealer will fill any tiny cracks.
- Fill cracks up to 1/2 inch wide as soon as you spot them—before frozen precipitation can cause more damage. Clean out the crack with a wire brush. Then fill it with driveway crack filler sold in caulk-gun cartridges. If the crack is deeper than 1/4 inch, partially fill it with sand, then finish filling with caulk and smooth with a trowel.
- Patch cracks wider than 1/2 inch with a sand and sealer mix. First clean out the crack with a wire brush. In a disposable pan, combine the sand and sealer until it is the consistency of putty. Use a trowel to pack the mixture into the crack and to smooth the top.
- Patch big holes with cold-mix asphalt compound. Have extensive damage repaired by a pro with hot-mix.

pest patrol

The most effective way to deal with pest infestations in your home is to block them from occurring. Insects look for food, water, and shelter. Deny them these, and you'll stop the problem before it happens.

- After cleaning the sink, wipe the sink area until it is almost dry.
- Wipe down counters after each food preparation; wipe out cabinets regularly.
- Wash out garbage cans regularly; empty the kitchen garbage once a day.
- Caulk cracks and crevices in walls, floors, and foundations. Don't overlook any gaps around pipes.
- Repair tears and holes in window screens.
- Top your chimney with a spark-arresting screening.

DANG!

do-it-yourself
Damage Control

HOME REPAIRS CAN EAT UP A CHUNK
OF YOUR INCOME IF YOU CALL SOMEONE
EVERY TIME THERE'S A PROBLEM.

doors that stick

If a door is sticking, first check the weather. Dampness can cause wood to swell. On a dry, cool day, check the door again; your problem may have gone with the humidity. If not, try the following:

- First, check the screws in the hinges and the strike plate. They may need to be tightened or reinforced.
- Second, make sure the hinges are properly mounted. If not, open the door and slip a wedge under the bottom edge to hold the door steady at the right height. If the door is sticking along the top edge, remove the screws from the bottom hinge on the side attached to the door frame (not the door). Slip a piece of cardboard (a shim) under the hinge to raise it slightly and then reinsert the screws. If the door is sticking along the bottom, insert a shim behind the top hinge on the frame side.
- If the door still sticks after shimming the hinges, sand or plane the door edge along the area that's sticking.
- If the door still sticks, remove the door from the frame and plane the entire edge, always working with the grain. Plane from the outer edge toward the center. After planing, check the edge you trimmed down with a straightedge, and sand any irregularities you find.
- Once the door opens and shuts smoothly, sand its edges, then prime and repaint the door to prevent it from absorbing moisture and swelling again.

slip-sliding doors

- A sliding door that rattles when you open or shut it may have faulty bottom door guides, or they may be missing altogether. Replace them if necessary.
- A sliding door that sticks may have dirt in the track. Try vacuuming the track

first. If this doesn't work, slip an old sock over the head of a flat-head screw-driver and use that to probe into and clean the track.

● Do not use household oil to lubricate the tracks of sliding doors; only use spray silicone.

fixing the door warp

A door that has become slightly bowed in the center can be fixed in one of two ways:

● If the bow is slight, try adding a third hinge at the point at which the door is bowed. In time, the pressure may straighten the warp.

● If the warp is more pronounced, remove the door from its hinges. Place the door, bowed side up, on four support bricks or cement blocks. Place additional bricks over the warp and let the door lie there until the warp has straightened out.

rug repairs

These are amazing simple fixes to make, but work carefully.

small stain or burn in pile carpeting Use small scissors to trim away the damaged tufts. If this will leave a noticeable hole, cut matching tufts of the carpet from a hidden area of the carpet, such as a closet floor or under a bed or sofa. Use a toothpick to dab rubber cement both in the hole and on the ends of the tuft. Insert the tuft in the hole and press lightly into place. Work the tufts upright with a clean toothpick. When the cement is dry, use the toothpick to blend the fibers into the surrounding carpet.

deeper burn, hole, or worn spot Use a carpet knife to cut out a square or rec-tangle around the damaged part and cut a matching piece from a carpet scrap or from a hidden area. Spread a thick layer of carpet glue over the back of the patch and carefully place the patch in the hole. Let dry for several hours or overnight before vacuuming.

restoring resilience

Resilient floors (no-wax vinyl or standard vinyl) are amazingly forgiving if you take care of them.

stubborn stains or ground-in dirt Use a solution of 1 part household ammo-nia to 10 parts water and a plastic scouring pad to scrub the area lightly. Make sure the room is well ventilated and wear vinyl gloves. If this doesn't remove the stain, try an extra-fine (#0000) piece of steel wool. Once the stain is gone, use wax or polish to restore the shine.

black heel marks Rub with either silver polish on a soft cloth or white appliance wax (available at appliance stores). Remove any excess polish or wax with a clean soft cloth.

flattening curled tiles Occasionally, a vinyl tile will develop curled edges or corners. Set a steam iron on low and cover the curled area with a doubled cotton dish towel or rag. Gently press the warm iron on the towel and move it back and forth just until the glue underneath is softened. Carefully pull up the edge of the tile and apply fresh adhesive. Press the tile back into place, wiping off any excess glue, then place weights (bricks or books are good) over the reglued area until it is set.

chilling out

One of the most-used appliances in your house, the refrigerator-freezer must be kept in good working order to do its job of keeping the food you and your family eat safely cold.

check the gaskets Of all the parts on a refrigerator, the gaskets are usually the first to wear out and need replacing. To check yours, put a 150-watt floodlight

---

KEEPING YOUR COOL WHEN POWER GOES OUT

Power outages are more than just inconvenient. If they last for too long, food in your refrigerator and freezer can start to spoil. If you face this situation, try the following:

● Keep the doors closed. The fewer times the door is opened, the fewer chances the cool has to escape. A fully stocked freezer with the door kept closed should keep the food frozen for 48 hours. If the freezer is only partially full, the food may keep for only 24 hours.

● If the power outage has lasted 48 hours, and there is no sign of power returning, check with your local provider of clear ice to see if they stock dry ice. Wear heavy-duty gloves when handling dry ice, keep it in cardboard containers, and never let it touch skin or food. Twenty-five pounds of dry ice will keep an average 10-cubic-foot freezer cold for about three days.

● If you end up with lot of spoiled, unusable food, check your homeowner's policy. You may be covered for the losts up to a certain limit, like $200.

---

on an extension cord in the refrigerator or freezer compartment. Check one edge at a time. Point the bulb toward the suspect edge with the cord coming out the opposite edge. With the light on, the door shut, and the kitchen lights off, check for light coming through the edge. If any light leaks out, the gasket is worn and should be replaced.

repairing a cracked gasket If the crack is small, you can usually fill it with a little silicone caulk (check the directions carefully to be sure the caulk is approved for use around food). Roll the gasket back and fill the crack with a tiny bit of the caulk; be careful not to apply too much.

replacing gaskets Check with your local appliance store to see if they have the right gasket for your particular model in stock; if they don't, they can special-order it. Most gaskets are held in place by a retainer strip and screws, some by just a retainer strip and some just by screws. Roll the gasket back and remove the screws, then remove the old gasket. Thoroughly clean the area under and around the gasket. If the new gasket has kinks in it, soak it in some hot tap water to remove them. Beginning at the top of the door, slip the new gasket over the retainer, working from one corner to the opposite. Continue around the opening until the new gasket is in position. Carefully reinsert the screws and tighten them gently, starting with those in the center of each side, then the corners, and then in between; don't overtighten the screws.

cookin' with gas

A gas cooktop and oven are ignited either by separate pilot lights or electronic spark igniters. Pilot lights especially may need a little adjustment from time to time. Burners can also need adjustment. All you need is a screwdriver.

● A pilot light system has one or two continuously burning small flames that spark the burners; the oven has a separate pilot light. If your stovetop burners won't ignite because a pilot light keeps going out, the pilot light flame needs to be adjusted. To adjust it, follow the gas-supply tube from the pilot light until you find an adjusting screw near the front of the range. Gradually turn the screw—counterclockwise to increase the flame—until the flame is a sharp blue cone 1/4 to 3/8 inches high.

● To adjust the oven pilot light, take off the cover over the bottom of the oven. Look on the safety valve or under the thermostat knob for the adjusting screw. Adjust the flame as for the cooktop pilot light.

● If burners with electronic spark igniters won't light, the most likely cause is a lack of power. Before calling for service, check for an unplugged power cord, a tripped circuit breaker, or a blown fuse.

● If your cooktop burner's flame is uneven—either low, yellow, and sooty or too high and noisy—you may need to adjust the mixture of gas and air: Open the range top and look for the air shutter (usually a sleeve with an opening on the burner tubes). Loosen the screw that holds the sleeve. Then turn the burner on high and open the shutter until the flame is loud and flickering. Slowly close the shutter until the flames are a small circle of uniform, 1-inch-high, steady, blue flames with tiny orange tips. When the flames are right, tighten the retaining screw. Be careful working around open flames.

in your element

Ongoing upkeep, particularly keeping the elements and drip pans clean so they can work efficiently, will benefit the cook and the electric cook top.

● If one of the cooktops elements has a spot that gets redder than the rest of the ring, the ceramic insulation sheathing on the coil has broken down. You can usually remove an element that needs replacing by simply lifting it up and pulling it out of its socket. Some older elements are wired directly with screw terminals.

● If the bake or broil element in your oven burns out, save money and replace them yourself. Unplug the unit. Remove the screws that hold the element to the oven wall; then disengage any brackets holding the element and gently pull the element out until the terminals are visible. The wires will be attached to terminal screws or slip-on clips; disconnect each wire noting which terminal it goes to. Remove the old element and put the new one in place. Attach the wires to the appropriate terminals; then screw the element back in place.

just exhausted

Cleaning the kitchen exhaust fan may seem daunting, but it's not that hard, and it will add years of use to the fan.

● Turn off the power source (the circuit, not the switch). Detach a removable grill and soak it in a mild dishwashing detergent solution, or use a soapy sponge to wipe it clean.

● Unplug and remove the fan-and-motor unit and lay it on old newspaper. Wipe off the heavy grease with a soft, dry cloth. Do not immerse metal and electrical parts in water.

- Wipe out the fan opening with a soft, dry cloth (do not use water); then replace the clean fan-and-motor unit and plug it in. Dry and replace the grill if you've removed it. Turn on the power.
- If you can't remove the fan-and-motor unit, remove the grease filters. Soak them in a detergent solution. Clean the fan with the crevice tool of your vacuum. Wipe the hood with the solution before replacing the filter.

dishwasher in distress

- Yellow or brown stains on your machine's interior and on dishes? The problem may be iron in the water. To stop staining, install an iron filter in your water supply.
- Chalky deposits in your dishwasher? Start the machine without dishes or detergent on a rinse-and-hold cycle. During the fill, add 1 cup of white vinegar and let the machine finish the cycle. Then add detergent and run the empty machine through a cycle.
- Dish rack jammed? The rollers may be sticking. Turn them by hand to loosen them. If they are worn and no longer round, replace them. Some can be removed by taking out screws; most simply pull off. If a rack sticks because it is bent, replace it.
- Chipped rack prongs? Pick up some inexpensive rubber tip covers at a home center or dealer.
- Not sure the spray arm is working? Note the position of the arm at the start of a cycle, stop the machine during the wash, and check to see if the arm has moved.
- Clogged spray arm? Remove the racks, unscrew the hub cap holding the arm, and lift it off. Use a stiff wire to open the holes fully. Rinse the arm well under running water.
- Clogged filter screen? Remove the spray arm and any clips securing the screen. Hold the screen under running water and scrub with a stiff brush.

REPAIR HELP ON THE WEB

If you encounter a home repair problem that you're not sure how to handle, try these Web sites, which are filled with step-by-step instructions, hints and tips, and expert advice as well as catalogs of goods they hope to sell you.

www.doityourself.com

www.handymanusa.com

www.homedepot.com

www.home-repair.com

www.hometips.com

www.lowes.com

washing machines out of whack

Be sure to unplug your washer before attempting any repair. If you must move the washer, disconnect the water hoses first.

- Vibrations from running your machine can throw it off the level; you'll notice an increase in noise. Use a carpenter's level and adjust the leg heights until the machine is on an even keel again.

- If your machine's drive belt is loose, you may notice problems during the wash or spin cycles. Open the machine's rear access panel and press on the belt; if it bends more than 3/4 inch, tighten it. If it shows signs of real wear, replace it or have it replaced. (On a top-loader, loosen the motor's mounting nut and move the motor along the slotted opening, increasing tension on the belt. Then retighten the nut.)

- Check all the hoses while the water is running to spot leaks. If a hose is worn or has a leak, replace it.

- If your clothes are taking a beating in the wash, slip an old nylon stocking over your hand and run your hand lightly over the washer tub and agitator. If you find any sharp edges or rough spots, use fine sandpaper to smooth them.

- A cracked or broken vane on an agitator or a loose or worn agitator can be hazardous to your clothing. Replace the agitator or have it replaced.

do-it-yourself dryer fixes

speed thumps Rotate the drum by hand. Slow thumping that varies with the speed of the rotation often means the drive belt is worn out and needs replacing.

multithumps Rotate the drum by hand. Many thumps each time you rotate the drum usually mean a worn support roller. Replace it following the directions in your owner's manual or have it replaced.

leaky door Move a piece of tissue paper over the door's edge while the dryer is running; if the paper is drawn in, the seal needs to be replaced. Usually you can just pull or pry off the old seal, remove any old adhesive with mineral spirits, and attach the new seal with the special heat-resistant adhesive, which is usually sold with the seal.

an essential bit of dryer maintenance

To keep your dryer running efficiently, make it a point once a year to clean out the vent duct:

- Turn off the power to the dryer (usually two circuits) and remove the duct. Shake out any built-up lint. If necessary, run a wadded cloth on a stick through the duct.

- When replacing the duct, make sure to reseal the joints with fresh duct tape. Try to set your vent duct so that it is straight; dips and kinks collect water and lint, blocking air flow.
- Outdoors, clean the damper and its hinge by inserting a length of straightened coat hanger into the vent hood.

quick fixes for leaky pipes

Dripping water can pose an electrical hazard and can cause other damage, so even minor leaks should be repaired promptly by a licensed plumber. But leaks don't always happen at times when plumbers are available, so for some temporary quick fixes, try the following:

- Shut off the water supply to the pipe.
- Using steel wool, sand off any rust from the pipe, wipe the pipe clean, and dry.
- To seal a small crack or puncture in a waste pipe, wrap layers of electrical tape around the pipe from one side of the leak to the other.
- For a small leak, wrap a rubber pad around the leak and cover it with a hose clamp.
- For a larger leak, wrap a rubber pad around the leak, then cover the pad with a pipe clamp, and bolt or screw the clamp in place. Make sure the clamp is centered directly over the leak.

getting into hot water

Keep an eye and ear on your water heater to spot any problems early.

- If you hear a lot of noise when the hot water is running, the temperature may be too high, causing steam in the pipes. Reset the water temperature.
- Dirty hot water or a long wait until the water gets hot? Either of these could mean sediment in your water heater's tank. Turn off the gas or power and the cold-water inlet valve on the tank. Open a hot-water faucet in your tub. Attach a garden hose to the water heater's drain valve and empty the tank water into a floor drain; this may take several hours. Reopen the cold-water valve and let water run through the empty tank until the draining water is clear. To prevent sediment buildup, drain the tank two to four times a year.
- No hot water from your electric heater? Check the circuit breakers or fuses. If they aren't causing the problem, turn off power to the heater, remove the access panel, and press the reset button on the upper thermostat. Replace the access panel; then restore power and test.

reduce, reuse,
Recycle

TO ANYONE BENT ON SAVING A DIME,
CONSERVING ON ENERGY AND RESOURCES
AND REUSING THINGS IS SECOND NATURE.

insulation issues

A surefire way to lower your heating and cooling bills is to improve the insulation in your home. As you review your insulation needs, be sure to take into account walls or floors that separate living spaces from garages, basements, attics, or crawl space as well as outside walls.

- Check at a home center for the specific insulation recommendations for your area. Or try the Department of Energy's Web site (www.energy.gov), which gives recommendations by zip code. These recommendations are based on installation costs and energy savings. Don't put in more insulation than is recommended, because it won't save you extra money.

- Insulation is measured in R-values, which indicate the resistance to heat loss your insulation should have in ceilings, walls, and floors. The highest R-values are recommended in the North, because of their cold winters, and in the South, because of their hot summers.

- Fluffy fiberglass blankets in either batts or rolls are very popular, but there are also rigid foam sheets, as well as sprayed-in foam and blown-in loose-fill insulation. Any type you choose will require a vapor barrier to keep damp air from condensing inside the wall, causing damage. Some insulation has the vapor barrier built in; some vapor barriers must be installed separately. Always place the barrier so it is facing toward the heated interior wall. If you live in a hot, humid area, however, the barrier may need to face the exterior wall, or it may not be needed at all; check with a local builder.

- Urethane foam insulation is rapidly gaining in popularity, both in new construction and in retrofitting older homes. This insulation is pumped into existing walls through a small hole (less patching) or sprayed in new walls. Foam provides excellent insulation and forms its own vapor retarder, but a licensed contractor must install it.

weather stripping and caulking cut costs

Another excellent and relatively simple step toward reducing your energy bills is to add weather stripping to all doors and windows and to caulk all cracks and leaks. The average heating bill can be reduced by as much as 30 percent just by preventing outside air from seeping through miniscule cracks.

- The most common sources of air leaks are plumbing penetrations, chimneys, fireplace dampers, attic access hatches, recessed lights and ceiling fans, missing plaster, electrical outlets and switches, windows, doors, and baseboard moldings.
- One of the biggest culprits in heating or cooling loss (up to 15 percent!) is air loss around ductwork. Either contact a qualified licensed contractor or check all the accessible air ducts in your home and caulk any cracks or leaks.
- Before applying weather stripping, lay a bead of caulking; this acts as an adhesive and stops any drafts caused by surface irregularities.
- Another easy-to-use and effective option for plugging leaks is expanding foam sealant, sold in cans at hardware stores and home centers. Follow the manufacturer's directions carefully.
- Self-sticking weather stripping has a tendency to peel off eventually. Add a few tacks or staples to reinforce the weather stripping the next time you put some up.
- To weatherproof a door, tack metal-backed door weather strips along the stops on the jamb. Then screw a bottom strip with a sweep onto the door. Trim both strips with a hacksaw and be sure each fits snugly.

thrifty thermostats

Lowering your thermostat during the winter or raising it during the summer (if you have central air-conditioning), even just a few degrees, can appreciably reduce your energy bills. During the cold months, a thermostat that is set at 66° to 68° F is perfect; in summer, aim for 78° to 80° F. If everyone is out of the house during the day, it's prudent to invest in an automatic thermostat timer that brings the heat up about one hour before you get up, lowers it 5 to 10 degrees for the hours the house is empty, and then turns it back up just before you get

AUDIT YOUR ENERGY

**www.homeenergysaver.lbl.gov
or 1-800-654-2765**

....

If you want to maximize your heating and cooling efficiency (and find out where it's all going), you can visit the Energy Advisor at this Web site to get a customized estimated annual energy bill for your home. You'll also receive suggestions for upgrades you can make to improve your energy performance. Since your particular situation will dictate your energy usage (home size, climate, usage patterns, and appliances), it helps to have an audit that takes your lifestyle into account. You can also call the Energy Service for information about conserving energy (and lowering your bills).

home. (The settings would, of course, be different for the summer months.)

filter savings

Get into the habit of checking your furnace filter once a month during the heating season. And do the same with your air conditioner during the summer. Choose a specific day of the month or do it the day your bill arrives (highly motivating). Cleaning or replacing the filter monthly can help keep your heating and cooling systems working efficiently, since clogged filters waste energy and make your systems work harder and run longer—money out the window.

energy-efficient windows

The cost of replacing your old single-glazed windows with new double-glazed ones that have argon gas between the panes can be fairly daunting. The long-term benefit in lowered heating and cooling bills, especially with the cost of energy continuing to skyrocket, makes it worth considering.

● If your old windows are basically sound, consider adding permanent combination storm windows. Because they have sliding screens, you won't have to change your storm windows with the seasons. And they double the energy efficiency of windows. Look for solid construction, resilient pile weather stripping, and three tracks instead of two. Make sure they are easy to open and close—and to get at when you want to wash them.

● Have your older windows professionally treated with low-E (low-emissivity) film. A low-E coating blocks and reflects heat and usually lasts about five years.

● The least expensive option to seal windows against winter cold is to install clear sheets of plastic. You will not be able to access the windows once these are in place, and you will be putting tiny holes in the plastic at the points where you attach the sheets, but they will still help lower your heating costs to an extent.

● Make your curtains an ally in energy efficiency: Light-colored curtains will keep a room warmer than dark-colored ones because the light-colored ones let sunlight come into the room. Line the curtains with an acetate or acrylic fabric so that your warm air doesn't pass through the curtains and out the window.

here comes the sun

You can use passive solar energy to heat your house in winter, and these same tricks work in reverse to keep your house cooler in summer:

cold weather During the winter months, allow as much sun as possible into the house. Remove and store window screens. On sunny days, open blinds, shutters, and shades and tie back curtains. Trim evergreen trees and shrubs that shade the windows. As soon as the sun starts to go down, close the blinds to hold the heat inside.

hot weather In the summer take the opposite approach: Plant trees to shade the house and especially your air conditioner. (A shaded air-conditioning unit uses 10 percent less energy than one in direct sunlight.) In addition, install awnings over south-facing windows and close your curtains early in the day. (Leave them closed all day if you will be gone.) If it cools down after sunset, open up the house to take advantage of the breezes.

lighten up

Invest in compact fluorescent bulbs for frequently used fixtures. These produce the same amount of light and fit in the same sockets as an incandescent bulb but use only about one-quarter of the energy. They also last ten times as long as their incandescent cousins—double savings indeed.

small savings

Using small appliances can actually save energy (thus lowering your bills). A toaster oven can bake a potato or cook a small-size portion of food; a microwave can cook anything liquid in less time using less energy than a stove can. Look for models of small appliances that have a lower wattage rating to further your savings.

hot tips for water heaters

Except for your home's heating and cooling units, your water heater is your largest energy user. So it pays to control its cost.

● Unless you need a higher temperature for a dishwasher, set the thermostat on your unit at 120° F. This simple step can cut your hot water costs by as much

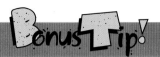

BAG IT!

The most economical and earth-friendly kind of bag is one you can use over and over again.

- Canvas shopping bags are ideal for grocery shopping. They hold anything and will not break. If they get dirty, you can just throw them in the washing machine.
- String shopping bags are great for keeping in your purse or briefcase to have when you're picking some things up on the way home, and they expand to accommodate a surprising amount.
- Paper bags are useful for collecting newspapers for recycling. Or you can unfold them and use the paper for wrapping packages, covering books, or anything else that requires heavy-duty paper.
- When you do end up with some plastic bags—they're unavoidable—reuse them as garbage pail liners. Or see if you can return them to the store for repayment. Some stores will pay 5 cents per bag.

as 50 percent! Turn the unit to the lowest setting if you will be gone a week or more.

- If your water heater runs out of hot water often, you may be doing tasks that consume a lot of hot water too close together. One bath, for example can completely use up a common 40-gallon tank, and it can take nearly an hour to reheat. To find out how quickly your water heater recovers, look for a plate on it that says how many gallons it can heat in an hour.
- If you have an electric water heater, find out if your power company offers off-peak rates. Then try to schedule bathing, laundering, and dish-washing for those periods, whenever possible.
- Unless you have a fairly new, superinsulated unit, buy an inexpensive water heater cover from your home center or hardware store. These covers come as kits and wrap around your water heater, keeping it insulated and the heat where it belongs. A cover can cut 15 percent off your hot water costs. If your unit is gas, be careful not to cover the top or to block the airflow to the gas burner at the bottom.

showered with savings

Installing inexpensive low-flow shower heads and faucets in your home is a simple fix you can do yourself and will reduce the amount of water you use by half, without decreasing the performance. Follow the manufacturer's instructions; you'll need only a wrench or pliers to do the job.

● Just taking a shower instead of a bath can save water: A three-minute shower uses one-fourth the water of a bath. With a low-flow shower head, you save even more.

● Check out shower heads with an off-on switch that lets you interrupt the flow while you soap up, shave, or shampoo and then resume the flow to rinse.

● Turn off the water while you soap your face or hands, shave, or brush your teeth. Get into the habit of turning off the tap when you're not continuously using it.

● Keep an old milk jug under each sink. When you have to run water to get it hot, use the jug to catch the water instead of letting it go down the drain. Then use the water in the jug for your houseplants or humidifier.

● When you replace a toilet, get a new low-flow model (which is now required in all new construction). These toilets use only 1.67 gallons of water per flush, compared with the 3.5 gallons the old type used.

● If you're not ready to replace your toilets, fill old plastic soda pop bottles with water and put one in each toilet tank to reduce the amount of water per flush.

appliance

DON'T buy the most expensive appliances automatically. Check for models with high energy efficiency and low water usage that are in the medium-price range. Really low prices may land you with a model that eats energy or water, costing you more in the long run.

DO look for dishwashers that have water-miser and no-heat drying features when you are shopping for a new one.

DO run dishwashers at night, when many power companies offer lower rates.

DON'T rinse off normally soiled dishes before you put them in the dishwasher. Just scrape off the food. Also, don't use your dishwasher's rinse-and-hold cycle except when dishes must be held overnight and odors may result.

DON'T use more detergent than you need in either your dishwasher or your clothes washer. Experiment to see how little you can use and still get things clean.

DO use nature for drying—a clothesline for laundry and the no-heat setting for dishes. (Open the dishwasher door while the dishes are drying to add humidity to a dry house.)

CHAPTER 10

Cheap Car Talk

- the best car buy

- car care

the best
Car Buy

IF YOU DO YOUR HOMEWORK
AND BARGAIN, YOU CAN GET
YOUR DREAM CAR FOR A LOT LESS.

research, research, research!

The first and most important step to selecting and buying a car is to gather as much information as possible about the models you are interested in.

- Don't limit yourself to one car manufacturer when you begin your research. That will automatically reduce your bargaining power. Instead, make a list of features that are most important to you (safety record, gas mileage, reliability, engine size, all-wheel drive). Then try to prioritize the list in order of importance.

- When you have a better idea of what kind of car you want, read magazines (such as Consumer Reports and Car and Driver), surf the Web (see Resources box, page 208 for good sites to check), and try to identify two or three manufacturers with models that fit your needs.

the real price

Once you've identified the car models you're interested in, the most valuable piece of information you can find out is the **wholesale price**—what the dealer paid for the car from the manufacturer. This price includes the base price as well as the "goodies" the manufacturer offered the dealer, including discounts, rebates, incentives, and special financing. There are a number of easy-to-access sources to find out a car's wholesale price, including Edmunds' New Cars & Trucks Prices & Reviews, a paperback book available in most local libraries. The same information is also available on-line at **www.edmunds.com**. Once you know what the dealer paid, you can tack on a modest profit—say $500—for the dealer and get yourself a terrific deal. You always want to start with the lowest price and bargain up. Never bargain down from the sticker price.

'tis the season

At the end of the year, most car dealers are eager to get rid of last year's models to make room for the new line. November and December are often great months to buy because dealers are more willing to negotiate aggressively in order to ensure you will drive an older model car off the lot. But never buy the upcoming year's models in November because you'll pay for the newness. Also, wait for bad weather. If the dealership has been a ghost town for a week because of the storm of the century, they will be more anxious to sell a car—at a better price for you.

it pays to shop around

When purchasing a car, most folks automatically think of the traditional dealer working out of a showroom. However, there are more places to shop for a car these days, and they're all worth checking out. It pays to know what these various options are offering because the more information you have at your fingertips, the better deal you're likely to strike on the car you want.

the dealer This option requires legwork and time as you go from one showroom to another, hearing sales pitch after sales pitch. If you're willing to do your home-work first and haggle fiercely, you can usually get an excellent price on the exact car that you want.

internet services On the Web, car shoppers can use a free dealer-referral serv-ice (see Resources box, page 208).

club services These are member-only car-buying services offered through price clubs and other organizations. They put you in touch with an affiliated dealer, who then offers prospective buyers a pre-arranged quote with a flat markup above the invoice. While convenient for those who can't bring themselves to haggle, you'll probably end up paying more for the privilege of using a buying service.

car talk terms

Learning the lingo can really help keep you on top of the bargaining process:

base price This is the cost of a particular model of automobile without any additional options at all (the standard package plus factory warranty).

invoice price This is how much the manufacturer initially charged the dealer for the car. The invoice price is generally higher than the dealer's final cost because car dealers often get rebates, allowances, discounts, and incentive awards from manufacturers. Also, the invoice price will often include freight charges—check this point carefully if you're using the invoice price as your base price. You don't want to be charged for the freight if it has already been paid for!

dealer sticker price This sticker is affixed to the window of the car by the car dealer. It shows both the Monroney sticker price (described below), and the suggested retail prices of any dealer-installed options, plus the charges for preparation and undercoating.

monroney sticker price (msrp) Federal law requires this sticker to be on every new car's window, and only the purchaser can legally take it off. It lists the base price, the manufacturer's installed options with suggested retail prices, the transportation charge, and the fuel economy of the vehicle (mileage per gallon based on city and highway driving).

the dos and don'ts of haggling

Unless you want to pay more than you should, you will need to learn how to haggle for a car. It is expected and it is necessary.

don't wait to shop until your current car is on its last legs. Being in need puts you in a very bad bargaining position.

do be prepared. Have your research firmly in your head or at your fingertips.

don't worry about bargaining too hard and offending the dealer. They take care of themselves. You can be friendly. In fact, making a buddy of the dealer can work to your advantage.

do be discreet. If you have your heart set on a particular car, continue to bargain as if you are undecided between two or three.

don't do the salesperson's work. During the course of bargaining, a salesperson may ask you to name a reasonable profit. Don't take the bait. That isn't your job, that's their job, and it's their problem!

do be willing to walk away. Trust your gut instinct if the deal isn't good enough or if some of the details don't feel right.

don't glide over the details. Most contracts include a charge for paperwork or an advertising fee. If you have agreed on a good price, ask the dealer to waive these fees. If they won't do that, suggest free servicing or complimentary extras (floor mats, for example) to offset the fees.

don't pay any mind when the salesperson asks, "What amount would you like your monthly payment to be?" It's one of the oldest dealer tricks and one of the most effective. Paying $219 a month is no kind of deal if the payments stretch on for an extra 24 months.

NETTING THE BEST DEAL

www.consumerreports.org
or 1-800-205-2445

Consumer Reports offers comprehensive pricing information and charges $12 for the first report; $10 for each additional one. Here are some other helpful sites:

For model and price info:

www.bbbonline.org
(Better Business Bureau)

www.carfax.com

www.carbargains.org

www.carprice.com

www.edmunds.com

www.kelleybluebook.com
or www.kbb.com

www.intellichoice.com

www.nadaguides.com

For dealer referrals:

www.autobytel.com

www.autovantage.com

www.autoweb.com

www.carmax.com

do keep your trade-in out of the negotiation until the end. Many clever salespeople will give you a huge bargain on the new car; then fleece you on the trade-in. Get a firm price on the new car first, then get the best price you can for your old one (you will do better selling it privately if you are willing to make the effort).

no deposit, no return

There are dealers who, once the deal is just about made, will press you to put a deposit on a car. Unless you know for certain that this is The Car, don't put any money down. Ignore threats of the car getting away. You could end up making a commitment you'll regret.

let's make a deal

If possible, try to close a deal on a Saturday at the end of the month. At some dealerships, the sales personnel can make a bonus for hitting a sales number (usually determined weekly or monthly or both).

signing on the dotted line

You've done your homework, you've haggled with the best, you're ready to sign the contract. Wait. Consider these:

- Be sure there is a clause in the contract that allows you to void the agreement if something goes wrong, such as a delay in delivery.
- Once you've read over the contract and agree with it, be sure the manager or general manager signs the contract with you. A salesperson will not have the authority to make certain contractual changes so you want the highest official signature possible.

lose the lease

Think twice about leasing a car. It's often a bad financial decision. Over time, you will end up paying more leasing than you would buying. You pay the big payment at the end rather than a larger down payment at the beginning. Lease payments are tax-deductible only if the car is used exclusively for work.

secondhand sensations

A good used car can be the best bargain of all. Just make sure to check reliability ratings in Consumer Reports or on-line at www.edmunds.com.

venues Independent used car lot, new-car dealership that also sells used cars, auctions, used car superstore, or private seller.

cost vs. worth Always know the market value of the car before negotiating (Kelley's Blue Book is an excellent source, either in print or on-line; see Resources box, opposite). Make your first bid slightly lower than the market price and go up from there, but set a limit for yourself and don't go above it. As with new cars, it is almost impossible to bargain down.

get a history A nonnegotiable requirement for buying a used car should be a detailed service history. This should list any potential problems including past accidents, damages, and odometer discrepancies. You can obtain a history on your own using the 17-digit VIN (vehicle identification number) from the state or a private company specializing in vehicle history reports. Search on the Web for "vehicle history."

get a check-up Have your mechanic check out the car before you buy it.

SAFETY FIRST

**www.nhtsa.gov or
1-888-DASH-2-DOT
(1-888-327-4236)**

The National Highway Traffic Safety Administration maintains a Web site and a toll-free phone number to offer the public information about the safety features of vehicles, any recalls, crash tests, and other auto safety topics.

1-800-424-9393

If you are thinking of buying a used car, call the number above first. This is the U.S. Department of Transportation's Auto Safety Hotline. By calling, you can find out if there have been any recalls on the vehicle model that you're considering.

car
Care

BECAUSE A CAR IS SUCH
A BIG INVESTMENT, IT PAYS
TO KEEP IT IN THE BEST POSSIBLE SHAPE.

the ins and outs of auto insurance

Trying to find the best auto insurance can be an overwhelming process. There are a lot of choices out there. Depending on where you live, the insurance rules in your state, and your driving record, the options will be many and varied. A few rules of thumb from the United States Office of Consumer Affairs, however, can help you make the right choice and get the most for your insurance dollars:

shop around Insurance premiums on identical policies can vary by hundreds of dollars. For unbiased information about auto insurance companies, ask family and friends for recommendations or call your state insurance department or an insurance-rating firm like A.M. Best. Consumer guides can tell you which companies offer the lowest rates, but cost should not be the only determining factor. You want to make sure that you are getting good service for your insurance dollars. If you should ever need to use your policy, you want an agent or company who's on your side and makes it easy for you.

up your deductible To lower the monthly cost of car insurance, offer to increase your deductible—the amount you would pay in the case of collision, fire, or theft before the insurance company has to pay anything. This can lower your insurance costs considerably.

less coverage on older cars At some point, having a lot of insurance on a car that is no longer worth that much invokes the laws of diminishing returns. Drop, or significantly lower, both collision and comprehensive (fire and theft) on any car that is worth less than $1,000.

check for double coverage Chances are you already have good health insurance, so you don't need this type of coverage in your auto insurance. Check with your state insurance department. Getting rid of duplicate coverage could lower your auto policy's personal injury protection (PIP) cost by up to 40 percent.

opt for the ordinary A car that is listed as "high theft" or that is expensive to repair generally will cost a lot more to insure than one that isn't. Be sure to check the insurance rates before you buy a high-end car.

low miles, low cost Ask your insurance company if they give discounts for low mileage—if you don't drive that much, why pay more?

good drivers get good rates Most insurance companies offer discounts for drivers who are over 50 years of age and for those with good driving records (no accidents in three years). Some will reduce rates if you've taken a driver's education course and will even offer discounts for student drivers who have gotten good grades. All of these discounts can add up to big savings.

safety first discounts The other area that might net you a discount on auto insurance is the safety of your car. Do you have automatic seat belts, air bags, an antitheft device, or antilock brakes? Does your car rank high on safety features with Consumer Reports? Ask your insurance agent if these features could mean lower rates for you.

three months or 3,000 miles

Memorize the above—it's the formula for oil changes. The most important fluid in your car is that dark, syrupy liquid that lubricates your engine. Perhaps the most critical thing you can do to keep your engine working well is to change the oil regularly. Be sure to use the correct weight and grade of oil recommended for your particular vehicle. If you use a heavier oil, it won't lubricate the bearings; if you use too light an oil, it can cause hammering in the engine when you start it cold—and that can eventually damage the engine. The exception to the three months or 3,000 mile rule is if you are using synthetic oil. Then the formula changes to every six months or 7,500 miles. When your car's oil is changed, make sure to check the car's other fluids (brake fluid, power steering, transmission, and such) replace the oil filter, and check all the belts and hoses.

batteries not included

The battery in your new car was installed at the factory and is probably not a top-rated battery. They don't usually last that long, so don't be surprised when yours suddenly quits working. Don't let your battery lose too much power before you replace it. This can cause the charging system to work way too hard and the starter motor to overheat. Save money (and wear on your engine) by planning ahead and start checking your battery at least six months before the warranty runs out.

- Buy the longest-lasting battery your car can take. It'll help prevent problems with the starting, charging, and electrical systems in the long run.
- Check the cold-cranking amp (CCA) rating! If you're replacing a battery, get one with the same or greater cold-cranking amp rating (the temperature at which the battery can be charged for 30 seconds at 0° F). Be sure the rating is measured in Fahrenheit, not Celsius. This is important because 0° C is actually 32° F. Making a mistake could mean the battery wouldn't be guaranteed to work at a lower temperature.

fuel facts

Some people have the idea that premium gas is better than regular unleaded. Not necessarily. If your car's engine isn't designed for high-test fuel, buying premium gas is a big old waste of your cash. With the exception of a few high-end cars, most cars today are designed to run on regular unleaded fuel. Cars requiring high-test fuel will say so under the gas gauge found on the dashboard. Unless the car manufacturer requires it, premium fuel is not better, it doesn't produce more power, improve engine performance, save fuel, or contain any additives that help your car. It just costs more.

maximizing the mileage

You want to aim at getting the mileage per gallon estimated by the government for your vehicle. If you're close, you're doing fine. If you're not, one of the following could be the culprit. With the price of gas today, it's worth taking steps to improve your car's fuel efficiency.

- If your brakes are even slightly rubbing, you can burn extra fuel without even noticing the excess heat or wear on your brakes.
- Every time you switch on an electrical device (headlights, for example, or defogger), you use a little more gas. But the greatest gas-sucking device of all is your car's air conditioner. The more you use it, the worse your mileage.
- The type of tires and their air pressure can affect your car's fuel efficiency. Big tires have more contact with the road resulting in more friction and more gas burned. During cooler months, your tire pressure may go down more rapidly than you notice. A tire that is inflated correctly at 70° F will be under-inflated by as much a five pounds per square inch (PSI) at 20° F. This also produces more friction with the road.
- A faulty transmission linkage means the information that the car needs to

work efficiently is not getting to the computer and, especially at highway speeds, this can significantly reduce fuel economy.

- Harsh wind, weather, and terrain can lower your car's fuel efficiency, as can a heavy load, stop-and-start traffic, and rough road conditions.

- Distance matters when it comes to fuel economy. Short trips of five miles or less reduce mileage and are harder on your engine, especially in cold weather. That doesn't mean you should drive farther, but it does mean you should take the time to warm up your car before you get started.

parts for pennies

Okay, you can't really get new car parts for pennies, but you can cut down on repair costs if you have a little information on your side. The most important distinction to remember when purchasing new parts is that between original equipment manufactured (OEM) and after-market parts. The OEMs tend to cost from 15 to 20 percent more than the after-market variety. So what's the difference? It's similar to the difference between name-brand drugs and generic ones.

SNOWBIRD DISCOUNTS

If you spend a good portion of every year away from home and are not driving a particular car, ask your insurance company about dropping coverage during the time the car is not in use. This could end up saving you a pretty penny.

- After-market parts are generally produced under the same standards as OEMs; however, the after-market parts come with mounting hardware that allows them to be installed in a number of similar vehicles, not just one or two. This helps lower the cost of the after-market part.

- The warranty on OEMs is usually twice as long as that of after-market parts and if the part goes bad, the OEM is replaced by the car dealer for nothing, including installation. Basically, if a longer warranty and the newest gizmo are important to you, go with OEMs; if you want to save money, use after-market varieties.

- Car dealers usually get the "latest and greatest" parts from the manufacturer; it may take longer for an after-market version to become available.

CHAPTER 11

Money-Savvy Medicine

O **medical insurance**

O **doctors and hospitals and HMOs, oh my!**

O **drugs for less**

medical
Insurance

HEALTH INSURANCE IS A MAJOR BUDGET
ITEM FOR EVERY FAMILY. HERE ARE SOME WAYS TO
MAKE THE MOST OF YOUR COVERAGE.

finding the best hmo or ppo

If you are buying a health plan on your own instead of getting it through your employer, choosing an HMO or PPO is an area where using a licensed insurance agent might save you money. Because of the great number of options and rapid changes in the systems, it can be tricky to decide what's best on your own. Here are a few key points to keep in mind:

- Health is more important than saving money. You can't put a price on your health, so go for the best, not the cheapest, plan you can afford.

- Check out the plan thoroughly. You want to be sure the insurance company and its network have a good track record. The Better Business Bureau, your state's department of insurance, and other policyholders can help you evaluate a company's performance.

- Preventive medicine should be included in the plan. If the National Committee for Quality Assurance **(www.ncqa.org)** gives a plan a high rating, it means the plan provides extensive screening (cancer, diabetes, and the like) to catch conditions early, when they are more likely to be easily and successfully treated. A low rating means the plan's records include an inappropriately high number of heart bypasses and angioplasties, indicating that the plan's emphasis is on fixing damage after it's done rather than on preventing damage. Clearly, preventing problems is better than fixing them, both for your health and your pocketbook.

- Does the organization have staying power? Look for a group that's been around for 15 to 20 years.

- Do you have a wide choice of doctors? Are they located reasonably near you? Are most of them taking new patients? You want to have a choice of doctors, but you don't want to have to travel far in an emergency. And you want a plan in which about 90 percent of the doctors are accepting new patients.

- What do you do if you need to see a specialist? Make sure the plan offers an adequate choice of specialists.
- Are doctors unhappy with the organization? If there is high turnover (10 percent or more), it usually means the doctors don't like dealing with this organization.
- What if you have a pre-existing condition? Are there restrictions on your coverage?
- What can you do if you don't agree with a doctor's diagnosis or treatment plan and want a second opinion? What recourse do you have?

an umbrella for my umbrella?

If your employer offers only hospital coverage, it's a good idea to look into buying an HMO or PPO plan for yourself and your family. Look for a plan with the best doctors and most convenient features, but don't worry about the hospitalization coverage, because you're already covered for that.

retiree recommendations

- Don't depend entirely on Medicare. It has way too many gaps in coverage, and the gaps are always changing and are not always easy to figure out.
- Don't just drop your major medical insurance when you retire. As you're approaching retirement, check with the program you're in; if you continue the coverage, the insurer will often keep it at the lowest possible rate. If you let your major medical drop and then try to get new coverage, it will be much more expensive and, after age 65, hard to get. Your major medical should cover any gaps in your Medicare.
- Scrutinize any policies that claim to supplement Medicare; some actually cover the same stuff. You want a policy that fills the gaps.
- Use group power. Organize a group of 50 seniors and approach a doctor. Offer a written agreement whereby the entire group will use only that doctor as its primary physician if the doctor will accept whatever Medicare agrees to pay. The physician may agree if the guaranteed patient volume seems to make the deal worthwhile.

medicare hmo?

This works just like a regular HMO. You sign up and agree to use a network of approved doctors. Then you don't need to buy Medigap coverage, and you only pay the usual small copayment. Medicare reimburses the other expenses. But be warned: In many states, insurance companies are closing Medicare HMOs because they are not profitable enough.

long-term care insurance pros and cons

We never want to think we'll end up in a nursing home, but there are no guarantees in life. Long-term care insurance can help protect you and your family by covering the costs of care where Medicare leaves off. But think twice before signing up for long-term care insurance.

⦿ Although widely promoted as essential for everyone, this form of insurance is mainly of real value for people who have considerable assets that they want to preserve for their families and who want to avoid depleting their wealth on nursing home bills.

⦿ Before buying this kind of insurance, analyze whether you can pay the premiums for the rest of your life; many policyholders on fixed incomes are forced to cancel their long-term care policies as they grow older and their premiums increase. They can no longer pay the premiums—just when they are more likely to need long-term care.

⦿ If you do want a long-term policy—and you no longer have dependents— you might want to consider converting your life insurance to long-term care insurance.

fighting back

Though insurance companies sell peace of mind, when it comes to actually shelling out payments, they can become mulish in the extreme. And the higher the amount of your claim, the more likely the insurer is to put up a struggle. Common problems include the following:

scenario: You've had surgery that was approved. You file a claim. Mr. Insurer sees the big bill and orders an audit of your medical records to see whether you made any mistakes on your application so that he can deny the claim or cancel your policy.

best defense: Avoid the problem in the first place by filling out your applications yourself, being careful to provide all of the information requested.

FLEXIBLE SPENDING ACCOUNTS

If your employer lets you set aside money tax free in a flexible spending account, it can be a great deal. You can use this money to reimburse yourself for many medical, dental, and vision expenses not covered by other plans, such as expensive dental work, eyeglasses, or a hearing aid. It saves you money by reducing your taxable income. For example, if you're in the 28 percent tax bracket and set aside $1,000, this will save you $280. The catch: You must spend the money in the year you set it aside or else you lose it. So use it only for an expense you know you are going to have.

scenario: You put in a claim, and Mr. Insurer wants to keep costs down, so he denies it without a full investigation.

best defense: Get written statements from your doctors to help support your claim. If Mr. Insurer still balks, appeal again with more documentation or to a higher level.

scenario: Your doctor says a procedure or treatment is necessary. Mr. Insurer gets his own doctor to say it isn't and therefore he doesn't have to pay for it.

best defense: Get a second opinion! And before you go for treatment, make sure your doctor is willing to fight for you in this kind of situation.

scenario: You're a writer who develops severe carpal tunnel syndrome, which prevents you from using a keyboard. You file a disability claim because you can no longer do your job. Mr. Insurer denies the claim, saying you can do other jobs.

best defense: Be sure your policy covers you for your specific line of work, not just any job. Tell your doctor what it is you do at work and why you can't do it anymore.

scenario: Your doctor says you need a certain operation. You call the insurance company, and the nice lady you talk to says OK. You have the operation and file a claim. Mr. Insurer denies the claim, contending that it's not the standard treatment and that the nice lady was only a clerk, not someone qualified to give approval for treatment.

best defense: Get the approval for treatment in writing from a claims adjuster. Be sure the adjuster includes his or her name, title, the specific procedure, and amount covered.

doctors and hospitals and
HMOs, Oh My!

GETTING THE MOST FOR YOUR
MEDICAL DOLLAR IS NOT SIMPLE.
BUT THERE ARE WAYS TO CONTROL COSTS.

back-to-school bargains

Because medical schools are generally up to date on the latest research, technology, and techniques, you can benefit from excellent care at discount prices at clinics run by medical schools and teaching hospitals. And you will be helping these young doctors develop exemplary bedside manners—good for them and good for you.

a word of caution If you are in a hurry, avoid teaching hospitals (medical school–affiliated) in the month of July. Why? July is the beginning of the medical year, so all the new residents and medical students are just starting. Though you will get excellent treatment, it will probably take longer because of the learning curve.

call me!

Instead of running to your doctor's office when you have a nonemergency problem, try calling first. Many medical offices keep nurses on staff just to talk to patients over the phone. Sometimes they can give you immediate information, and sometimes they consult the doctor and call you back.

● Most cities have information lines that you can call with questions about health care. Look in the Yellow Pages under the listings for Health Resources, Health Education, or Health Information.

testing, testing

A sad fact of life is that doctors who work for large private practices order about twice as many chest X rays and electrocardiograms as do their counterparts at HMOs or PPOs. It's a money thing: Tests make money for the practice, and each doctor's fee structure is based on how much income he or she brings in—which can encourage a doctor to order needless tests. HMOs and PPOs generally use a fixed prepayment structure, so there's less pressure to order expensive tests.

surgery cents

It has been estimated that about a fourth of the surgical procedures performed in the U.S. each year are not really necessary. Protect yourself by asking your doctor:

- Why do I need this operation now?
- Are there alternatives that do not involve surgery?
- What are the risks of the surgery versus not having it?
- Can I have a same-day surgery?
- If not, how long will I be in the hospital?
- What can I expect during recovery as far as pain?
- Will I require rehabilitative care?
- Will there be any residual effects of the surgery?
- When can I resume my normal routine?

the price of a second opinion

Getting a second opinion can save you money and pain. This is not a rejection of a good doctor you like and trust; it is just plain common sense.

- Avoid the old-boy network trap. Though most doctors will refer you to someone they feel is well qualified to answer your questions, there are those who will refer you to colleagues they're confident will simply back them up.
- Call a medical school or teaching hospital and ask for the department of surgery. Ask the administrative assistant if the department has referral lists for second opinions.
- If a teaching hospital isn't available in your area, call a local hospital that's not affiliated with the doctor.
- The American College of Surgeons (633 N. Saint Clair Street, Chicago, IL 60611, www.facs.org, or 312-202-5000) can provide you with the names of board-certified surgeons in your area.
- Ask the second doctor the same questions that you asked the first one. (See list above.)
- If the two opinions conflict, it is probably a good idea to seek a third and maybe even a fourth opinion.
- If you want to eliminate any question of whether the surgery is necessary, get an opinion from a medical doctor who isn't a surgeon; he or she would have nothing to lose by being honest.

check-in costs

Never check into a hospital on a weekend for tests or elective surgery (unless medically necessary). Chances are you will lie in bed for the weekend at a cost of up to $1,000 a day! Doctors try to discharge patients by Friday, so hospitals want to fill up the empty beds (which cost them money) on weekends. For your monetary and physical health, insist on checking in as close to the test or surgery time as possible. The same rule applies to holidays.

rub out billing errors

The most errors in hospital billing tend to be found in the following areas:

respiratory therapy After you stopped using an oxygen tank, the equipment charge continued to go on your bill.

pharmacy charges You actually didn't need a particular drug, so it was returned to the pharmacy, but no one bothered to remove the charge from your bill.

lab tests A lab test was canceled, but the cost still went on your bill.

central supply A staff person ran out of something for your roommate and borrowed it from your supply. They meant to note it in your chart but forgot, and it went on your bill.

avoid overbilling

write it down Bring a notebook and keep track of everything that you use, that's given to you, or that's done to you during your stay.

question everything Ask about anything that is given or done to you—tests, medications, therapies. If the doctor doesn't answer to your satisfaction, ask a nurse.

itemize When you are checking out, ask for an itemized bill that lists every service and charge so you can check it carefully against your own record.

double-check data Examine the room-and-board charges, make sure the number of days and type of room are correct, and check the rates.

don't overlook extras Scrutinize charges for phone calls and TV rental. Again, check the number of days.

examine the doctors' bills Many doctors don't prepare their own bills, and changes in visitations or in-office services are not always conveyed to the billing agent.

get an estimate in writing Whenever possible, ask ahead of time for a written estimate of what everything will cost.

drugs for
Less

THERE ARE WAYS TO KEEP DOWN
THE COST OF BOTH PRESCRIPTION
AND OVER-THE-COUNTER MEDICATIONS.

make your doctor
your penny-pinching partner

When your doctor prescribes a brand-name drug, ask why. Tell him or her that you are trying to keep your drug expenditures down, and ask if there is a generic form of the drug available that could treat your problem just as well. The drug may still be under exclusive patent, so there may not be a generic form available yet, and your doctor may not have another drug available that would produce the desired result. But it is important to ask, because generic drugs are often half the price of name brands.

sample these savings

You can often get free drugs simply by asking for them. Salespeople from drug companies regularly visit doctors and leave samples of new or favorite drugs they want the doctor to prescribe. Most doctors are happy to give you a starter dose from these samples. If you're starting a new medication, the samples give both you and your doctor an opportunity to see whether you will experience any side effects before you invest in a full prescription.

when half is half as much

If you take a prescription medicine that comes in solid pill form, ask your doctor about prescribing them in a higher-dosage size so that you can cut the pills in half. Pill cutters can be bought at most drugstores and are fairly inexpensive. And doubling the dosage and the halving the pill can result in a significant discount.

do a brown bag check

If you take a number of prescription medicines or regularly take an over-the-counter drug, put all of them in a brown bag and take them along on your next appointment with your primary care doctor. This is particularly important if you are seeing several doctors. Your primary care physician needs to know about all the medications that you're taking to make sure there are no dangerous or debilitating interactions. This also gives your doctor the chance to review the drugs to see whether there are any that you no longer need to be taking and whether there are newer, less expensive versions of the drugs that are now available.

mail order from aarp

If you are over 50 and are a member of AARP, check with the group about filling your maintenance prescription by mail. A maintenance prescription is one for any medicine that you take regularly for a chronic condition, such as high blood pressure or high cholesterol. Though this process takes a little longer, you may see a significant reduction in costs, because the drugs are ordered wholesale and the savings are passed on to you. Call 1-800-424-3410 or visit their Web site at **www.aarp.com** for more information.

otc generic gains!

Don't fall into the trap of buying brand names on your nonprescription over-the-counter (OTC) drugs, either! Store brands of OTC drugs are almost always less expensive than the name brands, and the key ingredient is the same. Read the labels of your preferred OTC remedies and learn to recognize the key ingredient. Then read the labels of the store brands, and you'll find out they are the same. But cheaper! See the box on page 225, for some money-saving listings of brand names and their generic equivalents.

big bottle bargains at big box stores

Price clubs such as Costco and Sam's Club offer OTC drugs in really big bottles. Do a cost comparison with a smaller bottle at your drugstore. You may find that buying that really big bottle of acetaminophen (which you use fairly frequently and always want to have on hand) is the much better buy, both in terms of cost per pill and convenience. But always do the cost comparison to make sure that you're getting the best buy.

a penny pinch of caution

Although generic drugs are usually the cheapest alternative available, it is not always true. Pharmacies pay less for generics, but some mark them up more than they mark up brand-name drugs. And if you have a good coupon, you may get the better deal buying the brand name. Each time you shop you should do some research and do the math instead of assuming that you'll always save by picking the generic.

combo costs

It is tempting to buy an all-in-one concoction to treat your cold or sinus headache, but it's often a waste of money and, worse, you could end up overdosing on one ingredient. Acetaminophen (Tylenol, etc.) overdoses are particularly worrisome because they can result in liver failure. Overdosing can occur from taking a multisymptom medication, such as Nyquil, which contains acetaminophen, and then an extra dose of acetaminophen on top of that.

You have two choices: Purchase only single-ingredient medications and take them to treat each symptom. For example, if you have a sinus headache, you can take a normal dose of acetaminophen, aspirin or ibuprofen, plus a decongestant such as pseudoephedrine. Or, purchase a multi-symptom medication and just take the recommended dose of that; do not supplement it with other medications. The first choice may well save you money since generic versions of basic medications usually cost less than name-brand multisymptom medications. However, many drug store chains produce low-price generic versions of multisymptom medications, so you have to do the math and choose the approach that works best for you.

throw it out!

Though we love to save just about everything, even the most devoted penny pincher knows to throw out the following:

- ● Any medicine past its expiration date.
- ● Prescription medicines from a former illness.
- ● Aspirin that has developed a vinegary odor.
- ● Over-the-counter drugs that you are no longer taking.
- ● Anything without a label or not in its original container.

Toss them in a bag and take it to your next doctor's visit. Ask them to dispose of the medications as hazardous medical waste (flushing them puts them into the water supply, and throwing them into the garbage puts them in landfills).

DECIPHERING OTC DRUG LABELS

Whether you are looking for a quick nonprescription remedy for a cold, an upset stomach, or a rash, you can save a lot by buying generic store-brand over-the-counter drugs instead of the brand names. Here is a list of some of the more common brand-name OTC drugs and the generic name of their main ingredient. With these and many others, all you have to do is compare the ingredients listed on the store brand with the ones on the brand name. Also make sure that the amount of the active ingredient is the same. They usually are. The generic brands are nearly always complete knock-offs of the brand names. Indeed, many drugstores put them side by side, and generic packages often are designed to resemble brand names.

Brand name	Generic name	Brand name	Generic name
Advil	ibuprofen	Gas-X	simethicone
Afrin	oxymetazoline	Imodium	loperamide
Alka-Seltzer	aspirin, citric acid, and sodium bicarbonate	Kaopectate	attapulgite
		Metamucil	psyllium
Aleve	naproxen	Midol	acetaminophen, caffeine, and pyrilamine maleate
Bayer	aspirin		
Benadryl	diphenhydramine		
Bufferin	aspirin	Motrin	ibuprofen
Chlor-Trimeton	chlorpheniramine	Sudafed	pseudoephedrine
Cortaid	hydrocorisone	Sudafed Sinus Headache	acetaminophen and pseudoephedrine
Cortizone	hydrocorisone		
Contact	pseudoephedrine	Tagamet HB	cimetidine
Dimetapp	brompheniramine and phenyl propanolamine	Tavist-D	clemastine and phenyl-propanolamine
		Tinactin	tolnaftate
Excedrin	aspirin, acetaminophen, and caffeine	Tums	calcium carbonate
		Tylenol	acetaminophen
Excedrin P.M.	acetaminophen and diphenhydramine	Tylenol Sinus	acetaminophen and pseudoephedrine

Frugal Finances

○ the working life

○ home accounting 101

○ retire like royalty!

the working Life

a working check-list

Most people work for someone else. If you are an employee, you have already found lots of ways to save money on work-related expenses in earlier chapters about clothing, insurance, cars, commuting, food, and even that morning cup of commuter cappuccino. Here's a quick review of what we've covered earlier as it applies to work:

clothing If you have a uniform, you are actually lucky. You spend almost nothing on working clothes. For the rest of us: Buy the best quality clothing you can afford and take good care of it so that it will last. Avoid impulse shopping and be sure any clothing or accessories you purchase can work with your current wardrobe.

commuting If at all possible, use public transportation, carpool, walk, bike, or find alternatives that will save you on commuting costs. Driving alone to work is a cash drain.

food Eating out is an enormous waste of money. To get an idea of just how much buying lunch at work costs, keep a written account of what you spend on each bagel, sandwich, or salad for just one week. You'll be surprised at how quickly it all adds up. Instead, save your money for a nice dinner or lunch out with a coworker or friend, and start carrying lunch (and breakfast, if necessary) to work. Most workplaces have a refrigerator, coffee maker, and microwave available to employees, so your brown-bag options are pretty broad. Not only will you save money by bringing food from home; you'll probably eat healthier compared to the fast food you can buy at work. If you feel as if you're missing out, make a date with a work colleague to eat your sack lunches together at the park or in the office. If you prefer to go solo, bring a great book you're dying to finish while you eat.

coffee Oh, what we will pay for a cup of Joe. We don't know whether to laugh or scream when we look at the prices for these so-called gourmet cups of coffee. It is easy and a lot less expensive to make and tote your own in a thermal mug.

There are many pros to having a home-based business, but there are also many cons — especially when you can't leverage a large company discount for things like medical insurance and bulk mailings. The Home Office Association of America (HOAA) is trying to change all that. Through the combined clout of the association, you can purchase insurance (medical, disability, life, dental) at a group rate, obtain a discounted schedule from the United Parcel Service, access collection agencies, get a credit card, receive hotel and other travel discounts, purchase insurance for your equipment, and more.

It's even cheaper to buy the instant special coffees and make them at the office.

another alternative If you really feel deprived at the thought of not eating out or buying that gourmet cup, at least cut down. Make lunch out a Friday event. Or have one special cup on Monday morning to start off the week.

maximize your paycheck

Many people sign a contract with their employer and leave the details of their paycheck to the accounting or human resources department. Don't make that big mistake! It's up to you to be in charge of the money you earn. Only then will you be sure that every penny is working for you.

scrutinize your withholdings Ideally, when tax time rolls around, you want to make sure you've paid the right amount in taxes with every paycheck. You don't want to owe money and you don't want to get any money back. Although it may feel great to get a big tax refund, this actually means you've been lending your money to the government, not putting it to work for you. That $2,000 tax refund could have been in a CD or money market account earning you interest.

inspect your insurance Make sure the coverage offered through the company is cost effective by checking with an insurance agent you know and trust. You'll want to check if you're paying too low a deductible or have more insurance coverage than you need. This is especially important for married couples who both work and have insurance.

take charge of retirement planning (see pages 243–249 for details) More and more companies are shifting the responsibility of retirement planning from the company to the individual. This will only benefit you in the long run, especially given the number of corporate scandals involving employee pension plans that have made headlines recently. If your company sponsors a 401(k) plan where it matches your contributions, it still may be a good investment. But never put all your retirement eggs in one nest. Diversify! Be sure to spread your assets around to safeguard your future. And keep a careful eye on how your plan is doing (see page 244 for tips on protecting your pension).

automatic savings

If your employer offers it (and most do), sign up for automatic deposits of your paychecks. Many banks will lower or even drop checking fees entirely if you use direct deposit. This method of payment is faster, safer, and the money is available to you immediately.

working at home

Saving money while working at home is an entirely different subject. If you're planning to set up a home office, either to supplement your outside work or as the base of operations for your own business, you can save yourself time, aggravation, and money by the choices you make.

office space

If you want to claim your office as a deduction, you can't just designate a corner of the family room as the office. The IRS is getting more and more particular about this deduction. A better and more professional option is to set aside a room as your office or create a semiprivate area in the home that is used exclusively for business. If you see clients, having a real office will look more professional. If you have ongoing projects that you need to organize and spread out, you'll be less likely to lose important documents with a real office. Ideally, your office should have a door, enough electrical outlets, and at least one phone jack.

TEN DEDUCTIONS FOR HOME-BASED BUSINESSES

Be sure to keep records of your purchases and payments and to follow the IRS guidelines for business expenses (see Publication 334 at www.irs.gov).

1. Office space (must be used only for business)
2. Car (mileage, parking fees, tolls)
3. Utilities (share of phone and electricity used)
4. Computers and related items (printer, scanner, Internet service)
5. Software (word processing, spreadsheets, databases, and such)
6. Professional books and subscriptions
7. Office equipment (fax machine, answering machine, etc.)
8. Educational expenses (courses related to your business)
9. Travel (airfare, hotels, meals, and so on)
10. Office supplies

going-out-of-business breaks

Keep your eyes open as you drive around town, and check newspapers or junk mail for office supply stores that are going out of business and selling everything. You can pick up desks, chairs, filing drawers, staplers, hole punches—at a big discount. Don't forget to check out restaurants and stores that are going out of business; they usually have office equipment as well, which you can pick up for pennies.

supply trick

If you have a home office, you'll need to stock it with basic supplies. The big office supply stores are often your best bet because you can buy everything you need to conduct your business in bulk. One trick to keep in mind: Look for damaged boxes. Office supply stores will often give you a discount on a damaged box if you ask for one (folks simply won't buy a damaged box even if it contains something that can't be hurt by the exterior flaw).

○ Price clubs stock a large assortment of office supplies; it's a major part of their business. Troll the aisles and pick up yellow legal pads, pencils, pens, dry-erase markers, bulletin boards, file cabinets, tape, and much more, in really big amounts. Just be sure you have the space at home to store these items.

surge saver

Do yourself a favor and invest in a good quality surge protector. You can pick them up at superstores, hardware stores, home improvement centers, and office supply stores. They usually aren't very expensive, but they can save your investment in computer equipment. If you use your phone line for your Internet connection, get a protector that protects against surges through your phone line as well.

computer costs

Fortunately, computers are a lot cheaper today than they were five years ago. You can pick up a basic model for about $500, which can link you to the Internet, provide you with e-mail, and allow you to play games, run word-processing programs, spreadsheet programs, and more. The more expensive computers will offer more features and run faster. It's easy to pay too much for a computer, especially when all the high-tech bells and whistles look so fun and exciting. In order to avoid overpaying for a computer, you'll need to think honestly about the way you will actually use it, what features are necessary, which are fun, and which you will never use and can live without.

read, read, read There are bookstores full of books devoted to every type of computer, software, and accessory imaginable. Computer magazines can also be a terrific source of information when you're researching which computer or components to purchase. And of course the Internet is filled with information about computers and accessories as well as shopping sites that will do instant comparisons of different models of computers.

salesperson standards If you're shopping in a store, make sure the salesperson listens fully to your list of needs before offering his or her ideas on what system might be best for you. If you sense a salesperson is trying to steer you to a "bigger, better, more expensive" system, find someone else to work with who is interested in actually helping you. A smart salesperson knows that a happy and satisfied customer usually comes right back when ready to upgrade or buy more components.

twice as nice (or nasty)

Buying used computers is tricky. It is almost impossible to know how much actual wear and tear a computer has been exposed to and whether it will work well for you. That being said, we picked up a relatively recent-model hard drive at a university sale for $50. At such a cheap price, it can be cost effective to take the risk on a used computer. If you are not a computer whiz, try to enlist a friend or relative who's well versed about various systems to help you shop.

⊙ American Computer Exchange is a well-respected service that offers an index of used computers and their prices. They will even try to match buyers and sellers for a small fee. To find out more, call 1-800-786-0717.

frugal phone facts

There are so many phone service options available now that it can really be confusing to choose the best option for you and your home business. Depending on the size of your business, it may be a good idea to keep your home and business services separate for ease of deductions at tax time. Here are some general hints:

review rates About every six months, sit down with all your telephone bills and list how many local, toll, long distance, and international calls you make. Once you've assessed how you use your phone, call several services and ask them to come up with a calling plan that meets your needs. Compare the plans and the rates to find the least expensive option.

wireless wonders We know a couple from Montana who lived in New York while one of them was doing postgraduate training. They made a lot of long-distance calls to family back home and their cheapest option turned out to be their wireless service. They paid for local service through the local phone company, but all long-distance calls were made on a cell phone. With all the competition between wireless companies these days, this may be your best option, too.

ax the options Phone companies are very fond of selling you service options you don't need or use. Scrutinize your bill to be sure you're not paying for an option you don't want. Each one you drop could save you over $40 a year or more.

the scoop about on-line services

The above comments for phone services could almost be repeated word for word when you're shopping around for online service providers: the choices are many and varied. At one time, America On Line (AOL) was the only way to go, but times have changed. Today, there are a host of companies large and small vying for your dollars and you should use this to your advantage. Make a list of the features you are looking for in an on-line service, then call at least five companies and see who offers the best deal. One caution with smaller providers: You often get better, more personalized customer service from a smaller company, but it is not unusual for these firms to be bought out by a larger company. If that happens, it may impact the service that they're willing to provide you.

discounting disability

Disability insurance provides income in the event you are unable to work at your job due to injury or illness. Unfortunately, it is one of the most overlooked types of insurance. Most disability policies will cover between 60 to 80 percent of your former income; if your employer only offers a policy covering 60 percent, you should consider a secondary policy to cover the remaining 20 percent.

make extra money with your hobbies

green thumb If you're a talented gardener, offer your expertise for a fee to community businesses or to your horticulturally challenged neighbors.

chef for a day If you're a whiz in the kitchen, utilize your gourmet skills and start your own small catering firm. Cook for parties and special occasions, make cakes for birthdays and weddings, or make takeout for time-stressed individuals.

sew simple Sewing is fast becoming a lost art. Use your sewing talent to do alterations, make custom children's clothes, fancy curtains, or create special quilts for newborns.

be handy Do you spend your free time puttering around the house doing fix-its? Take your handyman skills and charge others for your know-how and services.

knock on wood If you are good at building things with power tools, hire yourself out to make custom bookcases, cabinets, desks, tables, or anything else someone wants to commission.

number cruncher Are you really good with numbers? Come tax time, sell your services and help folks prepare their returns; or provide customized budgets.

sunday driver Hire yourself out as a part-time delivery driver or offer to display advertising on your vehicle.

animal lover Help people on vacation or at work care for their cat or dog by feeding, walking and playing with their animals.

tutor time Start tutoring or helping children with their homework. Call area schools to see if you meet their requirements and ask if they can recommend you to parents.

party on If you love to entertain or know how to throw great kids' parties, you can start a business as a party planner.

caution Before starting a business, consult with a lawyer or tax adviser about taxes, bookkeeping, licenses, and liability.

HELP FOR SMALL BUSINESS IS ON THE NET

The U.S. Small Business Administration bills itself as "America's Small Business Resource," and that is precisely what it aims to provide: information about starting, financing, and running your small business successfully. Affiliated with the SBA is the Service Corps of Retired Executives (SCORE), an organization that offers experienced business people as mentors to new entrepreneurs. It even offers direct e-mail counseling that provides advice on business plans, financial matters, marketing, human resources, and more. You can find links to several other organizations that maintain Web sites just to help small businesses at these two sites.

**www.sba.gov
or 1-800-827-5722**

....

**www.score.org
or 1-800-634-0245**

home accounting 101

calculate your net worth

Let's start at the beginning: Before you do anything else, it's essential to figure out just how much you are worth. The easiest way to do it is to get a pad and pencil and make two lists—one of your assets and one of your liabilities.

your assets Start by adding up the current value of everything that you own or have coming to you:

- Cash: Total of your checking and savings accounts, money-market funds, and CDs (certificates of deposit)
- House: The market value of your home.
- Other things of value: This includes jewelry, automobiles, home furnishings, art, vacation home, and such.
- Insurance: Figure out the cash value of all your policies.
- Investments: The current value of stocks and bonds, any rental properties, real estate partnerships, oil and gas partnerships, gold and silver, company stock options, personal collections (stamps, coins, antiques, and such), notes receivable, and the book value of a business.
- Retirement savings: IRAs, Keoghs, pension and profit-sharing plans, 401(k)s, any deferred compensation, and company savings plans (only count the money you could take if you left the company tomorrow).

your liabilities Now add up all your debts—the amounts that you owe to others:

- Mortgage: Be sure to include home equity loans.
- Loans: Bank, car, and any other loans or notes.
- Credit card balances or any other outstanding debts.

your net worth Once you have your two lists and have totaled them up, subtract your total liabilities from your total assets. The result is your net worth. Write that figure down. Memorize it. That's the number that will tell you when you can retire and how far along your are toward reaching your financial goals. Chances are your net worth is more than you think; however, if you find out that you are worth less than you think, let it serve as a wake-up call to revise your budget fast.

get with the budget

Every household should have a written budget. Some people have the feeling that if they balance their checkbook regularly that should suffice. But focusing only on your checkbook is not a realistic, safe, or forward-thinking way to approach your financial well being. It is also crucial to be honest about your budget, even when you overspend. Again all you need is a pad and pencil.

total income Add up all the money that you can expect to receive during the year:
- Regular paychecks and bonuses
- Part-time or freelance income
- Interest
- Dividends
- Other income: Rent on properties, benefits, and so on

fixed expenses Next add up all the payments that you make on a regular basis during the year:
- Mortgage payment or rent
- Electricity, gas, and water
- Telephone: Home and cell phone
- Internet service
- Garbage
- Alarm service
- Cable or satellite dish
- Insurance: Life, medical, dental, disability, homeowners, and auto-mobile
- Debt payments: Home equity and car loans
- Commuting expenses: Tolls, train or bus tickets, and such

variable expenses Now add up all the payouts you make that vary more widely from month to month:
- Food and beverages
- Paper goods: Toilet paper, paper towels, and so on
- Car maintenance: Gas, oil, upkeep
- Home maintenance and other improvement
- Furnishings and appliances
- Clothing

- Personal grooming: Haircuts, beauty products, etc.
- Recreation: Dining out, sports or cultural events, movies, museums
- Vacation
- Gifts and contributions
- Health care not covered by insurance

the moment of truth Subtract all your annual expenditures from your total annual income. If the total expenditures are less than the total income, you are living within your income; if the expenditures are more than the income, you need to go through your variable flexible expenditures—and some of your fixed expenditures as well—and reduce your spending.

think small to build big

A lot of people only think in big terms for savings—feeling that if they're not putting away $500 a month, then the effort is just not worth it. That kind of thinking is really destructive. If you're not used to putting away any money for savings, start small. Can you find $25 a month to go into a savings account? Most people can find that much just by cutting out a movie, a dinner out, or even a really lengthy long-distance phone call. If you can free up $25 per month to go to savings, you'll be $300 a year richer; if you can free up $25 a week for savings, you'll be $1,300 a year richer. Because the money you put aside will be earning interest, you'll be surprised at how fast even small amounts of savings will grow. Put it in perspective: If you save just $1 a day, by the end of the year you'll have $365. In an account with a four percent interest rate, that would actually become $372 (you've made $7 by doing nothing). In ten years, you'll have saved $3,650 or, at the same interest rate, $4,487. As you can see, over time it all adds up.

sneaky savings

Another trick to help you save more (or pay down debt much faster) is to take an amount from a debt payment that has been paid off and continue paying it—either into a savings account or into another debt. For example, let's say you have two car payments, one for $300 and one for $230. Once you pay off the lesser debt, just begin adding the $230 to thesecond debt and make new payments of $530. You'll be amazed how quickly you pay off the second debt (and save on the loan's interest as part of the bargain). Once that second debt is paid off, try tucking that payment into a money market savings account and watch your savings take off. Because you are already budgeting for the $530 to be unavailable to you each month, this strategy may be the most painless way to build up your savings.

safety margin

Conventional wisdom dictates that you set aside three to six months of living expenses in case of an emergency. To safeguard this critical safety net fund, you'll want to put the money into a money market account or short-term certificate of deposit (CD). That way you won't be tempted to dip into it. Only bank your money with institutions that are insured by the Federal Deposit Insurance Corporation (FDIC), which will protect your money up to $100,000. If you have more than this amount, spread your money among different banks so all your savings will be covered.

d is for diversify

As we discussed in the Working Life section, you never want to have all your assets in one place. The safest approach to saving and making your money grow is to diversify—invest your money using several different strategies so that if one fails, you are not back to square one. The fiasco at Enron proved the danger of putting all your retirement eggs in the company basket. Most companies administer their pension plans honestly and carefully, but even so, you need to approach money management with a well-thought-out plan to cover contingencies.

savings accounts This is where you should have your liquid emergency and contingency money. Savings accounts are insured by the FDIC (up to $100,000) and are easy to access when you need your money. Savings accounts pay interest, but the rates tend to be on the low side.

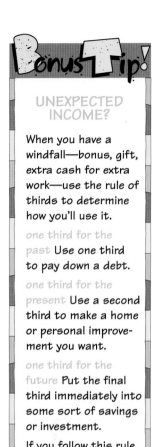

Bonus Tip!

UNEXPECTED INCOME?

When you have a windfall—bonus, gift, extra cash for extra work—use the rule of thirds to determine how you'll use it.

one third for the past Use one third to pay down a debt.

one third for the present Use a second third to make a home or personal improvement you want.

one third for the future Put the final third immediately into some sort of savings or investment.

If you follow this rule, you'll see your debt shrink, your savings grow, and you won't feel deprived.

money market deposit accounts These accounts pay slightly higher rates of interest than a savings account and will allow you to withdraw money relatively easily with a few restrictions. You may be required to deposit no less than $1,000, and there may be a limit on the number of withdrawals per year.

money market mutual funds This is similar to a money market in that it is relatively easy to access your money (they often have a few checks linked to the account) but it is administered by a large family of mutual funds. Often this type of account is tax free and offers even higher rates of interest than a money market deposit account.

certificates of deposit (cds) These usually earn higher rates of interest, though the rates vary with the time frame or terms of the account (the longer the term, the higher the interest). CDs are considered very low risk and are insured by the FDIC. But there are penalties for early withdrawal.

stocks When you buy stocks, you acquire a share of a company's profits. This is a riskier investment because, as we all know, the stock market can be volatile. However, in a diversified portfolio, you should have some investment in stocks because they can give you the highest returns, too. Think of stocks as a long-term investment where you can ride out the roller coaster of the market until you decide it is profitable to sell your shares.

bonds When you buy a bond, you are lending money to a company or to the federal, state or local government. The loan is for a fixed period of time ("term") and you are promised repayment on a set date with a set rate of interest. Bonds are lower in risk than stocks because bondholders are paid first if a company goes under. However, if interest rates have gone up since you bought your bond, you will earn less than the rate of inflation.

mutual funds This represents a pool of money from many investors that is managed by a professional. The money in a mutual fund can be invested in stocks, bonds, money markets, and other securities. The fund manager determines when it is best to invest and sell. By combining your money with that of other investors, you reduce individual risk.

annuities These are financial contracts made with an insurance company. A "deferred" annuity focuses on accumulating money for retirement; an "immediate" annuity offers regular income during retirement. Annuities can be very complex and are best approached with a professional's help.

your home This is often the single greatest investment a family makes over a lifetime. Your home's value can fluctuate over time based on its condition, square

footage, yard, features, style, surrounding neighborhood, school district, and even stores and businesses moving in and out of the area.

savings at the bank

Fees, fees, fees! They are the way that your bank makes money, and they add up fast. Unless you scrutinize your bank's statements (which you do, as a good penny pincher), you might not even be aware of some of them.

○ Scout around for a bank that will give you a checking account with a low or no minimum balance requirement—then make sure you keep that amount in the account. Some banks will allow the minimum balance to be that of the combined checking/savings accounts. This means you can park more money in savings and have it earn interest before you need it to pay bills.

○ Ask for a detailed list of all the bank fees, including ATM fees. If there is no fee for using your own bank's ATM, avoid using ATM machines from other banks so that you won't be charged every time you withdraw your money. Take out larger amounts of cash, if need be, to avoid using other banks' ATM machines.

○ Ask if your bank will drop or lower your checking fees if you use it for the direct deposit of your paycheck (or your Social Security or pension check)—many banks will, but only if you ask them.

go for broker

Once you make the decision to begin investing in stocks and/or bonds, you will need to use a

TEN MOST COMMON MISTAKES IN PERSONAL FINANCE PLANNING

① Only one family member is involved in financial affairs.

② Life goals are not put down on paper.

③ There is no budget for the family.

④ There is insufficient cash available to handle emergencies or new opportunities.

⑤ The family has no excess liability (or umbrella) insurance.

⑥ Contents of home are not insured up to their replacement value.

⑦ Employee benefits are poorly understood and mismanaged.

⑧ Investments are not diversified.

⑨ Tax reduction is used as a goal and no projections are made.

⑩ Income earners do not have adequate life or disability insurance.

broker or join an on-line service. A broker (discount or full-service) is licensed to monitor investments and give paid advice on stock purchases. Broker's fees can be a percentage of your portfolio or a set amount for each transaction. They can also make commissions on some of their products. Because you're giving a broker a lot of power over your money, you'll want to make sure that your broker is a member of the Securities Investor Protection Corporation (SIPC). This nonprofit organization can protect investments up to $500,000 if the broker goes out of business.

○ Call the National Association of Securities Dealers' (NASD) at 1-800-289-9999. They have records of disciplinary actions against brokerage firms or representatives.

○ If you decide to use an on-line service, be sure you are willing to do the homework. With this option, you will be buying your own stocks, bonds, and mutual funds for much lower fees than with a broker. But you will also be taking on added risk because you are making all your own investment decisions. Research any service you're thinking about using thoroughly: the fees, the research provided, the quality of customer service, the commission schedules, and whether the quotes are delayed or real-time.

good money advice

Financial planning can be daunting for the lay person. It can be tempting just to turn your financial planning over to a "professional" but be careful: Unless you do significant research, you may end up paying more for advice than you make in investments. If you feel you need financial advice from a pro, here are some guidelines:

personal financial advisor A certified financial planner (CFP) and a chartered financial consultant (ChFC) are essentially the same. In order to be certified, a planner or consultant has to take courses in financial planning and pass a simple exam. They also need at least three years of experience and should continue to take courses to keep abreast of financial trends and economic changes. But beware: Many planners and consultants get commissions for the investment products that they sell. To find a "fee only" financial advisor, someone who charges a flat rate for each service and doesn't get commissions for products sold, try www.napfa.org or 1-800-366-2732 or write to:

The National Association of Personal Financial Advisors
355 West Dundee Road, Suite 200
Buffalo Grove, IL 60089

certified public accountant A CPA can be a real help if your portfolio and tax

preparation is very complicated. They go through significant training and a rigorous examination to obtain their credentials. They also have to take a number of courses every year to maintain their license. Their fees can vary dramatically, depending on the area or the size of the company they work for. Many (though not all) will also provide financial advice on a fee only basis. To locate a CPA, try www.aicpa.org or 1-212-596-6200 or write to:

The American Institute of Certified
Public Accountants
1211 Avenue of the Americas
New York, NY 10036-8775

(Note: There are also offices in New Jersey, Washington, D.C., and Texas.)

double checking duty

One of the biggest mistakes a couple can make is for only one person to be the manager or keeper of the money. Though the practice may have been common when most wives stayed at home, it is not a wise arrangement. Both partners need to be actively engaged in meeting financial needs and plans.

○ In most couples, one person ends up managing daily finances or paying bills. If that's the case, the other partner should take on the balancing act: When the bank statement comes in, he or she takes the checkbook and balances it against the statement. By doing this, the non-bill-paying partner gets to see exactly where the money goes each month. If both partners are involved, they are much more likely to catch errors. Working together this way is also a perfect opportunity to discuss purchases and figure out discrepancies.

CREDIT CHECK

It is wise to check your credit rating, if for no other reason than to remind yourself how precious a good rating is, especially when it comes time for major purchases such as a home or car. Since more than one credit bureau may have a file on you, try the three majors first:

EQUIFAX
P.O. Box 740241
Atlanta, GA 30374
1-800-685-1111
www.equifax.com

EXPERIAN
(formerly TRW)
P.O. Box 949
Allen, TX 75013
1-888-397-3742
www.experian.com

TRANS UNION
P.O. Box 390
Springfield, PA 19064
1-800-916-8800
www.tuc.com

TEN SOLID TIPS FOR INVESTORS

- **Shop around:** Compare fees and investment options at a variety of banks, credit unions, planners, brokers, and investment houses.

- **Question authorities:** Be sure you understand every investment, especially the risks and benefits. Ask questions until you feel satisfied. Ask yourself: If you can explain the investment and how it works?

- **Get it in writing:** Have everything pertaining to your investment in writing, particularly fees, services, and the investment product itself.

- **Get educated:** Too many people assume they won't be able to understand complex investment or financial matters. Nonsense! Start with books written for the layperson, like the Dummies or Idiot's guides. Then branch out to investment and financial publications such as the Wall Street Journal, Money, Smart Money, and Investor's Business Daily.

- **See a specialist:** A financial advisor, accountant, or tax advisor can help you set goals and grow your money with less risk. Their knowledge can especially help you with tricky investment products and negotiations. But be sure any financial advisor charges a set fee for services, rather getting a commission for selling you a product.

- **Just hang up:** Never buy a financial product from a salesperson over the telephone. And, never let a salesperson pressure you into making an immediate decision. Ask for any information in writing and tell them you'll call back if you're interested.

- **It's too good to be true:** If it sounds too amazing, start running and don't look back. Salespeople who offer the moon (or an incredible rate of return) are scamming you, pure and simple.

- **Gimme a "D":** diversify, diversify, diversify. It's safe, financial planning.

- **Don't get it, don't bet on it:** If after reading all the literature and talking to the salesperson, you still don't understand how a product works, don't invest in it. It's your money.

- **Regular maintenance:** Give your financial planning regular reviews, especially when you've had a major life change (marriage, birth, divorce, family death, job change, house move, and so on). Because you have to start gathering financial information in January to prepare your taxes, this might also be a good time to review your financial plan.

retire like Royalty!

YOU NEED TO USE ALL YOUR MONEY-SAVING TRICKS TO MAKE YOUR RETIREMENT YEARS ENJOYABLE.

retirement reality check

The first—and probably hardest—step toward a financially secure retirement is to come up with a realistic figure of what you'll need after you stop working. Some experts estimate the average person will need 70 percent of their pre-retirement income, and lower-wage earners will need up to 90 percent or more, just to live with some degree of comfort and security. However, the statistics are frightening: Less than half of Americans today are putting away money just for retirement. Many workers who have access to a 401(k) plan through their employer aren't taking advantage of it—even though the average person spends 18 years in retirement! These sobering statistics should make you stop and think.

security check

Most people see the FICA deduction in their paycheck and don't give it a second thought. Fact is, the Social Security Administration is a huge organization run by an enormous number of people, and like all organizations, mistakes in accounting do occur. The only one who can catch and correct these errors is you. And don't wait until you're on the verge of retirement. You can do it at anytime. Here's how to check:

○ Call your local Social Security office or call 1-800-772-1213, and ask for a Personal Earnings and Benefits Estimate Statement (PEBES). You can also download a request form at www.ssa.gov. The report is free and will be sent to you about five weeks after your request.

○ If you find a discrepancy, dig out your old tax returns and W-2 forms and take them to your local Social Security office. After you support your claims, the agency should make an adjustment to your records.

employee advantage

Recent corporate scandals involving employee pension funds have made caution the word for anyone considering employer-sponsored plans. But you should definitely take advantage of them—especially if the company adds to or matches the money you invest in the plans. To protect yourself, make sure you remember to diversify your retirement funds.

pension plans Usually only pretty big companies or government agencies offer a defined-benefit pension plan—where you receive a set monthly amount during retirement based on how many years you worked for the company. Ask your employer for an individual benefit statement to see what your current benefit is worth. If you're thinking of changing jobs, be sure to find out what becomes of the money already invested in the pension fund. Call previous employers and ask if you are eligible for benefits from them (that is, if you worked long enough to qualify).

401(k) In recent years, many employers have shifted corporate contributions for retirement away from traditional pension plans in favor of a tax-sheltered savings plans called 401(k)s. Under this plan, you can automatically contribute a portion of your paycheck's gross income up to a maximum of $12,000 per year (increasing up to $15,000 in 2006). This can be a terrific savings opportunity because, in many cases, your employer will also contribute or even match your investment up to a limit. Money in a 401(k) plan can be invested in stocks, bonds, mutual funds, and CDs. You defer paying income tax on the money until you begin to withdraw, and the interest earned is also tax deferred. There are penalties for early withdrawal, though some plans allow withdrawals for "hardship" reasons such as medical emergencies. Last, but not least, because you're contributing from your gross income, your taxes are lower in the years you are investing in a 401(k). A definite win-win scenario.

403(b) Also known as tax-sheltered annuities, these plans are similar to 401(k)s, but are set up to serve nonprofit organizations such as schools, hospitals, or social service agencies. Again, you can set aside pretax money that is tax-deferred until you begin making withdrawals. The maximum amount you can contribute in a given year is determined by how long you've worked, how much you make, and how much you've already contributed.

protect your pension

The past few years have been a wake-up alert that trusting your company for your retirement may be a gamble you can ill afford to take. This means you have

to be an active watchdog. Luckily, there are places to go for help.

get in the know Federal law requires each company or union to publish a Summary Annual Report, a yearly overview of how the company has managed employee funds. It details the amount in the fund, profits or losses for the past year, and administrative costs. If you see big investment losses or high adminis- trative costs, you may be spotting trouble ahead. You can demand a more detailed summary (Form 5500), which will specify where all the money is or has gone.

spoiling the sport If you find anything that sends up red flags, contact the Department of Labor's Pension and Welfare Benefits Administration (PWBA). If there is anything illegal going on, this is the agency to attack it. The national office is in Washington, D.C, (202-219-8776), or you can look in your phone book for a local bureau.

free publication *Protecting Your Pension—A Quick Reference Guide*, pub- lished by the PWBA, is available by calling 1-800-998-7542. This explains Form 5500 in detail and offers other ways to safeguard your retirement funds.

web site The Department of Labor Web site, www.dol.gov, offers information about your rights, retirement, and more.

do-it-yourself accounts

One of the best ways to set aside money for retirement is to set up an individual retirement account (IRA).

regular ira Currently, you can put up to $2,000 a year into a regular IRA (this amount will go up to counter inflation in coming years). You pay no taxes on the interest earned until you retire. If you are 50 or older, you contribute even more. Depending on your income and whether you are contributing to other retirement plans, you may also be able to deduct your IRA contribution from your income tax and not pay taxes on the amount until you withdraw it.

roth ira Money put in a Roth IRA is not tax deductible and must come from income you've earned. But the interest earned by the Roth is not taxable when you withdraw it. There are no age limitations and you don't have to start with- drawing at any particular age. After an initial five year period, there are also fewer restrictions on withdrawing. For example, you can withdraw money from a Roth IRA to make a down payment on a first house. Whether you can set up a Roth depends on your income. It's best to consult with a financial advisor to determine if you are better off with a Roth or a conventional IRA.

self reliance

If you are self-employed or work for a company with no retirement benefits, consider these plans for your future:

sep-iras Simplified Employee Pension Individual Retirement Account, better known as SEP-IRAs, are just that: simple. There is little paperwork, fuss, or bother to set one up and they let you set aside 15 percent of your earnings. One great feature is that you can change the amount you contribute each year. In a good year, you can contribute the maximum; in a less-profitable year, you can contribute whatever is comfortable. For a self-employed person whose income varies greatly from year to year, this flexibility is a real plus.

keogh plans Another separate retirement account, Keoghs usually require a bit more paperwork to set up, but you can contribute more to them in any given year. You can usually put up to 25 percent of your net income, up to a maximum of $30,000 tax-deferred, into a Keogh plan.

analyzing annuities

For most folks, annuities are an option to consider when you have reached your maximum limit on contributions to 401(k)s and IRAs. There is no cap on contributions to annuities. You buy an annuity from an insurance company, either with a lump sum or with payments. The insurance company guarantees to grow your investments at a specific rate, on a tax-free basis. On an agreed date, you begin to receive regular payments from the annuity that will continue for the rest of your life. The size of the payments are based on how much you invested over the years, how long you left the money in the account, the agreed rate of return on your investment, and whether your spouse or other heir continues to receive some payment after you die. Basically, annuities are part investment and part insurance.

○ Contributions to a nonqualified deferred annuity are not tax deductible; however, a qualified annuity supporting an IRA, 401(k), 403(b), or other qualified plan, may allow contributions before tax or be tax deductible. Taxes on the interest earned in either case are deferred until you begin receiving payments.

○ Immediate annuities allow you to invest a large sum of money, then immediately begin receiving payments on a monthly or other regular basis.

○ Deferred or immediate annuities can be paid out based on a fixed or variable interest rate. A fixed annuity will pay you at a fixed rate of interest. Fixed annuities protect your investment from dips in the market, but won't allow you to take advantage of upswings. Variable annuities are designed to take advantage of upswings in the market and, hopefully, make you more money over time if the interest rates are high. But if the market dips significantly, your investment isn't protected.

insuring financial freedom

Many folks don't think about insurance when planning their financial future, but it can be one of the most important retirement investments you can make. From insuring your health and life to insuring your home, these policies should protect you from the unexpected and provide for your family in the event of a long-term illness and death. Do your research so you can make the right choice for you and your family.

that's life

Life insurance can provide for your loved ones and help their financial future. It is important to have life insurance if you are married and critical if you have dependents.

term life The most straightforward type of life insurance, it guarantees a fixed payment to your beneficiary if you die during the policy's term. Premium cost goes up as you age.

whole life Instead of coverage for a fixed term, this is a lifelong policy that guarantees a benefit when you die, as long as you have paid the premiums. Some whole life policies claim to pay increasing dividends based on the accrued cash value of the policy, but often these increases are not guaranteed.

DISCOUNTS

Believe or not, some people don't like to be offered the senior discount. How silly! If you've put in the years, you deserve every treat, rebate, discount, honor, bargain, break, and any other perk that someone wants to give you.

- Discount clothing chains such as Kohl's offer 10 percent discount to seniors 55 or older on Tuesdays. The discount applies to their already reduced prices on everything from clothing to home furnishings.

- Most movie theaters offer a senior discount; usually the same price as a child's ticket. Now, you can take your grandchildren and have a ball!

universal life A variation on whole life with a bit more flexibility, universal life insurance allows the policyholder to set the premium amounts and payment frequency (with certain restrictions), and to adjust the policy as life needs change. The policyholder accrues interest from the premiums and cash value of the policy.

variable life Somewhat similar in flexibility to universal life insurance, variable policies provide even more decision-making power to the holder by allowing them to select where their investments will go; however, this form of insurance is subject to greater fluctuation in cash values depending on how the selected investments perform.

safe house

Having a good homeowner's policy will protect one of the biggest retirement investments of your life—your home. If your home is damaged or its contents are ruined, a good policy will cover repair or replacement. The policy may also protect you if someone has an accident on your property. Be sure your policy covers the most common natural disasters for your geographic region, including protection from earthquakes, floods, brush fires, and tornadoes. If at all possible, try to buy a policy that covers 100 percent of your home's contents and replacement costs.

a will is the way

Because many people don't want to think about death, they expose their partners or dependents to unnecessary financial risk. A will that is legal and binding is essential to protecting your loved ones and equally crucial to protecting your interests. Without a will, the state will decide who raises your children and how to distribute your estate (for a fee). Features of a thorough will should:

- Include specific instructions if you and your spouse die together, including designating legal guardians for your children and distribution of property.
- Include a no-contest clause which requires anyone who feels you didn't leave enough for them to forfeit his or her share if they decide to contest your will.
- Try to leave each beneficiary a bequest that takes into account his or her particular situation and age. For an adult this may mean outright cash, and for a minor it may mean a trust fund.
- Try to avoid leaving joint ownership of anything, especially when one partner is clearly more powerful.
- Specify percentages of your estate to be left rather than exact dollar figures, which may change with inflation. This is especially important if you are young and want your will to stay current over a number of years.
- Include a living will that spells out the care you descritically ill and instructs your family how to proceed with such issues as life support measures.

GIVE SOMETHING BACK

Years ago, when a person retired it meant the time had come to give something back to the community, primarily through volunteer work. For retirees, volunteer work can be a tremendous opportunity to use their skills to help others and add real meaning to their days. No matter what your age, volunteer work can be wonderfully enriching. Some groups that need volunteer help:

- **American Red Cross (1-800-HELP-NOW):** Help with disaster relief, blood drives, collections, and more. One lively 80-year-old we know used his talents as a former engineer to repair the dummies used by the Red Cross to teach CPR.

- **Habitat for Humanity (1-800-422-5913):** Help build housing for those who can't afford to buy a decent home. There are ongoing projects all over the U.S., and there is a special band of retirees, the Habitat Gypsies, who travel around the country in their RVs offering their help at various sites.

- **Teach for America (1-800-832-1230):** Dedicated to bringing teachers to underserved regions, both rural and urban, this organization offers paid positions.

- **Peace Corps (1-800-424-8580):** You don't have to be a college age student to go off to an exotic region and help carry out this organization's mission. From teaching to farming, there are many opportunities for a wide span of age ranges in underserved areas or countries.

- **National Forest Service (1-800-281-9176):** You can help maintain hiking trails throughout the United States or work on archeological digs. Another alternative is to call or check Web sites for the National Park Service and your state's parks to find additional volunteer opportunities preserving our national treasures.

- **National Trust for Historic Preservation (1-800-944-6847):** Volunteers can help with everything from fund raising to hands-on restoration of America's historic homes and public buildings.

If this list doesn't inspire you, create your own. There is no shortage of organizations that need volunteer help. Think about the kind of work that you would enjoy doing; then identify local or national groups that would be a good fit for you.

index

a

AARP, medications and, 223
Accessories, clothing, 38–43
Acne, 45, 47
Aerobic exercise, benefits, 75
Air conditioner filters, 200
Air fresheners, 84–85
Air shows, 163
Air travel, 168–70
Airport transportation, 171
Allergy remedies, 57
American Automobile
Association (AAA), 162
Anniversary gifts, 148
Annuities, 238, 246–47
Antique furniture, 96
  appraisers, 100
Ant
  killer, 85
  traps, 188
Aphid spray, 85
Appliances
  energy efficiency with,
    201, 203
  bread machines, 15
  clothes dryers
  buying, 86–87
  dry-cleaning in, 89
  repairing, 196–97
  troubleshooting, 88–89
  hair dryers, 52
  handheld blenders, 24
  kitchen, buying, 22
  refrigerator-freezer repairing,
    19293
  shopping, energy ratings and,
    82
  washing machines
  buying, 86–87
  maintaining, 87
  repairing, 196

using efficiently, 87–88
Appraisers of antiques, 100
Art supplies, 119
Arthritis remedies, 57
Asparagus, buying and
  preparing, 14
Asphalt shingle repairs, 185–86
Athletic shoes, 73–74
Auctions, for furniture, 95–96
Automatic paycheck deposits,
  229
Automobiles. *See* Cars

b

Baby-care products, 109
Baby food, 109
Baby needs, 103–10
Baby powder, 106
Babysitting co-ops, 109
Baby wipes, 106
Baking pans, 24
Baking soda, uses for, 81
Baking with kids, 122
Balloons, for parties, 127
Banking, 239
Baskets
  as bassinets, 107
  gift, 149
  in kids' rooms, 114–15
Bassinets, 107
Bathing, 53–54
  babies, 108
Bathroom cleaning, 83–84
Batteries, for cars, 211–12
Beading, 41–42
Beans, buying and preparing, 14
Beds, 97–98
  for kids, 114
Beef, buying, 13
Beer, 128
  for weddings, 136
Belts, 39

Berries, buying and preparing, 15
Beverages
  for parties, 128
  for weddings, 135–36
Bibs, 107
Bicycling for exercise, 72–73
Birth announcements, 104
Black spot killer, 85
Blankets, baby, 108
Blemishes. *See* Acne
Blender, handheld, 25
Bonds, 238
Board games, 121, 128
Bookstores, 164
Bookcases, 99–100
  for kids, 116
Booster seats, 115–16
Botanical gardens, 162
Bowling, 120
Box stores
  for baby needs, 103
  for clothing, 29, 112
  for cookware, 23
  for furniture, 94
  for medications, 223
  for office supplies, 230
  professional decorators
    and, 92
Bread, buying and preparing, 15
Bread machines, 15
Brokers, financial, 239
Budgets
  household, 9, 235–36
  for wedding, 130–31
Bulk buying
  art supplies, 119
  foods, 12, 111
Buttons, 40

c

Cake(s)
  decorating bag, 24–25

decorating with children, 122
wedding, 135
Calamine lotion, for blemishes, 45
Camping, 181–82
as children's party theme, 129
Canada, travel in, 183
Candles, 125–26
Carpets and rugs
buying, 92
caring for, 77–78
cleaning, 79–80
repairing, 191
Car(s)
batteries for, 211–12
buying, 205–9
gasoline for, 212
insurance, 210–11, 213
leasing, 209
mileage, maximizing, 212–13
oil changes, 211
online resources for, 208, 209
parts, 213–14
rental, 175–76
Caulking, 199
Certificates of deposits (cds), 238
Chalk, 120
Changing pad for baby, 107–8
Chanukah decorations, 140–41
Cheese buying, 15
Children('s)
clothing, 112–13
dining out with, 153
entertaining, 117–23
family vacations with, 181–83
furniture, 115–16
party themes, 129
room decorating, 114–16
Christmas
cookies, 145
decorations, 141, 142
luminarias, 126
trees, 142
Citrus fruit, buying and
preparing, 15–16
Cleaning. See also Stain removal
bathrooms, 83–84
butcher blocks, 24

canvas sneakers, 36
dishwashers, 82
house, 77–85
gutters, 186–87
masonry, 187
rags, 82
with shaving cream, 79–80
siding, 187
wallpaper, 78–79
walls, 78
windows, 78
Cleansing cloths for skin, 45
Clearance sales
for baby needs, 104
for cars, 205–6
for clothing, 27–28, 29, 112
Clothes dryers
buying, 86–87
dry-cleaning in, 89
repairing, 196–97
troubleshooting, 88–89
Clothing, 26–43
for babies, 103–4
sizes, 105
basic, 26
for children, 112–13
coats, 32
for exercise, 73
extending life of, 31
Halloween costumes, 144–45
line-drying, 87
restoring, 33, 35
signs of quality, 31
stain removal, 88
stores, 27–28
wedding, 133–34
work, 227
Coats, 32
Coffee
buying and preparing, 16–17
at work, 227–28
Cold and flu remedies, 57–59
Cold packs, homemade, 64
College performances, 118,
156–57
College sports, 159
Color in house decorating, 90–91

Community cultural events, 156
Commuting to work, 227
Comparison shopping,
cars, 206
supermarkets, 10
Computers for home business,
230–31
Congestion remedies, 59–60
Consignment stores for clothing,
29–30, 112
Constipation remedies, 59
Construction materials for
children, 121
Convenience foods, avoiding, 12
Cookies for Christmas, 145
Cookware
buying, 22–25
cutting boards, 22–23
knives, 24
utensils, 23–24
Cooling the house, 199–200
with shading, 201
Corn and callus remedies, 59
Cornstarch, as baby powder, 106
Cosmetics, 46–50
Cough remedies, 60
Coupons
for car rentals, 175
for clothing, 30
for dining, 150–51
for makeup, 46
for supermarket items, 10–12
Courier, traveling as, 170
Credit rating, checking, 241
Cribs, 107, 110
Cruises, 178–80
Culinary schools for discount
dining, 151
Cultural events, 118, 154–57
Currency exchange, 177
Cutting boards, 22–23

d

Dancing for exercise, 74
Dandruff treating, 51
Decks, building, 187

Decorating
  cakes, 24–25, 122
  for Easter, 145
  for Halloween, 144
  house, 90–93
    for holidays, 140–41
    kids' rooms, 114–16
    for Thanksgiving, 143
Denim restoring, 35–36
Dental care for babies, 109–10
Denture cleaning, 60
Deodorants, 54–55
Department stores
  for cookware, 23
  for kids' clothes, 112
Detergent, amount to use, 88
Diapers, 105–6
Dining in, 117
Dining out, 150–53
Disability insurance, 232
Discounts on clothing, 30–31
Discount superstores. See Box
stores
Dishwasher
  cleaning, 82
  repairing, 195
Diversifying assets, 237
Door repairs, 190–91
Drain cleaner, 85
Drawer liners, 108
Driveway repairs, 189
Drugs. See Medications
Dryers
  buying, 86–87
  dry-cleaning in, 89
  repairing, 196–97
  troubleshooting, 88–89

e

Ear remedies, 60–61
Early-bird restaurant specials, 150
Easter, decorating for, 145
Education, 119
Eggs, buying and preparing,
  13, 17
Elderhostel, 176
Emergencies, supplies for, 65

Employee pension funds,
  243–44
Energy rating
  appliances, 82
  washers and dryers, 86–87
Enrichment classes, 119
Entertaining, 125–29
  party themes for kids', 129
  supplies for, 128
Entertaining children, 117–23
  party themes, 129
Entertainment discounts, 157
Equipment. See also Appliances
  exercise, 73, 74–75
Essential oils, 53
Estate planning, 248
Ethnic communities, visiting, 183
Ethnic potluck, 129
Exercise, 72–75
Exhaust fan, kitchen, repairing,
  194–95
Eye makeup, 49
Eye care, 47

f

Fabric
  for holiday decorations, 140
  for upholstery, 100–1
Facials, 48–49
Fairs and festivals, 163–64
  online resources, 165
Family Adventure Magazine, 183
Family memberships for cultural
  institutions, 118–19
Family vacations, 181–83
Farmers' markets, 20
Farms, pick–your–own, 162–63
Fertilizer for houseplants, 85
Filters, furnace and air
  conditioner, 200
Financial planning, 234–42
Fingerpaint formula, 120
Fireplace cleaning, 80
Fish, storing, 17
Flea markets for furniture
  shopping, 95
Flexible medical spending

accounts, 218
Floors
  finishing, 91–92
  restoring, 191–92
Flowers
  as fashion accessories, 38–39
  as gifts, 147
  for parties, 126–27
  for weddings, 134
Food. See also specific kinds
  for babies, 109
  as gifts, 147–48
  for parties, 127–29
  at sporting events, 158–59
  for Thanksgiving, 143
  for weddings, 134–35
  at work, 227
Food shopping, 9–21
  package sizes, 111
Foot ache remedies, 61
Formulas
  for facial masks, 48–49
  for fingerpaints, 120
  for laundry aids, 89
  for papier-mâché, 122
  for play clay, 123
  for skin toner, 45
Freezers. See Refrigerator-
freezers
Freighter cruises, 180
Fresh foods, buying, 11–21
Fruit, buying and preparing,
  15–16, 18
Funnels, 23
Furnace filters, 200
Furniture
  buying, 94–101
  caring for
    removing candle wax
      drippings, 79
    removing water rings, 79
    scratch repair, 101
  for babies, 107, 110
  for kids, 115–16
  polish, 85
  purchasing options, 101
  refinishing, 96

g

Games
  animal cracker race, 121–22
  board, 121, 128
  story sack, 122
Garage sales
  for baby needs, 104
  for furniture, 94–95
  for holiday decorations, 140
  for kitchen items, 22
Gardening with children, 123
Gasoline, 212–13
Generic medications, 223, 225
Gifts, 146–49
  wedding favors, 137–38
Gingerroot, buying and
  preparing, 18
Gloves, buying and caring for, 39
Glue guns, 42
Golden Age Passport, 182
Guests, for wedding, 131
Gutter cleaning, 186–87

h

Haggling, 207–8
Hair care, 50–52
  after swimming, 52
  dandruff treatment, 51
  highlights, 50–51
  rollers for, 48
  shampoo, 50
Haircuts, 50
Halitosis remedies, 61
Halloween, 144–45
  decorations, 142
Hand care, 52–53
Handheld blenders, 25
Hangover remedies, 61–62
Hats, caring for, 38
Headache remedy, 62
Health care, 219–21
Health insurance, 215–18
Heartburn remedies, 62
Heat exhaustion remedies, 63
Heat rash remedies, 62–63
Heating the house, 199–200
  with solar power, 201

Herbs, storing, 18
Hiccup remedies, 63
Highchairs, 115–16
Hive remedies, 63
HMOs, 215–18
Hobbies, turning into
  home-based businesses,
  232-33
Holiday(s), 140–49
  gift giving, 146–49
Home. *See also* House
  -based businesses, 227,
  228, 229–233
  improvements, 185–203
  as wedding location, 131–32
Homeowner's insurance, 248
Honey, 25
Honeymoons, 138
Hospital costs, 221
Hot-water heater
  energy efficiency with, 201–2
  repairing, 197
House
  as investment, 238–37
  cleaning, 77–85
  insulation, 198–99
  rentals, 182
  repairs, 185–91
  swapping, 175, 177
Household aids, 85
Houseplant fertilizer, 85

i

Individual retirement account
(IRA), 245
Insect bite remedies, 63–65
Insulation for house, 198–99
Insurance, 247
  auto, 210–11
  discounts for travelers, 213
  disability, 232
  from employer, 228
  homeowner's, 248
  life, 247–48
  medical, 215–18
Investment tips, 242
Invitations, for wedding, 133

j

Jewelry, restoring, 41, 43
Juice
  for babies, 108
  buying, 13, 111

k

Keough Plans, 246
Kids
  clothing for, 112–13
  decorating rooms for, 114–16
  entertaining, 117–23
  dining out with, 153
  family vacations with, 181–83
  furniture, 115–16
  party themes, 129
Kitchen
  children's activities in, 122
  renovating, 92–93
  setting up, 22–25
Kitchen exhaust fan, repairing,
  194–95
Knives, buying and caring for, 24
Kool Aid, for cleaning
  dishwashers, 82
Kwanzaa decorations, 140–41

l

Laundry, 86–89
Leather care, 32–33, 37, 39
Libraries, 165
Life insurance, 247–48
Light fixtures, 201
Line-drying for clothes, 87
Lipstick, 49–50
Living will, 248
Location, for wedding, 131–33
Lodging, 173–75
  house rentals, 182
Long-term care insurance, 217
Luminarias, 126
Lunches
  at restaurants, 153
  for school, 111–12
  at work, 226

m

Makeup, 46–50
Markers, 120
Masks, facial, 48–49
Masonry cleaning, 187
Mattresses, buying and maintaining, 98
Medical care, 219–21
Medical insurance, 215–18
Medical schools for bargain health care, 219
Medications, 222–23
  discarding, 224
  generic, 224, 225
Membership discounts, 157, 172, 173
Menopause remedies, 65
Mexico, travel in, 183
Mileage per gallon of gasoline, 212–13
Milk, buying, 19
Mirrors, 93
Modeling clay, formula for, 123
Moisturizers for skin, 45
Money market accounts, 238
Mothballs, 85
Motion sickness remedies, 65
Movies, 117–18, 128
Museums, 118–19, 155–56
Mushrooms, buying and preparing, 19
Music
  performances, 118, 156
    opera, 155
    for weddings, 136–37
Musical instruments, 119–20
Mutual funds, 238

n

Natural materials for holiday decorations, 141–42
Nausea remedies, 65–66
Net worth, calculating, 234–35
Newspapers
  for price comparisons, 10
  for restaurant discounts, 152

Nosebleed remedies, 66
Nuts, storing, 19

o

Odor removing, 84–85
Office supplies, buying, 230
Online resources
  art supplies, 119
  car buying, 208
  car safety, 209
  cookware buying, 23
  cruises, 178, 179
  festivals and fairs, 165
  holiday decorations, 142
  home repair, 195
  house swapping, 177
  for kids, 115–16
  knife buying, 24
  museums, 157
  parks and natural areas, 164
  party supplies, 128
  restaurants, 152
  safety for children, 112
  for small businesses, 233
  sports injuries, 70
  supermarket coupons, 11
  travel, 167, 171
  weddings, 135
Online service providers for home-based businesses, 232
Osteoporosis remedies, 66–67
Outlet stores
  for clothing, 28–29
  for kids' clothing, 112
Oven
  cleaner, 85
  cleaning, 80–81
  gas repairing, 193–94
Over-the-counter drugs (OTC), 222–23

p

Package tours, 172
Paint
  fingerpaint formula, 120
  softener, 85

Paintbrush cleaner, 85
Panty hose and tights, 34
Papier-mâché recipe, 122
Parking near airports, 170–71
Parks, national and state, 164, 181–82
Parties, 125–29
  supplies, 125
  themes, 128–29
Peaches, for skin care, 45
Peppers, sweet, buying and preparing, 19–20
Perfume and cologne, 54
Personal gift certificates, 146–47
Pest control, 85, 188, 189
Pet spray, 85
Phone service, for home-based business, 231–32
Photographers, for weddings, 137
Picnics, 117
Pill-taking, 67
Pillows, 115
Play clay, formula for, 123
Plumbing repairs, 197
Poison oak or ivy remedies, 67
Postcards, 120
Potlucks
  ethnic, 129
  Thanksgiving, 143
Power failures, 192
PPOs, 215–18
Premenstrual syndrome (PMS) remedies, 67–68
Prescription medications, 222–23
  discarding, 224
  generic, 224, 225
Price clubs
  for baby needs, 103
  for clothing, 29
  for furniture, 94
  for groceries, 12–13
  for parties, 127
  for medications, 223
  for office supplies, 230
Produce. See also specific kinds
  shopping for, 9–10

Professional sports, 158–60
Purses, buying and caring for, 37

r

Rags for cleaning, 82
Range
   cleaning, 80–81
   repairing, 193–94
Recipes, 121
   facial masks, 48–49
   fingerpaints, 120
   laundry aids, 89
   papier-mâché, 122
   play clay, 123
   skin toner, 45
Recycling
   for children's projects, 121
   shopping bags, 202
Refinishing furniture, 96
Refrigerator-freezers
   defrosting, 81
   repairing, 192–93
Remedies, 57–71
   allergies, 57
   arthritis, 57
   colds and flu, 57–59
   congestion, 59–60
   constipation, 59
   corns and calluses, 59
   coughs, 60
   denture cleaning, 60
   ears, 60–61
   foot ache, 61
   halitosis, 61
   hangovers, 61–62
   headaches, 62
   heartburn, 62
   heat exhaustion, 63
   heat rash, 62–63
   hiccups, 63
   hives, 63
   insect bites, 63–65
   menopause, 65
   motion sickness, 65
   nausea, 65–66
   nosebleeds, 66
   osteoporosis, 66–67

pill-taking, 67
poison oak or ivy, 67
premenstrual syndrome
   (PMS), 67–68
sleep, 68–69
snoring, 69
sore throat, 69
splinters, 69–70
sports injuries, 70
sunburn, 70–71
toothache, 71
Rental cars, 175–76
Repairs
   clothes dryers, 196–97
   dishwasher, 165
   house, 185–91
   kitchen exhaust fan, 194-95
   plumbing, 197
   refrigerator-freezer, 192–93
   washing machines, 196
Resale shops
   for baby needs, 103
   for kids' clothing, 112
Resources. See also Online
resources
   for financial planning, 240–41
Restaurant(s)
   coupons, 150–51
   dining out with children at, 153
   lunches, 153
   specials, 150
Retirees. See also Senior citizens
   AARP, medications and, 223
   medical insurance for, 216–17
   Social Security, 243
Retirement planning, 228–29,
   243–48
Roach repellent, 85
Rollers for hair, 48
Roofing, 185–86
Root vegetables, buying and
   storing, 20
Rubbing alcohol for cleaning
windows, 78
Rule of three for clothing, 26

s

Safety net fund, 237
Sales. See Clearance sales
Saving accounts, 236–39
Scarves, 39–40
Screens, window, repairing,
   188–89
Second opinions for medical
treatment, 220
Senior citizens. See also Retirees
   AARP, medications and, 223
   discounts for, 247
   Elderhostel, 176
   Golden Age Passport, 182
   medical insurance for, 216–17
   medications, 223
SEP-IRAs, 246
Shampoo, 50
Shaving, 55
Shaving cream, for cleaning,
   79–80
Shawls, 39–40
Shoe(s)
   for babies, 105
   buying and caring for, 34–35,
36
   for exercise, 73–74
   for kids, 113–14
   shining, 36
Shopping, bags for, 202
Shower cleaning, 83
Shower curtains, cleaning, 83
Siding
   cleaning, 187
   repairs, 186, 187
Sightseeing, 173
Skiing, 161
Skin care, 44–49
   for babies, 109
Sleep remedies, 68–69
Sneakers, cleaning, 86
Snoring remedies, 69
Soap, 44
Social Security, 243
Sofas, buying and maintaining, 97
Solar energy, 201
Soot and cinders, cleaning, 80

Sore throat remedies, 69
Splinter remedies, 69–70
Sponges, cleaning, 80
Sporting events, 118, 158–61
Sports, 160–61
Sports injury remedies, 70
Stain removing, 88
  from carpets and rugs, 77
  from clothing, 88
  from gloves, 39
  from leather, 33
  from upholstery, 79
Stickers for kids, 123
Stockings, 35
Stocks, 238
Store courtesy cards, 10
Store special events, 165
Story sack, 122
Stove cleaning, 80–81
Suede shoes, caring for, 36
Sugar, 20
Sunburn remedies, 70–71
Supermarkets, 9–13
Superstores
  for baby needs, 103
  for clothing, 29
  for cookware, 23
  for furniture, 94
  for kids clothing, 112
  professional decorators and, 92
Surge protectors, 230
Surgery, 220
Swapping houses, 175, 177
Sweat clothes, 74
Swimming for exercise, 73
Swimsuits, 32

t

Tax deductions for home-based
  businesses, 229
Tax withholding, 228
Telephone service, for home-
  based businesses, 231–32
Terms, car sales, 206–7
Thanksgiving, 143
Theater, 118, 156

discounts, 154–55
Theme parks, 163
Thermostat setting, 199–200
Thrift stores, 29–30
  for furniture, 94
  for kids' clothing, 112
Tile cleaning, 83
Times for shopping at
  supermarkets, 10
Tipping, 177
Toilets, cleaning, 83–84
Tomatoes, buying and
  preparing, 21
Toothache remedies, 71
Toothbrushes, uses for, 49
Tours, organizing, 172–73
Toys, 120–21
  household objects as, 121
Train travel, 176–77
Travel, 167–83
  discounts, 172–77
  off-season, 150
Tub cleaning, 83

u

Unexpected income, 237
Upholstery
  cleaning, 79–80
  fabric for, 100–1
Used cars, 209
Used musical instruments, 119
Used wedding gowns, 133
Utensils, kitchen, 23–24
  for cake decorating, 24–25

v

Vases, 127
Vegetable. *See also* specific
  kinds
  buying and preparing, 19–21
Vegetables, root, buying and
  storing, 20
Vinegar, uses for, 84
Volunteering, 249
  for cultural events, 157

w

Walking for exercise, 72
Wallpaper, cleaning, 78–79
Walls
  cleaning, 78
  decorating, 90–91
Washing machines
  buying, 86–87
  maintaining, 87
  repairing, 196
  using efficiently, 87–88
Water, reducing usage of,
  202–3
Water pipes, repairing, 197
Weather stripping, 199
Wedding favors, 137–38
Weddings, 130–39
  anniversary gifts, 148
  planning, 139
Wicker furniture, 99
Wills, 248
Windfall spending, 237
Window(s)
  energy efficient, 200–1
  repairs, 187–88
  storm, 188
  washing, 78
Wine, 128
  for weddings, 136
Witch hazel, for blemishes, 45
Wooden shingles and shakes,
  repairing, 186
Working at home, 227,
  228, 229–33
Wrapping gifts, 148–49
Wrapping paper, as drawer
  liners, 108

y

Yogurt, for skin care, 44

z

Zoos, 162
Zucchini, buying and
  preparing, 21